Technologies for Sustainable Global Higher Education

Digital technologies are influencing the way we learn, live, work, and exist in different contexts of society in the digital age. There are a variety of learning systems that support innovative digital approaches, and universities and organizations around the world are investing in building their own e-learning platforms. Digital technologies are enabling wider access to education and new markets for student recruitment, resulting in increased income prospects for global higher education institutions. Technology enables numerous data and information sources, which give greater access to information and data. It also enables highly virtual environments, which impact teaching and the classroom. The widespread use and application of digital technologies in the teaching and learning process provoke pedagogical inquiry and mediation. It is in this context that **Technologies for Sustainable Global Higher Education** focuses on analyzing the application of digital technologies in the teaching–learning process.

The chapters in this edited collection seek to answer questions relevant to the context of higher education, such as:

- What is the concept of digital technologies?
- How is digital technology used to mediate the learning process?
- What technologies are used to qualify education in higher education?

This book provides answers to these questions by focusing on issues central to improving education through digital technologies, digital learning, and pedagogical practices in digital education. It also provides case studies of higher education institutions.

Advances in Computational Collective Intelligence

Edited by
Dr. Subhendu Kumar Pani
Principal, Krupajal Group of Institutions, India

Published

Applications of Machine Learning and Deep Learning on Biological Data
By Faheem Syeed Masoodi, Mohammad Tabrez Quasim, Syed Nisar Hussain Bukhari, Sarvottam Dixit, and Shadab Alam
ISBN: 978-1-032-214375

Artificial Intelligence Techniques in Power Systems Operations and Analysis
By Nagendra Singh, Sitendra Tamrakar, Arvind Mewara, and Sanjeev Kumar Gupta
ISBN: 978-1-032-294865

Technologies for Sustainable Global Higher Education
By Maria José Sousa, Andreia de Bem Machado, and Gertrudes Aparecida Dandolini
ISBN: 978-1-032-262895

Forthcoming

Artificial Intelligence and Machine Learning for Risk Management of Natural Hazards and Disasters
By Cees van Westen, Romulus Costache, Dimitrios A. Karras, R. S. Ajin, and Sekhar L. Kuriakose
ISBN: 978-1-032-232768

Computational Intelligence in Industry 4.0 and 5.0 Applications: Challenges and Future Prospects
Joseph Bamidele Awotunde, Kamalakanta Muduli, and Biswajit Brahma
ISBN: 978-1-032-539225

Deep Learning for Smart Healthcare: Trends, Challenges and Applications
K. Murugeswari, B. Sundaravadivazhagan, S. Poonkuntran, and Thendral Puyalnithi
ISBN: 978-1-032-455815

Edge Computational Intelligence for AI-Enabled IoT Systems
By Shrikaant Kulkarni, Jaiprakash Narain Dwivedi, Dinda Pramanta, and Yuichiro Tanaka
ISBN: 978-1-032-207667

https://www.routledge.com/Advances-in-Computational-Collective-Intelligence/book-series/ACCICRC

Technologies for Sustainable Global Higher Education

Edited by
Maria José Sousa
Andreia de Bem Machado
Gertrudes Aparecida Dandolini

CRC Press
Taylor & Francis Group
Boca Raton London New York

CRC Press is an imprint of the
Taylor & Francis Group, an **informa** business

AN AUERBACH BOOK

First edition published 2024
by CRC Press
2385 NW Executive Center Drive, Suite 320, Boca Raton, FL 33431

and by CRC Press
4 Park Square, Milton Park, Abingdon, Oxon, OX14 4RN

CRC Press is an imprint of Taylor & Francis Group, LLC

© 2024 Taylor & Francis Group, LLC

Reasonable efforts have been made to publish reliable data and information, but the author and publisher cannot assume responsibility for the validity of all materials or the consequences of their use. The authors and publishers have attempted to trace the copyright holders of all material reproduced in this publication and apologize to copyright holders if permission to publish in this form has not been obtained. If any copyright material has not been acknowledged please write and let us know so we may rectify in any future reprint.

Except as permitted under U.S. Copyright Law, no part of this book may be reprinted, reproduced, transmitted, or utilized in any form by any electronic, mechanical, or other means, now known or hereafter invented, including photocopying, microfilming, and recording, or in any information storage or retrieval system, without written permission from the publishers.

For permission to photocopy or use material electronically from this work, access www.copyright.com or contact the Copyright Clearance Center, Inc. (CCC), 222 Rosewood Drive, Danvers, MA 01923, 978-750-8400. For works that are not available on CCC please contact mpkbookspermissions@tandf.co.uk

Trademark notice: Product or corporate names may be trademarks or registered trademarks and are used only for identification and explanation without intent to infringe.

ISBN: 978-1-032-26289-5 (hbk)
ISBN: 978-1-032-54371-0 (pbk)
ISBN: 978-1-003-42454-3 (ebk)

DOI: 10.1201/9781003424543

Typeset in Adobe Garamond Pro
by SPi Technologies India Pvt Ltd (Straive)

Contents

Preface vii
Editors ix
Contributors xi

    Introduction: Is a Seamless Learning Experience Design
    Framework an Answer to Attaining Quality Digital Learning
    in Higher Education? 1
    HELGA HAMBROCK

1 A Comprehensive Review of the Literature on Digital Higher
    Education Pedagogies 9
    ANDREIA DE BEM MACHADO, GERTRUDES APARECIDA DANDOLINI,
    AND MARIA JOSÉ SOUSA

2 Digital Education Knowledge from Theory to Teaching
    Experiences in Three European Universities 33
    ANDREA BRAMBILLA, TIANZHI SUN, ERICA ISA MOSCA,
    MARCO GOLA, ALEXANDER ACHILLE JOHNSON,
    MARIA JOSÉ SOUSA, SYLVIE CHEVRIER,
    AND STEFANO CAPOLONGO

3 Skills for Safety, Security, and Well-Being in the DigComp
    Framework Revision and Their Relevance for a Sustainable
    Global (Higher) Education 45
    ANÍCIA REBELO TRINDADE, DEBBIE HOLLEY,
    AND CÉLIO GONÇALO MARQUES

4 Digital Technologies as a Key Driver of Sustainable Global
    Higher Education 77
    SAID JABOOB, MOHAMMAD SOLIMAN, BALAJI DHANASEKARAN,
    AND SAMSKRATI GULVADY

Contents

5   Higher Education: Networks and Technology – The Complex World of Sustainability 95
LOURDES CARAÇA

6   Artificial Intelligence and Blockchain in Higher Education Institutions: A Bibliometric Review 105
ANDREIA DE BEM MACHADO, GERTRUDES APARECIDA DANDOLINI, JOÃO ARTUR DE SOUZA, MARCO TULIO BRAGA DE MORAES, AND MARIA JOSÉ SOUSA

7   Educational Strategies in Smart and Sustainable Cities for Education in the Post-Covid Era 121
ANDREIA DE BEM MACHADO, JOÃO RODRIGUES DOS SANTOS, ANTÓNIO SACAVÉM, MARC FRANÇOIS RICHTER, AND MARIA JOSÉ SOUSA

8   Accounting Education: New Pedagogies and Digital Approaches Based on the Research Agenda 143
HUGO PALÁCIOS AND MARIA JOSÉ SOUSA

9   International Mobility Challenges in Higher Education in the Digital Era 187
MARIA DO CARMO BOTELHO, NUNO NUNES, CATARINA FERREIRA DA SILVA, ISABEL MACHADO ALEXANDRE, MARIA DAS DORES GUERREIRO, AND MARIA JOSÉ SOUSA

10   Artificial Intelligence: Applicability of This Technology to Higher Education – A Scoping Review 211
ANDREIA DE BEM MACHADO, GERTRUDES APARECIDA DANDOLINI, JOÃO ARTUR DE SOUZA, MILTIADES DEMETRIOS LYTRAS, AND MARIA JOSÉ SOUSA

11   Case Study of Two Higher Education Institutions in the Use of a National MOOC Platform toward Sustainable Development 237
PEDRO BARBOSA CABRAL, CÉLIO GONÇALO MARQUES, INÊS ARAÚJO, JOSÉ MIGUEL PADILHA, FRANCISCO VIEIRA, AND LUÍS CARVALHO

Index 259

Preface

Knoweldge is not a virus
Susanna Sancassani – Head of the Unit "Innovative Methodologies and Technologies for Learning" at Politecnico di Milano
Daniela Casiraghi – Project Manager and Instructional Designer at "Innovative Methodologies and Technologies for Learning" at Politecnico di Milano

Knowledge is not a virus; it can't be transmitted like viruses. Nor is it transferred like a courier *delivery*. It would seem obvious.

And yet, we note that the instructivist–behaviorist paradigm, for which learning consists in the reception of the contents presented by the teacher, as "faithfully" as possible and without distortions or disturbances, and their "retention" verifiable through the measurement of the ability to reproduce them, again "faithfully", is still very much ingrained and absolutely prevalent.

Hence, the metaphor of the teaching–learning experience as "transmission of knowledge" or, worse, "transfer of knowledge", is by far the most frequently used expression in any forum where education and its future are discussed.

Unfortunately, this has nothing to do with how human beings work when they learn, something we still know very little about, but not that little.

We have already known for almost a century that learning is a recursive and active process, stimulated by a social context and the environment in which it takes place: learning sees a progressive "accommodation" of our cognitive structures in the creation of ever-new mental representations and the connections between them, in an applicative perspective too.

Suffice it to think how, after a lesson, active work (which we call "study") is indispensable for the narrated contents to become knowledge or skills, or, in the most fortunate cases, to be integrated to form competences and usually requires much more time and effort than the lesson itself. The metaphor of "knowledge transfer", therefore, is not only inappropriate with respect to the phenomenon it seeks to represent but is highly misleading because it considers the teacher's responsibility as focused on the delivery of content. In practice a "knowledge courier", whose responsibility ends with the delivery on the doorstep.

The learning experience has, on the contrary, a prevalent systemic dimension. In its simplest terms, the systemic approach is based on the idea that the interconnection between things is a fundamental aspect of understanding any phenomenon and devising effective strategies for intervening in it.

Learning is a transformative process that occurs in a system made up of parts that interact with each other in a life cycle: it has structure, function, performance, and behavior. But above all, it has characteristics of the "system level" (emergent properties), which are properties of the system as such, not simply the sum of the attributes of the individual parts. It's a complex system in which we can observe a mutually influential relationship between content, the activities of individuals (from note-taking, to study, reflection, repetition, and exercise) and groups, physical or virtual contexts outside the strict teaching context, channels supporting interaction, but also the spatial (in physical presence or online) and temporal dimensions (at the same time or at any time) in which exchanges and activities unfold.

If we reason in these systemic terms, the teacher's synchronous or asynchronous narration of content, the "lesson", whether it takes place in the classroom or online, synchronously, or asynchronously, is only one of the inputs, and not necessarily the most crucial one.

And from this reflection raises the main challenge to be met by the Higher education community in becoming "digital" or "blended": this is to ensure that the learning experience leads the student to acquire the knowledge and skills that we consider fundamental for the chosen pathway, through a systemic learning experience, in which peer collaboration, knowledge application, active exploration, and fruitful discussions are fully integrated, well designed, and communicated.

In the meantime, we can't forget how, in recent times, the need to think about all the processes necessary for our existence in a sustainable perspective has become urgent and indispensable. Strangely, little attention is paid to the issue of knowledge sustainability, understood as the design and implementation of processes for the creation, formalization, and dissemination of knowledge that enable the achievement of the goals of our communities in ways that are compatible and consistent with environmental, social, and economic dimensions.

We need to develop digital education with these two main focuses: a systemic learning approach.

Editors

Maria José Sousa is a University Professor at ISCTE, a research fellow at the Business Research Unit, and a collaborator of IPPS-ISCTE. She is also an expert in digital learning and digital skills, as she has assumed a Post-Doc position from 2016 to 2018, researching that field, with several publications in journals with high impact factors (*Journal of Business Research*, *Journal of Grid Computing*, *Future Generation Computer Systems*, and others). She is collaborating as an expert in digital skills with Delloite (Brussels) as per request of the European Commission for the creation of a new category regarding digital skills to be integrated with the European Innovation Scoreboard (EIS).

Andreia de Bem Machado holds a doctorate of philosophy degree in Engineering and Knowledge Management from the Federal University of Santa Catarina (UFSC), Florianópolis, Brazil, and a master's degree in Scientific and Technological Education from UFSC. She is a specialist in graduate studies in pedagogy at Santa Catarina State University, Florianópolis, and in management processes. She currently participates in the Athena Project and is part of postdoctoral studies at the UFSC.

Gertrudes Aparecida Dandolini is a professor at the Federal University of Santa Catarina (UFSC), Florianópolis, Brazil. Previously, she was a professor at the Federal University of Pelotas, Brazil, between 2003 and 2007, where she was a course coordinator. She is currently the leader of the Research Group on Intelligence, Management and Technology for Innovation (IGTI) and a member of ENGIN-Engenharia da Integration and Knowledge Governance.

Contributors

Isabel Machado Alexandre
Instituto Universitário de Lisboa (ISCTE-IUL), IT-Iscte
Lisboa, Portugal

Inês Araújo
LIED, Polytechnic Institute of Tomar
Tomar, Portugal

Andreia de Bem Machado
Federal University of Santa Catarina
Florianópolis, Brazil

Andrea Brambilla
Design & Health Lab, Department of Architecture Built Environment Construction Engineering, Politecnico di Milano
Milan, Italy

Pedro Barbosa Cabral
NAU Project, FCCN
Lisboa, Portugal

Stefano Capolongo
Design & Health Lab, Department of Architecture Built Environment Construction Engineering, Politecnico di Milano
Milan, Italy

Lourdes Caraça
Instituto Politécnico de Santarém
Santarém, Portugal

Maria do Carmo Botelho
Instituto Universitário de Lisboa (ISCTE-IUL), CIES-Iscte
Lisboa, Portugal

Luís Carvalho
Nursing School of Porto
Porto, Portugal

Sylvie Chevrier
Management Research Institute, Université Gustave Eiffel
Champs-sur-Marne, France

Gertrudes Aparecida Dandolini
Federal University of Santa Catarina
Florianópolis, Brazil

Balaji Dhanasekaran
University of Technology and Applied Sciences
Salalah, Oman

Maria das Dores Guerreiro
Instituto Universitário de Lisboa (ISCTE-IUL), CIES-Iscte
Lisboa, Portugal

Marco Gola
Design & Health Lab, Department
  of Architecture Built Environment
  Construction Engineering,
  Politecnico di Milano
Milan, Italy

Samskrati Gulvady
University of Technology and Applied
  Sciences
Salalah, Oman

Helga Hambrock
Concordia University Chicago
River Forest, IL, USA

Debbie Holley
Bournemouth University
Poole, England

Said Jaboob
University of Technology and Applied
  Sciences
Salalah, Oman

Alexander Achille Johnson
Design & Health Lab, Department
  of Architecture Built Environment
  Construction Engineering,
  Politecnico di Milano
Milan, Italy

Miltiades Demetrios Lytras
Effat University
Jeddah, Saudi Arabia

Célio Gonçalo Marques
LIED, Polytechnic Institute of Tomar
Tomar, Portugal
and
University of Coimbra
Coimbra, Portugal

Marco Tulio Braga de Moraes
Universidade Federal de Santa
  Catarina
Florianópolis, Brazil

Erica Isa Mosca
Design & Health Lab, Department
  of Architecture Built Environment
  Construction Engineering,
  Politecnico di Milano
Milan, Italy

Nuno Nunes
Instituto Universitário de Lisboa
  (ISCTE-IUL), CIES-Iscte
Lisboa, Portugal

José Miguel Padilha
Nursing School of Porto
Porto, Portugal

Hugo Palácios
University of the Algarve
Algarve, Portugal

Marc François Richter
Universidade Estadual do Rio
  Grande do Sul
Porto Alegre, Brazil

António Sacavém
Universidade Europeia
Lisbon, Portugal

João Rodrigues dos Santos
IADE/Universidade Europeia
Lisbon, Portugal

Catarina Ferreira da Silva
Instituto Universitário de Lisboa
  (ISCTE-IUL), ISTAR-Iscte
Lisboa, Portugal

Mohammad Soliman
University of Technology and Applied Sciences
Salalah, Oman

Maria José Sousa
ISCTE – University Institute of Lisbon
Lisbon, Portugal

João Artur de Souza
Federal University of Santa Catarina
Florianópolis, Brazil

Tianzhi Sun
Design & Health Lab, Department of Architecture Built Environment Construction Engineering, Politecnico di Milano
Milan, Italy

Anícia Rebelo Trindade
University of Coimbra
Coimbra, Portugal

Francisco Vieira
Nursing School of Porto
Porto, Portugal

Introduction: Is a Seamless Learning Experience Design Framework an Answer to Attaining Quality Digital Learning in Higher Education?

Helga Hambrock
Concordia University Chicago, River Forest, USA

Contents

0.1 Introduction and Background 1
    0.1.1 Possible Solutions 4
    0.1.2 Proposing the SLED Framework 5
0.2 Conclusion 6
Resources 7

0.1 Introduction and Background

Offering high-quality digital education and selecting relevant content for the higher/tertiary education environment is an important goal for educational institutions to prepare students for the world of work in the time of the 4th Industrial

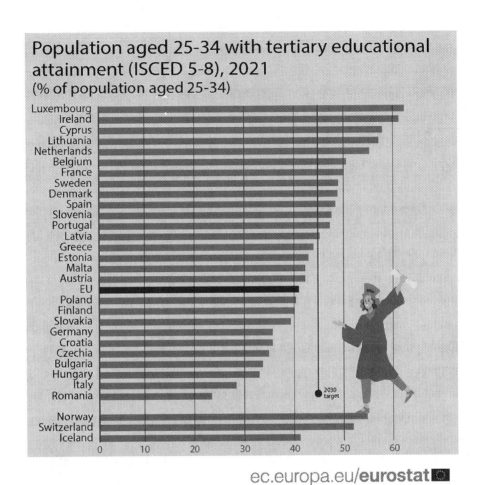

Figure 0.1 European tertiary educational attainment statistics 2021. https://ec.europa.eu/eurostat/statistics-explained/index.php?title=Educational_attainment_statistics

Revolution. Achieving this goal has become increasingly challenging, especially as technology and research have exponentially grown and will grow even faster in the future. Designers for learning experiences therefore need to ask important questions such as: Are traditional teacher-centered teaching methods still relevant or should students be offered choices and opportunities to think and make critical choices as active learners and how could students be prepared more effectively?

According to data, the population of students at tertiary institutions in the EU lies between 25% and 62% (see Figure 0.1), which indicates the interest of students to earn University degrees.

Data collected in the USA over the past 18 years also confirms an increased interest of students to study and be prepared for a profession (See Figure 0.2).

Introduction ■ 3

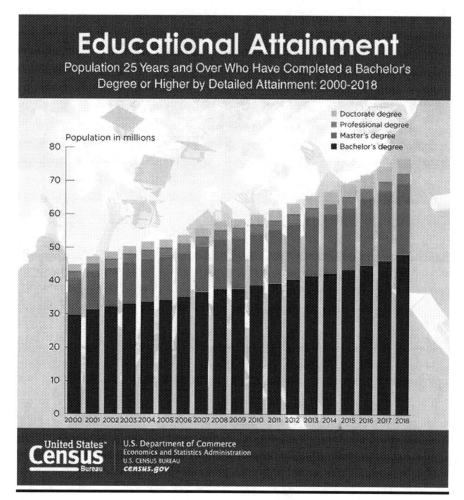

Figure 0.2 US population spotlight educational attainment.

Source: U.S. Census Bureau, 2000–2018 Annual Social and Economic Supplement to the Current Population Survey. https://performance.commerce.gov/stories/s/U-S-Population-Spotlight-Educational-Attainment/na47-j74r/

However, according to data from 2021 where earning and unemployment rates by educational attainment were compared, it is clear that it is not a given that students can be certain of a job when they complete their studies.

The graph indicates that unemployment increases the less educated the population is. These statistics may not be a representation of the world's population but can be considered as a trend in Europe and the USA. It means that students are interested in being educated (Enyama, et al. 2022).

Degrees are believed to prepare students for the job market but from the data in Figure 0.3, the high percentage of unemployment of graduates with College and

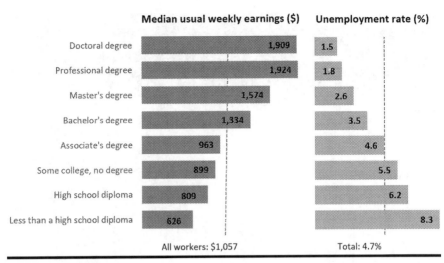

Figure 0.3 US Earnings and unemployment rates by educational attainment 2021.

Note: Data are for persons age 25 and over. Earnings are for full-time wage and salary workers.

Source: U.S. Bureau of Labor Statistics, Current Population Survey. https://www.bls.gov/careeroutlook/2022/data-on-display/education-pays.htmT

Bachelor's degrees is concerning and the question remains if higher institutions are providing the quality needed for students to reach their goals.

0.1.1 Possible Solutions

When all schooling moved online during COVID-19, the unthinkable happened to most traditional educators. They had to use technology for teaching their students online. They may have continued to use technology with a teacher-centered approach which means that they were still the "sage on the stage" instead of being "the guide on the side", but during their online teaching experience, they also became familiar with applications such as discussion boards, groups work for collaboration, journals and wikis. When they realized that students do not all have access to technology, they had to come up with other approaches to distribute the knowledge. When teachers realized that not all students have access to technology, they had to reformulate their pedagogical methodologies and invent other approaches to distribute knowledge. In developing countries like South Africa and Malaysia, students were given free data for their phones, and they could receive and submit their assignments via these channels.

Now that the restrictions for in-classroom teaching have been lifted and students are back in face-to-face classes, it is rather interesting how some educators are still using technology for student-centered activities but also that some have sunk back in their teacher-centered approaches.

0.1.2 Proposing the SLED Framework

Through my involvement with the International Association of Mobile Learning in 2018 and leading the Global Research Project (GRP), the possibilities of designing quality seamless learning experiences for higher education caught my attention and thus my research in this area began.

While I was leading the GRP from 2018 to 2020 and 2020 to 2022, two projects and two books were published on the topic of Seamless learning design. The first project included researchers from five countries: the Netherlands, Malaysia, South Africa, the USA and New Zealand. For the second project, researchers from 11 countries worked together. They were from Malaysia, the USA, South Africa, Canada, Portugal, Denmark, Sweden, Turkey, Egypt, Saudi Arabia and India. During the first GRP project, the most important processes for implementing seamless learning were identified (Du Plessis, et al. 2022).

The findings amalgamated into a model that consists of a helpful five-concept matrix for assessing courses with the focus of improving and ensuring a quality student's learning experience. The model includes core concepts, practical concepts, physical concepts, human concepts and design concepts (Figure 0.4).

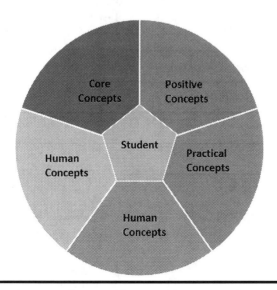

Figure 0.4 Seamless Learning Experience Design (SLED) framework (Hambrock & De Villiers (2022).

The Core concepts include the pedagogical approaches that can be included for a deep and rich learning experience, for example, selecting in and out of classroom learning over time and space by using teacher-centered, student-centered, behaviorist, constructivist, cognitive and socio-constructivist pedagogical approaches.

The Positive concepts include aspects that capture the students' attention and promote self-efficacy and motivation.

The Practical concepts include access to technology, inviting experts to classrooms and using Zoom and other tools or apps to improve an experiential and immersive experience.

The Human concepts include support for the student from parents to writing centers and study methods and management, instructors and the university.

The Design concepts include the design elements that are needed for quality design from analysis to evaluation based on Bloom's taxonomy of learning.

Each concept is unpacked in more detail in the second seamless learning book and is available as an open resource (https://pressbooks.pub/seamlesslearning2/).

0.2 Conclusion

To answer the question of this chapter: **Is seamless learning an answer to quality digital learning in higher education?**, a solution for the challenges of higher education is viewed from an instructional designer perspective. This means the instructional designer constantly revises the courses of the institution to be relevant and of high quality in order to provide the skills and tools students need for the learning experience.

Using a design model for course designs such as the ADDIE model where the context is analyzed, and the course is designed, developed, implemented and evaluated and by including relevant levels of learning such as Bloom's taxonomy are an important foundation for quality course designs.

Again, these models can be overwhelming and somewhat abstract. Thus, the SLED framework offers more tangible and specific direction to all stakeholders including the instructional designer, the content developer, the instructor, and management and also opens opportunities for feedback from students as well as feedback and involvement from the job market.

The SLED framework may not be the only solution for the challenges of Higher education today but can certainly be applied as a useful guideline to attain the 4th Sustainable Development Goal as mentioned by United Nations to provide the students with ongoing quality education in the 4th Industrial Revolution and thus offering the students the education they are hoping for when they register at our Universities and thereby contributing to the economy and the greater good of the world in a meaningful and excellent way.

Resources

Du Plessis, M., Jansen van Vuuren, C.D., Simons, A., Frantz, J., Roman, N., & Andipatin, M. (2022). South African Higher Education Institutions at the Beginning of the Covid-19 Pandemic: Sense-Making and Lessons Learnt. *Frontiers in Education*, 564. Frontiers, https://doi.org/10.3389/feduc.2021.740016

Enyama, D., Balti, E.V., Simeni Njonnou, S.R. et al. (2022). Use of WhatsApp®, for Distance Teaching during COVID-19 Pandemic: Experience and Perception from a Sub-Saharan African Setting. *BMC Medical Education* 21, 517. https://doi.org/10.1186/s12909-021-02953-9

Eurostat statistics explained (2021). Educational attainment statics. https://ec.europa.eu/eurostat/statistics-explained/index.php?title=Educational_attainment_statistics

Hambrock, H. & De Villiers, F. (2022). Proposing A Seamless Learning Experience Design (SLED) Framework Based on International Perspectives of Educators from Five Higher Education Institutions. *Electronic Journal for E-learning*. November, 2022. (In Press).

Hambrock, H., de Villiers, F., Power, R., Koole, M., Ahmed, M., Ellis, W., Abd Karim, R., Kurubacak, G., El-Hussein, M., Ossiannilsson, E., Sharma, R., José Sousa, M., & Wollin, U. (2022). Seamless Learning in Higher Education 2: Comparisons from International Educators of Changes During a Global Pandemic (H. Hambrock, F. de Villiers, R. Power, and M. Koole, Eds). *International Association for Mobile Learning and Power Learning Solutions*. ISBN 978-1-9993825-6-8. https://pressbooks.pub/seamlesslearning2/

Hambrock, H., De Villiers, F., Rusman, E., MacCallum, K., & Arrieya Arrifin, S. (2021). Seamless Learning in Higher Education: Perspectives of International Educators on Its Curriculum and Implementation Potential. https://seamlesslearning.pressbooks.com/front-matter/acknowledgements/e

OECD (2020). OECD Policy Responses to Coronavirus (COVID-19) Education responses to COVID-19: Embracing digital learning and online collaboration. https://www.oecd.org/coronavirus/policy-responses/education-responses-to-covid-19-embracing-digital-learning-and-online-collaboration-d75eb0e8/

OECD (2021). *Education at a Glance 2021: OECD Indicators*, OECD Publishing, Paris, https://doi.org/10.1787/b35a14e5-en

Schwab, K. (2016). The fourth Industrial revolution: What it means, how to respond. *World Economic Forum*. https://www.weforum.org/agenda/2016/01/the-fourth-industrial-revolution-what-it-means-and-how-to-respond/

US Department of Commerce (2018). Education Attainment 2000–2018. https://performance.commerce.gov/stories/s/U-S-Population-Spotlight-Educational-Attainment/na47-j74r/

US Bureau of Labor statistics (2021). Employment Projections. https://www.bls.gov/emp/chart-unemployment-earnings-education.htm

Chapter 1

A Comprehensive Review of the Literature on Digital Higher Education Pedagogies

Andreia de Bem Machado and
Gertrudes Aparecida Dandolini
Federal University of Santa Catarina, Florianópolis, Brazil

Maria José Sousa
ISCTE – University Institute of Lisbon, Lisbon, Portugal

Contents

1.1 Introduction	10
1.2 Digital Pedagogy	10
1.3 Methodological Approach	12
1.3.1 Methodological Procedures	13
1.3.2 Bibliometric Analysis	13
1.3.3 Bradford's Law	15
1.3.3.1 Lotka's Law	16
1.3.4 Zipf's Law	16
1.3.5 Countries	17
1.3.6 Relevance of Publications by Author	18
1.3.7 Main Scientific Sources	18

1.3.8 Most Impactful Authors 18
1.3.9 Three-Field Plot 21
1.3.10 Word TreeMap 24
1.4 Digital Pedagogy in Higher Education 24
1.5 Final Considerations 29
References 29

1.1 Introduction

The educational landscape has undergone a substantial transformation as a result of education and new technology. The educational context that, in the pandemic year of 2020, suffered a significant alteration with the usage of information and communication technologies is studied through a pedagogy that is infused with scientific and technical knowledge. Such scientifically based knowledge aims to explain instructional practices, methodological intervention procedures, and the coordination of knowledge and actions pertaining to the dissemination and appropriation of knowledge. Higher education is the subject of this research because it is necessary to rethink educational practices in all forms of teaching.

As a result, higher education institutions (HEIs) have been forced to redefine themselves and rethink in order to keep up with the technological challenges of the post-modern world in this scenario marked by the COVID-19 pandemics, linked to profound social, economic, and cultural transformations, and the accelerating development of digital information and communication technologies. In this context are contemporary pedagogical practices that use technological resources to make learning active. This form of teaching, known as digital pedagogy, combines the use of technology in teaching techniques with the adoption of more dynamic learning methodologies. Therefore, the chapter's central problem is: What are the primary digital pedagogies used in higher education? In order to address this, the primary digital pedagogies used in HEIs will be mapped. As a result, in addition to this introduction section, the article is divided into five further sections. The methodology presented in the next part uses the Web of Science, the biggest peer-reviewed collection of abstracts and citations from the scientific literature, to present in detail the bibliometric result from the scenario of scientific publications arising from this domain. The research challenge is addressed in the third section. The last thoughts are made in the fourth section, which comes before the sources that were cited throughout the text.

1.2 Digital Pedagogy

The use of methods and techniques for teaching and learning is only one aspect of pedagogy. It examines how each person's views and values interact and what it means for the teaching and learning process (Kreber 2010). It also highlights presumptions regarding how teaching and learning are related as well as approaches, tactics, and technology that should be applied in a classroom setting (Zhang and Yu 2021).

According to Anderson (2020), the pedagogical techniques and approaches addressed in digtial Pedagogy help students improve their intellectual, social, and personal resources so that they are prepared for lifelong learning. Digital technology was used to enhance online teaching and learning in 2020 as a result of the COVID-19 pandemic. As a result of the need for instructors to understand how to use these technologies in the classroom, new educational policies were inspired (Williamson 2019). As a result, cognitive and technical abilities were needed to be able to use information and communication technologies to search, assess, generate, and convey information (De León, Corbeil, and Corbeil 2021). Digital literacy is a term that the instructor started to use more frequently in the year 2020 and refers to these abilities. The need for technical proficiency among teachers in higher education is growing. The COVID-19 epidemic expedited the implementation of digital pedagogy; as a result, digital literacy alone was insufficient to fulfill the challenges that instructors and students faced (De León, Corbeil, and Corbeil 2021).

Given that it can be perceived from a variety of perspectives, the phrase "digital pedagogy" is challenging to comprehend (Väätäjä and Ruokamo 2021). Simply expressed, digital pedagogy is the application of technological aspects to improve or transform the educational process (Unesco 2019). Digital pedagogy is the ability to incorporate digital technologies into teaching in order to improve learning, teaching, evaluation, and curriculum, according to Kivunja (2013, p. 131).

Pedagogical orientation, pedagogical practices, and digital pedagogical skills are the three components of the digital pedagogy paradigm proposed by Väätäjä and Ruokamo (2021). A teacher's conception of how the learning process should be carried out, how people should learn, and how they should be instructed and advised is known as their pedagogical orientation. According to their instructional aims, it implements the teacher's suggested strategy. The instructional strategies employed by the teacher are referred to as "pedagogical practices". The abilities instructors need to have in order to successfully incorporate digital technology in the classroom are known as digital pedagogical competences (Väätäjä and Ruokamo 2021).

Competences in digital pedagogy include pedagogical, digital, and ethical skills, and awareness, according to Ryhtä et al. (2020), as shown in Figure 1.1.

As shown in Figure 1.1, Digital Pedagogy consists of three competences (Ryhtä et al. 2020): Pedagogical competence, which consists of having knowledge of the subject, experience in teaching methods, and expertise in professional life skills.

Digital competence, on the other hand, implies having knowledge of digital technology and having the ability to use it, understanding the potential of digital technology, and using digital technology in teaching.

Ethical competence, which consists of being aware of student equality, prioritizing the learning experience, and emphasizing digital literacy.

In this context, the competences proposed by Digital Pedagogy do not focus solely on the use of digital technologies for teaching, but also discuss and reflect

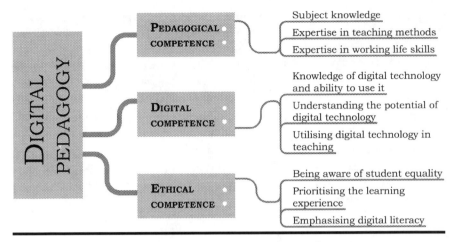

Figure 1.1 Competences of digital pedagogy (Ryhtä et al. 2020).

on approaches to technological tools and their use in the educational context. Therefore, it is as much about using digital tools thoughtfully as it is about deciding when not to use digital tools and paying attention to the impact of digital tools on learning (Masood and Haque 2021). As such, Digital Pedagogy not only promotes interaction and free exchange of knowledge between students and teachers but also inspires innovation and change.

1.3 Methodological Approach

A systematic search in an online database was employed as a method of literature search, and the findings were then subjected to an integrative analysis. As a result, it was attempted to work with the five steps of Torraco (2016), which were elaborated in the integrative literature review phase and are described below.

> formulation of the research problem is the initial stage;
> second phase: defining the sources of research;
> third phase: choosing conferences and articles;
> fourth stage: assessment of the choice; and
> The research problem's solution is in the fifth step.

To address the problem of the present research, the work was carried out from an exploratory-descriptive view with the inductive method, with the objective of mapping the theme and increasing the familiarity of the researchers. With this methodology, the objective was to delineate the theme and increase the researchers' familiarity with the fact, as well as, to clarify the concepts inherent to the subject under study.

1.3.1 Methodological Procedures

The integrative review contributes to the systematic visualization of the state of the art (Machado et al. 2020; Torraco 2016) on the research subject and its timeline to the level of production by area, avoiding minimization or repetition of studies, or even the tendency to bias when looking at a specific theme. For this analysis, the research was organized into five phases, namely: problem formulation, definition of research sources, article selection, screening evaluation, and analytical synthesis of the results.

The first phase is the formulation of the research problem that guides this study. This will answer the question: What are the main digital pedagogies applied to HEIs? To answer this question a database search was conducted; it started and was completed in October 2021.

In the second phase, the definition of research sources and some criteria for the selection of the research were defined, such as the delimitation of the research base. The Web of Science electronic database was chosen, considered relevant due to the number of its indexed, peer-reviewed abstracts and references, as well as its impact on the academic field in the interdisciplinary scope.

The third phase is the selection of articles and conferences. Accomplishing it meant delimiting the search terms or expressions: ("pedagogy* digital" OR "digital education") AND "higher education". The variations of the expressions adopted for the search are presented in a broader context, in the same proposal, because a concept depends on the context to which it is related and on its historical trajectory and conceptual analysis. As a basic principle of the search, it was chosen to insert the terms and expressions in the "Title", "Abstract", and "Keyword" fields. No restrictions of time, language, area of knowledge, or any other restrictions were allowed.

The fourth phase, evaluation of the selection, based on the previously defined criteria, totaled 156 papers published in indexed journals. This bibliometric analysis will be explained in the section "Bibliometric Analysis" (Section 1.3.2).

The answer to the research problem is in the fifth phase of the research. In this phase, the inclusion and exclusion criteria were used. Of the 156 articles, 68 were excluded because they did not answer the research question: What are the main digital pedagogies applied to higher education? First, the remaining 88 documents were selected only for abstract reading. After this step, 11 papers that answered the research question were selected to be read in full according to the online search and the open-access papers, in order to map the main digital pedagogies applied to higher education, thus establishing the schematic summary presented in Section 1.4, titled "Digital Pedagogy in Higher Education".

1.3.2 Bibliometric Analysis

RSudio software, the bibliometric package bibliometrix, and biblioshiny were used to analyze the data (Moral-Muñoz et al. 2020). The summary of this information is presented in Table 1.1.

Table 1.1 Main Information about Data

Description	Results
Main Information About Data	
Timespan	2005–2021
Sources (journals, books, etc.)	94
Documents	157
Average years from publication	2.7
Average citations per document	2.522
Average citations per year per doc	0.6966
References	5.023
Document Types	
Article	88
Article; early access	8
Article; proceedings paper	1
Editorial material	1
Meeting abstract	1
Proceedings paper	54
Review	4
Document Contents	
Keywords Plus (ID)	162
Author's Keywords (DE)	571
Authors	
Authors	465
Author appearances	479
Authors of single-authored documents	30
Authors of multi-authored documents	435
Authors Collaboration	
Single-authored documents	32

(*Continued*)

Table 1.1 (Continued)

Description	Results
Documents per author	0.338
Authors per document	2.96
Co-Authors per documents	3.05
Collaboration Index	3.48

For bibliometric data analysis, three laws were used, namely (Figueiredo et al. 2019):

1. Bradford's Law, which refers to the productivity of journals, identifying which journal has the greatest trends in publishing the topic of interest;
2. Lotka's Law, which checks the productivity of each author, interpreting it as the probability of productivity, in which the number of published works increases the probability of the publication of new works related to the same topic by the author; and
3. Zipf's Law, frequency of keywords in works with correlated subjects.

1.3.3 Bradford's Law

The analysis began by referencing the global growth rate in the annual number of scientific publications on higher education and digital pedagogy, which was 36.22%. The number of publications in the last four years analyzed (2017–2021) was 115 articles, significantly higher than in the previous period (2005–2015), which totaled only 41 articles. Figure 1.2 indicates the growing interest in the topic,

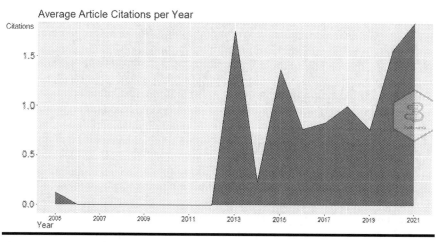

Figure 1.2 Annual scientific production.

16 ■ *Technologies for Sustainable Global Higher Education*

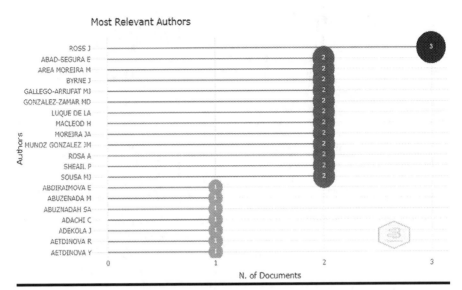

Figure 1.3 Most relevant authors.

also indicating the average number of citations received annually, that is, the impact of the publications.

According to Bradford's law, the degree of relevance of journals should be estimated by measuring the journal productivity (Figueiredo et al. 2019). The three journals with the highest publication productivity in the area of digital pedagogy in higher education are *Digital Education Review*, with 28 publications, *Digital Education: Out to the World and Back to the Campus*, and *Disco 2015: From Analog Education to Digital Education*, both with 6 publications in the area.

1.3.3.1 Lotka's Law

This analysis began by identifying the 20 most relevant authors on the subject of this research, which are explained in Figure 1.3.

The interpretation of Lotka's Law was based on the number of publications per author, in which 97.2% of the authors have only one publication, while 2.6% of the authors have two publications. The largest number of publications per author is three works by author Jen Ross, representing only 0.2% of the authors, as shown in Figure 1.4.

1.3.4 *Zipf's Law*

For the analysis according to Zipf's Law, the main keywords were classified according to the frequency of occurrence: the higher the frequency, the greater the area

Digital Higher Education Pedagogies: An Integrative Review ■ 17

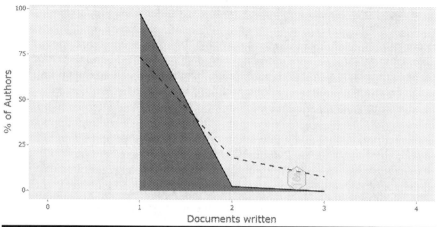

Figure 1.4 Author productivity by Lotka's Law.

Figure 1.5 Keyword cloud following Zipf's Law.

that a given word occupies in the word cloud. The words education, impact, and students are the most frequent words in the published works. Figure 1.5 shows a keyword cloud following Zipf's Law.

1.3.5 Countries

The countries that published the most about Higher Education and Digital Pedagogy were: Spain, with 37 publications, and Russia, with 19 publications. Figure 1.5 shows the intensity of publication by country and the relationship established between them, through citations between published works.

In Figure 1.6, the countries with the most publications on the subject of this study are highlighted in dark blue on the map, and those colored in lighter blue are the countries with fewer publications. The countries colored in gray are those that have no publications on the subject.

Figure 1.6 shows the flow of collaboration between countries. The thicker orange bands demonstrate an intense collaboration between Portugal and the countries of South America. The thinner bands represent less collaboration between countries in North America, Asia, and Oceania.

1.3.6 Relevance of Publications by Author

The productivity and relevance of the main authors' production over time are represented in Figure 1.7, in which the dot size represents the number of publications and the color intensity represents the number of citations of the annual publications. It is observed that the productivity and relevance of publications over time are dynamic.

Figure 1.7 refers to the production of the authors, showing in the larger circle in dark blue color the authors who had the highest number of publications and citations in the area: Emilio Abad-Segura, Mariana-Daniela González-Zamar, and Antonio Luque de la Rosa, the last two both with two articles published in 2020 and a total of 8 citations per year. Antonio Luque de la Rosa appears twice in Figure 1.7, with abbreviations of his name as follows: Luque de La and Rosa A. The larger circle in light blue refers to Manuel Area Moreira, who is the second most cited author in the area. He had two articles published in 2018 and got 1.8 citations per year.

1.3.7 Main Scientific Sources

The analyzed documents were published in 96 different journals, and among a total of 156 studies, 28 were published in a single journal, *Digital Education Review* journal, as shown in Table 1.2, which shows the 10 scientific sources most relevant on the topic "Digital Pedagogy" and "Higher Education".

Digital Education: Out to the World and Back to the Campus and *Disco 2015: From Analog Education to Digital Education* ranked second with six publications, while *Digital Education: At the Mooc Crossroads Where the Interests of Academia and Business Converge* scored five papers, followed by *Education Sciences* with four publications.

1.3.8 Most Impactful Authors

Figure 1.8 represents the co-citation network in three clusters. The cluster in blue indicates anonymous, Knox J., and Bayne S. as the most influential network in the area of Digital Pedagogy and Higher Education.

Digital Higher Education Pedagogies: An Integrative Review ■ 19

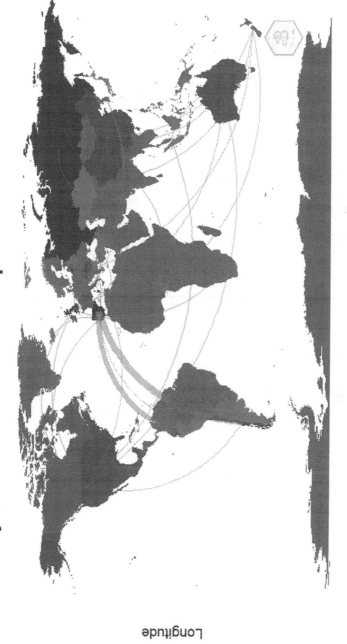

Figure 1.6 Country collaboration map.

20 ■ *Technologies for Sustainable Global Higher Education*

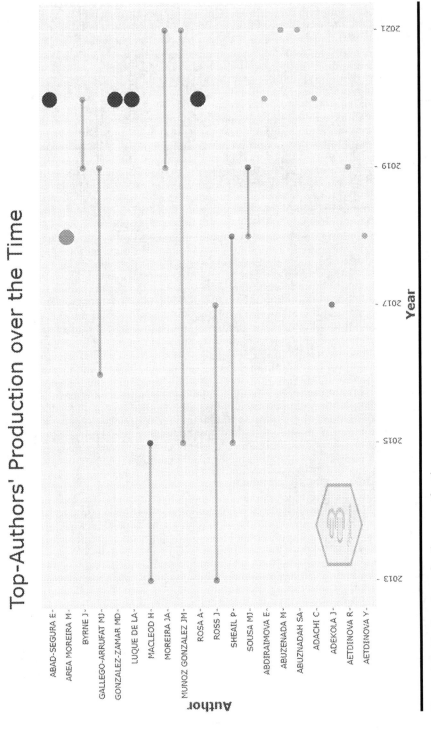

Figure 1.7 Authors' production over the time.

Table 1.2 Most Relevant Scientific Sources

Sources	Articles
Digital Education Review	28
Digital Education: Out to the World and Back to the Campus	6
Disco 2015: From Analog Education to Digital Education	6
Digital Education: At the Mooc Crossroads Where the Interests of Academia and Business Converge	5
Education Sciences	4
Edulearn18: 10th International Conference on Education and New Learning Technologies	3
International Review of Research in Open and Distributed Learning	3
Learning Media and Technology	3

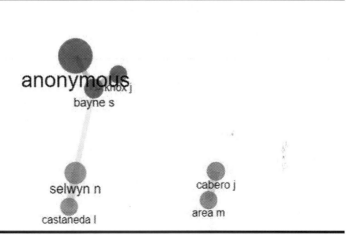

Figure 1.8　10-Node co-citation network of authors and institutions.

1.3.9 Three-Field Plot

Figure 1.9 represents an innovative three-field plot, in which in the observed columns, from left to right, the interactions between author keyword, authors, and most relevant countries were shown. It was possible to observe that most of the studies on Digital Education were published by Maria José Sousa, from Portugal, and J. António Moreira, from Canada.

Figure 1.10 shows a three-field plot, generated from countries (in the first column), keywords plus (in the middle column), and authors (in the last column).

22 ■ Technologies for Sustainable Global Higher Education

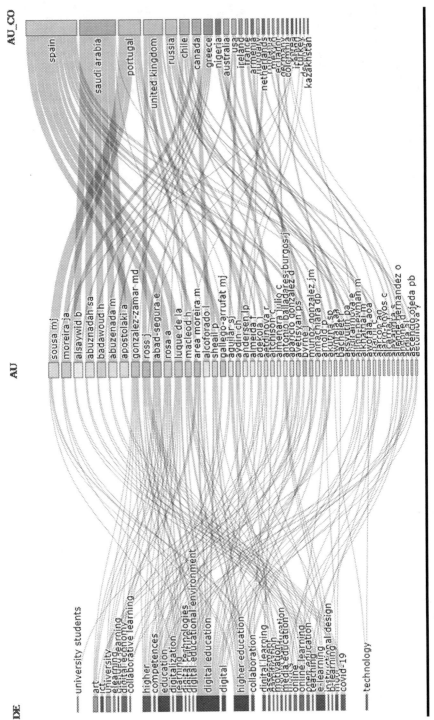

Figure 1.9 Three-field plot with author keywords vehicles, authors, and countries.

Digital Higher Education Pedagogies: An Integrative Review ■ 23

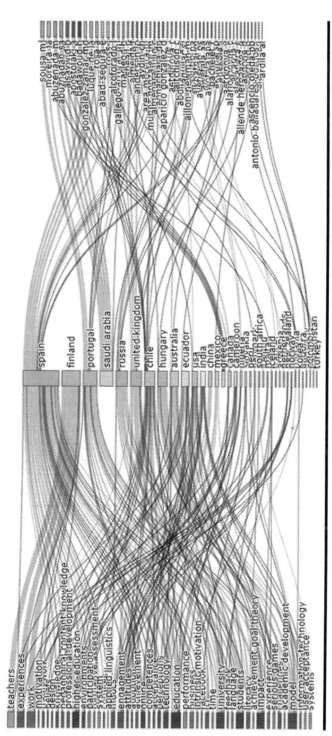

Figure 1.10 Three-field plot, with countries, keywords plus, and authors.

1.3.10 Word TreeMap

The set of rectangles represented in the TreeMap in Figure 1.11 shows, in a proportional way, the hierarchy of the sub-branches of the research. It is noticeable that themes such as education, impact, model, online, students, and higher education appear with some relevance and relate to digital pedagogy.

1.4 Digital Pedagogy in Higher Education

Education is the subject of pedagogy, a science that concentrates on the teaching–learning process. In the COVID-19 pandemic phase, when society was impacted by its spread, changes were needed across a number of societal domains, including education. It was necessary to reinvent the teaching process by requiring fresh and inventive teaching methods from educators. Teachers were rapidly confronted with new demands, and they were forced to adapt by coming up with fresh ways to carry out their didactic plans. In order to engage students in the learning process and to fulfill the goals set forth in the lesson plan, teachers should use digital languages and information and communication technology. This pedagogy that uses information and communication technologies is called Digital Pedagogy. In this research, a mapping was performed using the Web of Science database and, according to the fifth step proposed by Torraco (2016), the following articles answered the research question and were selected to compose the systematic summary (Table 1.3).

The main digital pedagogies applied to higher education are based on the development of mobile learning, smartphones, and computers, which facilitated changes in teaching models in all subjects. With the application of technology, teaching is no longer limited by time, space, psychological state, or geopolitical boundaries. In this way, it is possible to learn anywhere and to form a lifelong habit of learning (Xu 2019). Many national and foreign universities have built their own online teaching platforms in recent years, using the resources of the internet and digitization to offer students an interactive and personalized learning channel that is not limited to time and space for autonomous learning (Cornali and Cavaletto 2021). Learning is supported by mobile technologies and applications for tablets and smartphones (Sousa and Rocha 2020).

Technologies applied in the digital world such as gamification and MOOCs, among others, demonstrate that students learn new knowledge through instructional videos that include auditory and visual content (Lehmann 2019). In this way, limited time in the classroom can be used mainly for teaching activities that employ interaction or two-way communication, such as practicing, problem-solving, and discussions, to enhance the learning effects and realize the idea of student-centered education (Shen, Wu, and Lee 2017).

Digital Higher Education Pedagogies: An Integrative Review ■ 25

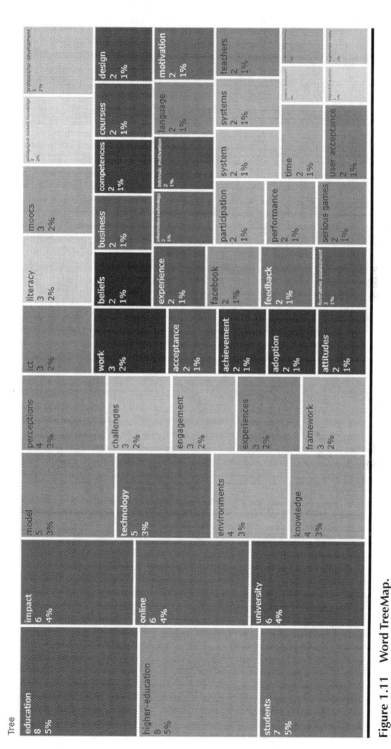

Figure 1.11 Word TreeMap.

Note: Graphical Parameters: Field: Keywords Plus; n° of words = 50; word occurrence measure: square root.

Table 1.3 Schematic Summary

Year	Authors	Title	What are the Main Digital Pedagogies Applied to Higher Education?
2017	Adekola et al.	Development of an institutional framework to guide transitions into enhanced blended learning in higher education	Digital Pedagogy applied to higher education must involve all university agents, adopting a holistic view in the search for a combined learning, that is, an optimized combination of online and on-site learning.
2017	Valverde-Berrocoso and Balladares Burgos	Enfoque sociológico del uso del b-learning en la educación digital del docente universitario	Blended learning or B-learning is an integrative educational program that combines computer-based activities with regular classes, to be used as a pedagogical tool.
2018	Area Moreira, San Nicolás Santos and, Sanabria Mesa	Virtual classrooms in face-to-face tertiary education: the student perspective	A Digital Pedagogy that adopts innovative pedagogical models of teaching through technologies.
2018	Aguilar, Holman, and Fishman	Game-inspired design: empirical evidence in support of gameful learning environments	Digital Pedagogy that involves games, through active student participation with the realization of study projects, through gamification, using the process of playful design, and using games as inspiration for changes in the type and structure of tasks given to students, with the aim of better supporting intrinsic motivation.

(Continued)

2019	Halkic and Arnold	Refugees and online education: student perspectives on need and support in the context of (online) higher education	The use of Massive Open Online Courses (MOOCs) as a resource of Digital Pedagogy in higher education.
2019	Sousa et al.	Creating knowledge and entrepreneurial capacity for HE students with digital education methodologies: Differences in the perceptions of students and entrepreneurs	Digital pedagogy that relies on ICTs so that the learning process is carried out through text, images and audio, and with this, each person can create their own story and engage in in-depth learning. Use of digital storytelling and digital problem-based learning.
2021	Decuypere and Landri	Governing by visual shapes: university rankings, digital education platforms and cosmologies of higher education	Use of a platform called U-Multirank as an educational platform.
2020	González-Zamar et al.	Digital education and artistic-visual learning in flexible university environments: research analysis	Digital pedagogy should use the internet, education, visual resources, computer programs, learning, digital media literacy, and educational technology.

(*Continued*)

Table 1.3 (Continued)

Year	Authors	Title	What are the Main Digital Pedagogies Applied to Higher Education?
2020	Bawa	Game on! investigating digital game-based versus gamified learning in higher education	Digital Pedagogy should use digital game-based learning (DGBL) and may include a variety of game types such as those designed for educational purposes, as well as digital education for games and those created for entertainment and commercial purposes such as massively multiplayer online games (MMOs).
2020	Avetisyan and Gevorgyan	Free educational environment as the basis of human capital and relationships between social sectors	Transforming the educational system into a single free space that enables the development of a country's intellectual human capital in the context of digitization. In this case, internationalization and digitization (as well as their interconnection) function as tools and conditions for the development of the modern educational system.
2021	Alsaywid et al.	Effectiveness and preparedness of institutions' e-learning methods during the COVID-19 pandemic for residents' medical training in Saudi Arabia: a pilot study	Digital pedagogy should be based on defined critical success factors (technical support, content enhancement, pedagogy, etc.) and, if possible, define priority levels, so that a more permanent e-learning practice is achievable.

1.5 Final Considerations

It was discovered that there was a shift in the pedagogical paradigm from traditional higher education on campus to digital and online higher education as a result of increased globalization and the emergence of digital learning. This allowed the main pedagogies and digital educational strategies applied to HEIs to be based on activities carried out through research projects that provide open and direct feedback. MOOCs, digitization, gamification, interaction design, and Blockchain, a data transmission security mechanism that enables the control of the educational process through its feedback, are the major technologies used in this scenario.

Digital education competencies are the skills that enable people to utilize digital media to seek information, analyze the information they receive from the internet, and communicate with others using a variety of digital tools and applications, such as social media and cell phones. As a result, having a strong understanding of information and communication technologies as well as having moral awareness and cognitive abilities all fall under the umbrella of having a digital competency. In this context, digital pedagogy should provide interaction between teachers and students through the effective use of technology for teaching and learning.

For future research, it is proposed to analyze the design of active methodologies for the digital teaching and learning process.

References

Adekola, J., Dale, V. H. M., & Gardiner, K. (2017). Development of an institutional framework to guide transitions into enhanced blended learning in higher education. *Research in Learning Technology*, 25(0). https://doi.org/10.25304/rlt.v25.1973

Aguilar, S. J., Holman, C., & Fishman, B. J. (2018). Game-inspired design: Empirical evidence in support of gameful learning environments. *Games and Culture*, 13(1), 44–70.

Alsaywid, B., Lytras, M. D., Abuzenada, M., Lytra, H., Sultan, L., Badawoud, H., Apostolaki, A. (2021). Effectiveness and preparedness of institutions' E-learning methods during the COVID-19 pandemic for residents' medical training in Saudi Arabia: A pilot study. *Frontiers in Public Health*, 9, 707833.

Anderson, V. (2020). A digital pedagogy pivot: re-thinking higher education practice from an HRD perspective. *Human Resource Development International*, 23(4), 452–467. https://doi.org/10.1080/13678868.2020.1778999

Area Moreira, M., San Nicolás Santos, B., & Sanabria Mesa, A. L. (2018). Las aulas virtuales en la docencia de una universidad presencial: la visión del alumnado. *RIED Revista Iberoamericana de Educación a Distancia*, 21(2), 179. https://doi.org/10.5944/ried.21.2.20666

Avetisyan, P. S., & Gevorgyan, N. M. (2020). Free educational environment as the basis of human capital and relationships between social sectors. *Economy of Region*, 16(2), 494–506. https://doi.org/10.17059/2020-2-12

Bawa, P. (2020). Game on!: Investigating digital game-based versus gamified learning in higher education. *International Journal of Game-Based Learning*, 10(3), 16–46. https://doi.org/10.4018/ijgbl.2020070102

Cornali, F., & Cavaletto, G. M. (2021). Emerging platform education: What are the implications of education processes' digitization? In *Handbook of Research on Determining the Reliability of Online Assessment and Distance Learning* (pp. 359–378). IGI Global. https://www.igi-global.com/chapter/emerging-platform-education/266557

De León, L., Corbeil, R., & Corbeil, M. E. (2021). The development and validation of a teacher education digital literacy and digital pedagogy evaluation. *Journal of Research on Technology in Education*, 1–13. https://doi.org/10.1080/15391523.2021.1974988

Decuypere, M., & Landri, P. (2021). Governing by visual shapes: university rankings, digital education platforms and cosmologies of higher education. *Critical Studies in Education*, 62(1), 17–33. https://doi.org/10.1080/17508487.2020.1720760

Figueiredo, R., Quelhas, O., Vieira Neto, J., & Ferreira, J. J. (2019). The role of knowledge intensive business services in economic development: a bibliometric analysis from Bradford, Lotka and Zipf laws. *Gestão & Produção*, 26(4). https://doi.org/10.1590/0104-530x4356-19

González-Zamar, M.-D., Abad-Segura, E., Luque de la Rosa, A., & López-Meneses, E. (2020). Digital education and artistic-visual learning in flexible university environments: Research analysis. *Education Sciences*, 10(11), 294. https://doi.org/10.3390/educsci10110294

Halkic, B., & Arnold, P. (2019). Refugees and online education: student perspectives on need and support in the context of (online) higher education. *Learning, Media and Technology*, 44(3), 345–364. https://doi.org/10.1080/17439884.2019.1640739

Kivunja, C. (2013). Embedding digital pedagogy in preservice higher education to better prepare teachers for the digital generation. *International Journal of Sustainability in Higher Education*, 2(4), 131–142.

Kreber, C. (2010). Academics' teacher identities, authenticity and pedagogy. *Studies in Higher Education*, 35(2), 171–194. https://doi.org/10.1080/03075070902953048

Lehmann, A. (2019) Problem tagging and solution-based video recommendations in learning video environments. *2019 IEEE global engineering education conference, EDUCON (2019)*, pp. 365–373.

Machado, A. de B., Sousa, M. J., Nawaz, F., & Martins, J. M. (2020). Impacts of the integration of Chinese managers in the Western economies the case of Brazil. *Transnational Corporation Review*, 12(3), 319–328. https://doi.org/10.1080/19186444.2019.1693203

Masood, M. M., & Haque, M. M. (2021). From critical pedagogy to critical digital pedagogy: a prospective model for the EFL classrooms. *Saudi Journal of Language Studies*, 1(1), 67–80. https://doi.org/10.1108/sjls-03-2021-0005

Moral-Muñoz, J. A., Herrera-Viedma, E., Santisteban-Espejo, A., & Cobo, M. J. (2020). Software tools for conducting bibliometric analysis in science: An up-to-date review. *El Profesional de La Información*, 29(1). https://doi.org/10.3145/epi.2020.ene.03

Ryhtä, I., Elonen, I., Saaranen, T., Sormunen, M., Mikkonen, K., Kääriäinen, M., Koskinen, C., Koskinen, M., Koivula, M., Koskimäki, M., Lähteenmäki, M.-L., Wallin, O., Sjögren, T., & Salminen, L. (2020). Social and health care educators' perceptions of competence in digital pedagogy: A qualitative descriptive study. *Nurse Education Today*, 92(104521), 104521. https://doi.org/10.1016/j.nedt.2020.104521

Shen, K. M., Wu, C. L., & Lee, M. H. (2017). A study on Taiwanese undergraduates' conceptions of Internet-based learning. *International Journal on Digital Learning Technology*, 9(3), 1–22.

Sousa, M. J., Carmo, M., Gonçalves, A. C., Cruz, R., & Martins, J. M. (2019). Creating knowledge and entrepreneurial capacity for HE students with digital education methodologies: Differences in the perceptions of students and entrepreneurs. *Journal of Business Research*, *94*, 227–240. https://doi.org/10.1016/j.jbusres.2018.02.005

Sousa, M. J., & Rocha, Á. (2020). Learning analytics measuring impacts on organisational performance. *Journal of Grid Computing*, 18(3), 563–571. https://doi.org/10.1007/s10723-018-9463-1

Torraco, R. J. (2016). Writing integrative literature reviews: Using the past and present to explore the future. *Human Resource Development Review*, 15(4), 404–428. https://doi.org/10.1177/1534484316671606

UNESCO. (2019). Rethinking pedagogy: exploring the potential of digital technology in achieving quality education. https://unesdoc.unesco.org/ark:/48223/pf0000372786

Väätäjä, J. O., & Ruokamo, H. (2021). Conceptualizing dimensions and a model for digital pedagogy. *Journal of Pacific Rim Psychology*, 15, 183449092199539. https://doi.org/10.1177/1834490921995395

Valverde-Berrocoso, J., & Balladares Burgos, J. (2017). Enfoque sociológico del uso del b-learning en la educación digital del docente universitario. *Sophia*, 23, 101.

Williamson, B. (2019). New power networks in educational technology. *Learning, Media and Technology*, 44(4), 395–398. https://doi.org/10.1080/17439884.2019.1672724

Xu, D. (2019). Research on new English mobile teaching mode under the impact of mobile internet age. *Open Journal of Social Sciences*, 07(05), 109–117.

Zhang, J., & Yu, S. (2021). Reconceptualising digital pedagogy during the COVID-19 pandemic: A qualitative inquiry into distance teaching in China. *Innovations in Education and Teaching International*, 1–11. https://doi.org/10.1080/14703297.2021.2000473

Chapter 2

Digital Education Knowledge from Theory to Teaching Experiences in Three European Universities

Andrea Brambilla, Tianzhi Sun, Erica Isa Mosca, Marco Gola, and Alexander Achille Johnson
Design & Health Lab, Department of Architecture Built Environment Construction Engineering, Politecnico di Milano, Milan, Italy

Maria José Sousa
Istittuto Universitario de Lisboa, Lisbon, Portugal

Sylvie Chevrier
Université Gustave Eiffel, Champs-sur-Marne,France

Stefano Capolongo
Design & Health Lab, Department of Architecture Built environment Construction Engineering, Politecnico di Milano, Milan, Italy

Contents

2.1 Introduction 34
2.2 Theoretical Framework 35
    2.2.1 Sustainable Digital Education at Instituto Universitário de Lisboa (ISCTE) 35
    2.2.2 Collaborative Online International Learning (COIL) at Université Gustave Eiffel (UGE) 36
    2.2.3 Online Learning and Offline Extended Classroom at Politecnico di Milano (POLIMI) 36
2.3 Education Pedagogy and Applied Technologies 36
    2.3.1 Digital Learning Pedagogies and Technologies from Theory 36
    2.3.2 Digital Learning Pedagogies and Technologies from UGE 37
    2.3.3 Digital Learning Pedagogies and Technologies from POLIMI 38
2.4 Evaluation Process 40
    2.4.1 Digital Education Assessment Techniques 40
    2.4.2 Assessment Practice from COIL Project 40
    2.4.3 Examination Typology of POLIMI 42
2.5 Final Considerations 43
Acknowledgments 43
References 44

2.1 Introduction

Educational methodologies and practices are in a state of constant evolution, reacting in tandem to changes in educational theory, classroom structures, and social dynamics. In the 21st century, the rapid development and implementation of education technologies in classrooms have been a primary force in reshaping our basic conception of what a classroom is. A key category of these education technologies is digital communication technologies (DCTs) that facilitate blended learning, experiential learning, and increased student collaboration. DCTs, previously utilized to varying degrees across educational systems, were suddenly catapulted into the forefront of global pedagogies in the wake of the coronavirus disease 2019 (COVID-19) pandemic as these systems adapted to avoid complete interruptions. As the globe continues to react to the ongoing pandemic situation, it is important that we reflect on the quality of online teaching and learning in an effort to enhance the delivery of remote education, improve student outcomes, and meet student needs (Dhawan 2020, Mukhtar et al. 2020). This is particularly true given that online learning will likely continue in a robust way post-pandemic (Schwartz et al. 2020). Additionally, a great challenge is posed by the increasing need for multidisciplinarity and synergies between different disciplines to train students to tackle complex contemporary problems (Azzopardi-Muscat et al. 2020, Gola et al. 2020).

The purpose of the Project University Goes Digital is to improve the digital skills of university teachers, to reinforce their capacity to respond to the challenges universities are facing during the COVID-19 pandemic or will face during future similar challenges. With the active involvement of the lecturers and students from the beginning of the project, ATHENA will create, test, and implement innovative digital practices, putting technologies into use to create new pedagogical approaches and achieve better learning and teaching experiences. The project seeks to foster cooperative learning environments, making them transformative and inclusive through the effective adoption of new technologies, such as e-learning, gaming platforms, and virtual and augmented reality, systematically modeled to activate key competencies in digital learning. The project will create templates that lecturers can adopt and adapt to their classes, using different pedagogical approaches.

This article describes the research of Instituto Universitário de Lisboa (ISCTE) and the teaching experience of Université Gustave Eiffel (UGE), and Politecnico di Milano (POLIMI) during the COVID-19 pandemic, explaining their educational frameworks, teaching pedagogies, adopted technologies, and evaluation processes. Reflecting on these experiences provides an opportunity for improvement within and across these universities.

2.2 Theoretical Framework

Prior to the COVID-19 pandemic, discussions and research on online teaching focused on its potential value as an educational strategy when compared to traditional face-to-face teaching methods, evaluating what role it may play educational systems (Means et al. 2009). In the setting of COVID-19 pandemic regulations, its implementation instead became necessary, shifting discussions to how online teaching can best be implemented on a mass scale. We detail the theoretical frameworks of three European universities as they began their pedagogical shift to an online-based classroom.

2.2.1 Sustainable Digital Education at Instituto Universitário de Lisboa (ISCTE)

Educators can use technology to incorporate students into the learning process, with numerous studies showing increased student interest when digital devices are integrated into the learning environment.

Strategies to include technology in the educational context are defined as Open strategy, establishing access to information and the production of knowledge for all with a focus on flexible content; Constructive strategy, integrating openness to new spaces of knowledge, with its progressive construction; and Interactive strategy, presupposing the development of the interactive processes that occur in the virtual environment (Sousa and Costa 2014, Sousa et al. 2017, Sousa and Rocha 2018).

These strategies become more important in the current global context, helping to develop a more inclusive, innovative, and effective educational system, while contributing to poverty reduction, all in line with the UN Sustainable Development Goals (1 – No poverty, 4 – Quality education, and 10 – Reduced inequalities).

2.2.2 Collaborative Online International Learning (COIL) at Université Gustave Eiffel (UGE)

Educators at UGE developed the COIL project as an opportunity to allow students to experience an international work environment while at home. This consisted of an international learning project carried out by mixed groups of students from two collaborating classes in France and the United States of America (USA). They collaborated through technological devices and developed joint deliverables.

This project exists within a broader series of educational practices grouped under the term internationalization at home and represents a key example of how online learning can be leveraged to extend education in ways that were not possible in the traditional classroom. A COIL project can take many forms but should always be organized around a central activity and involve multiple groups of students located in different countries. Students will exchange ideas, perspectives, and contexts specific to their country and culture, and in doing so develop intercultural skills and a global appreciation.

2.2.3 Online Learning and Offline Extended Classroom at Politecnico di Milano (POLIMI)

Changing regulations related to the COVID-19 pandemic resulted in two stages of digitalization at POLIMI. In the setting of government-mandated quarantines beginning in March 2020, POLIMI initially converted to an entirely online learning framework. This took considerable effort to realize this transition over a brief period, ensuring the university could maintain its extensive activities previously conducted in the classroom. As the pandemic and resulting regulations changed, the university consolidated newly utilized online teaching methods with more traditional methods into a blended learning framework.

2.3 Education Pedagogy and Applied Technologies

2.3.1 Digital Learning Pedagogies and Technologies from Theory

Digital learning assumed maximum relevance as educational systems across the globe defined and implemented policies to comply with social distancing measures – policies which centered around the online classroom. In this setting, utilizing a diversity of digital learning pedagogies and technologies at ISCTE by educators becomes critical (Table 2.1).

Table 2.1 Digital Pedagogies and Technologies

Scope	Topic
Digital Learning Pedagogies	Collaborative communities; Cooperative learning; Collaborative learning; Network participation; Flipped classroom using digital media; Experiential online development; Open educational practice; Online learning; e-Learning; Blended learning; Digital storytelling; Gamification
Digital Learning Technologies	Educational games; Augmented reality; Web-based video; Digital video; Webinars; LMS; YouTube; Facebook; Instagram; Wikipedia; Linkedin; Google; Websites; Learning object; Mobile learning; Learning Repositories; Blackboard; Moodle

2.3.2 *Digital Learning Pedagogies and Technologies from UGE*

The COIL project at UGE was conducted within a bachelor class of 28 students in International Management at the Université Gustave Eiffel in France and a class of 14 students from various disciplinary backgrounds in the honors college at the University of Texas at Dallas in the USA.

As shown in Table 2.2, the pedagogy of the COIL project has two stages: a) the Professors' Preparation Phase and b) the Implementation Phase. The first stage involves professors identifying classes to be matched and making any necessary organizational arrangements. In the second phase, the COIL project was presented separately to each class during the course introduction within which the COIL project was to take place. In a short video posted on Padlet for everyone to review, students were asked to prepare a brief oral presentation about themselves, to identify a common stereotype about the other country, and to identify one reason driving poverty in their respective country. At the same time, students from UGE started to review material provided on their learning platform concerning socio-economic inequalities and posted a critical review.

A first synchronous session was organized so that the two classes could see and engage with each other. The entire joint class was broken into small mixed groups via online break-out rooms where they could discuss what they had posted in their videos. Following the joint session, student project teams were composed of educators from a complementary perspective. Over the following weeks, the groups of students self-organized to meet virtually and to define their project topic. A second synchronous session was organized to introduce the chosen topics and to provide feedback on these topics. After three weeks of teamwork in autonomy, the COIL project culminated in synchronous final group presentations. One week later, a final synchronous session was held to receive student feedback on the experience and any suggestions to improve the process.

Table 2.2 Educational Pedagogy and Applied Technologies at UGE

Stage	Pedagogy	Technology
Professors' preparation	(1) Respective professors identify classes that can be matched, agree on learning outcomes and skills to be acquired, and start building the training program (2) Determine the organizational arrangements concerning the student team members, COIL calendar, resources given to students, details of the deliverables, and assessments	Communication tools (Padlet, Zoom) E-learning platforms Shared thematic or methodological video clips
Implementation	(1) Presentation of the COIL project (2) Brief oral presentation from each student (3) First synchronous session: small mixed groups in online break-out rooms for discussion (4) Student project teams were signed by teachers (5) Second synchronous session: topics reviewing (6) Third synchronous session: final presentations (7) Last synchronous session: feedback and suggestions	Useful websites Communication tools (WhatsApp, Zoom), etc.

2.3.3 Digital Learning Pedagogies and Technologies from POLIMI

For the academic year 2019–2020, prior to the start of the semester, several steps had been taken by POLIMI to switch entirely to online teaching. Table 2.3 presents the practice of digital learning in terms of pedagogy and technology at POLIMI.

During the online learning phase, the applied technologies depended on five identified classroom scenarios: (1) Computer/tablet + slide share; (2) Computer/tablet + screen share; (3) Microsoft Teams + tablet and pen; (4) Class with PC Microsoft Teams and webcam + blackboard; (5) Class with PC, Microsoft Teams and webcam + digital board.

The online platform chosen by POLIMI for lectures was Microsoft Teams. The personal pages of teachers and students were updated with links to this platform to provide a formal method to connect to each other with specific online meetings.

Table 2.3 Digital Pedagogy and Applied Technologies at POLIMI

Stage	Pedagogy	Technology
Online learning (Academic year 2019–2020)	(1) Identification of the synchronous collaboration tool to replicate the classroom in-presence time (Microsoft Teams) (2) Identification of the main classroom scenarios (3) Tutorials and basic technical support regarding the use of Microsoft Teams for teachers and students and methodological seminars (4) Constant monitoring and support	Slide share Screen share Microsoft Teams Webcam Blackboard Digital board
Extended classroom (Academic year 2020–2021)	In the design phase (1) Design of the classroom following the PST framework: pedagogical approaches, spaces, and technology (2) Classrooms with audio-video systems integrated with virtual rooms and therefore usable by both students in the classroom and those at home (3) Identification of different scenarios to understand which tools are necessary to equip in classrooms (4) Methodological support for teachers in the design of teaching and learning In the work phase A technological and methodological support to explain the technological equipment in the classroom and its use and the new web conference platform adopted for the management of the extended class	Cisco WebEx Camera Projector Blackboard Doc Cam Classroom console Students' devices

Once the semester began and was functioning completely online, the university teaching staff was provided with continuous monitoring and support.

In the first semester of the 2020–2021 academic year, POLIMI experimented with the extended classroom to accomplish a blended learning methodology. Prior to the introduction of the extended class, a design phase was needed to manage the extended classroom configuration. During the second phase, classrooms were configured with different technologies to allow for a blended teaching experience including a camera, projector, blackboard, Doc Cam, classroom console, and students' devices (Figure 2.1). In this case, the online platform used by POLIMI was Cisco Webex. At this time, the links for the meetings of the lesson were associated with each professor instead of the course. The rapid setup of several activities and innovative learning techniques was based on already existing strategies and methodologies developed at the METID Learning Innovation unit of Politecnico di Milano (Sancassani et al., 2019).

2.4 Evaluation Process

2.4.1 Digital Education Assessment Techniques

Selecting appropriate evaluation instruments compatible with new digital education practices involved several practical issues such as ease of administration, time required for administration, ease of communication and application of results, availability of equivalent forms, and costs. Other considerations by the ISCTE regarding assessments include evaluating the acquired knowledge and skills of students and determining individual progress. Table 2.4 outlines utilized assessment techniques.

2.4.2 Assessment Practice from COIL Project

The assessment of the COIL project was based on several deliverables. The assessment of the students from UGE included the following components: (1) an individual critical review of the material to gain knowledge on the content of the project; (2) a collective presentation and slide show; (3) individual comments on other teams' work; (4) and individual self-reports about their learning of intercultural work.

The first and the last deliverable were graded only by French educators based on the assessment of knowledge and analytical skills. In the final self-report, each student had to demonstrate their ability to work at distance in an intercultural environment by showcasing some of their actions and analyzing some of their behaviors during the work. This reflexivity makes it possible to formalize the learning achieved through the project.

The presentation and slides were assessed jointly by the two professors, considering multiple criteria including the relevance of the introduction and its ability to engage the audience, the quality of the USA/France comparison, the relevance and originality of the recommendations, the research incorporation, the use of proper resources, the teamwork and coordination of the team, and the quality of oral and written communications. Assessments between the professors typically converged, though in a few cases, different weights were assigned to the same element and resulted in different rates for one given criterion.

Digital Education European Universities ■ 41

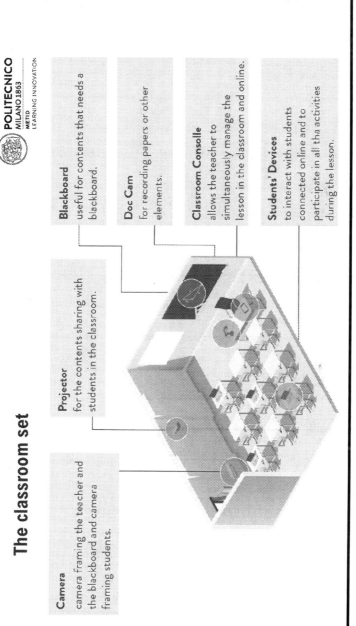

Figure 2.1 Extended classroom configuration with devices that allow the blended learning (METID, 2021).

Table 2.4 Learning Assessment Techniques

Assessment Technique	Objective	Description
Testing	Tests are used to evaluate student knowledge.	(1) Written: brief or extensive tests; tests with short response, alternative response, multiple choice, and combination (2) Practical: test of procedures or process tests
Reports	Seeks to obtain views of the student (in writing or verbally) about a given situation or to assess his/her knowledge and ability to communicate.	(1) Presentations (2) Questions (3) Reports
Observation	To assess psychomotor or social behavior (attitudes) of students.	(1) Records ("anecdotal records") – Brief descriptions of an individual's behavior (2) Checklist – to evaluate, step by step, the execution of a given task (3) Rating scales – to grade a particular quality or particular characteristic

2.4.3 Examination Typology of POLIMI

POLIMI explicitly asked for the student to be recognized by the educator by comparing the image of the student taken by the webcam with the photo in the student's file. Five typologies of exams were established and associated with specific online platforms relating to the need to fix a method followed by all educators.

The exam typologies with related platforms were defined as follows:

1. Delivery of paper, assignment, project, essay: Beep platform (used by POLIMI to exchange files between teachers and students for each course)
2. Oral exam: Microsoft Teams
3. Test with live supervision with closed and/or open answers or with specific applications: Microsoft Forms, Zoom, Moodle

4. Closed and/or open-ended tests with automatic "proctored" control: Moodle, Respondus + Lockdown browser
5. Written test on paper live supervision: Microsoft Forms, Microsoft Onedrive, Zoom

The management functions for the exams were activated on the teachers' personal pages, where different configurations were provided in relation to the exam's typology.

2.5 Final Considerations

According to the theoretical research from ISCTE, it is possible to create a more sustainable education using different pedagogies and technologies. The teaching experience of the COIL project and POLIMI show the possibility of digital learning practices from homes and classrooms, in the field of advanced and traditional education, both online and offline.

COIL can be used in many courses with different themes to contribute to internationalization at home. It contributes to the development of certain dimensions of intercultural competencies that cannot be developed through traditional education. COIL is not expensive. It is also very flexible and can be adapted to different contexts, but it requires preparation beforehand and above all requires good collaboration between the educators involved.

From POLIMI, the university created new online learning and extended classroom models, meeting different needs (lessons, exercises, workshops, group reviews, etc.) and adapting to the methodological approaches and style of educators. These experiences created in reaction to the COVID-19 pandemic can be an opportunity to transform traditional teaching into a higher teaching experience.

Acknowledgments

The authors would like to acknowledge this paper as part of a wider European Project Erasmus + 2020-1-PT01-KA226-HE-094833 Project ID: 1681945 Titled: "ATHENA - University Goes Digital for a Sustainable Global Education", main participants: ISCTE – Instituto Universitario de Lisboa (Coordinator), Université Gustave Eiffel, Sigmund Freud Privatuniversitat Wien GmbH, Politecnico di Milano. In particular, the authors would like to acknowledge Politecnico di Milano unit METID Learning Innovation "Methods and Innovative Technologies for Learning" for support in understanding the didactic strategies of the university with specific regards to Dr.ssa Susanna Sancassani and Dr.ssa Daniela Casiraghi.

References

Azzopardi-Muscat, N., A. Brambilla, F. Caracci and S. Capolongo. 2020. Synergies in Design and Health. The Role of Architects and Urban Health Planners in Tackling Kkey Contemporary Public Health Challenges. *Acta Biomedica*. 91(Suppl 3): 9–20.

Dhawan, S. 2020. Online Learning: A Panacea in the Time of COVID-19 Crisis. *Journal of Educational Technology Systems*. 49(1): 5–22.

Gola, M., A. Brambilla, P. Barach, C. Signorelli and S. Capolongo. 2020. Educational Challenges in Healthcare Design: Training Multidisciplinary Professionals for Future Hospitals and Healthcare. *Annali di Igiene Medicina Preventiva e di Comunità*. 32(5): 549–566.

Means, B., Y. Toyama, R. Murphy, M. Bakia and K. Jones. 2009. Evaluation of Evidence-Based Practices in Online Learning: A Meta-Analysis and Review of Online Learning Studies. In US Department of Education. US Department of Education. https://eric.ed.gov/?id=ED505824

METID Learning Innovation "Methods and Innovative Technologies for Learning", Politecnico di Milano. 2021. Online Learning and the Extended Classroom The Politecnico di Milano experience. Report.

Mukhtar, K., K. Javed, M. Arooj and A. Sethi. 2020. Advantages, Limitations and Recommendations for Online Learning during COVID-19 Pandemic Era. *Pakistan Journal of Medical Sciences*. 36(COVID19-S4): S27.

Sancassani, S., P. Marenghi, V. Baldoni and S. Malan 2019. *Spreading Educafé*. Milano, Politecnico di Milano – METID Learning Innovation. Report.

Schwartz, H. L., D. Grant, M. K. Diliberti, G. P. Hunter and C. M. Setodji. 2020. Remote Learning Is Here to Stay: Results from the First American School District Panel Survey. *RAND Corporation*. https://www.rand.org/pubs/research_reports/RRA956-1.html

Sousa, M. J. and E. Costa. 2014. *Formação ou aprendizagem? Mudança de paradigma*. Novas edições académicas.

Sousa, M. J., R. Cruz and J. M. Martins. 2017. Digital learning methodologies and tools–a literature review. *Edulearn17 Proceedings*. 5185–5192.

Sousa, M. J. and Á. Rocha. 2018. Corporate digital learning–proposal of learning analytics model. In *World Conference on Information Systems and Technologies*. 1016–1025. https://experientiallearning.net/wp-content/uploads/listing-uploads/file-up-to-1-document/2020/04/paper-digital-learning-methodologies-and-tools-EDULEARN17-FV.pdf

Chapter 3

Skills for Safety, Security, and Well-Being in the DigComp Framework Revision and Their Relevance for a Sustainable Global (Higher) Education

Anícia Rebelo Trindade
University of Coimbra, Coimbra, Portugal

Debbie Holley
Bournemouth University, Poole, England

Célio Gonçalo Marques
Polytechnic Institute of Tomar, Tomar, Portugal
University of Coimbra, Coimbra, Portugal

DOI: 10.1201/9781003424543-4

Contents

3.1 Contextualization 46
3.2 Theoretical Framework 48
    3.2.1 The European Digital Framework and the United Nations Sustainable Goals (UNSDGs) 48
        3.2.1.1 DigComp Framework and Sustainable Education 48
    3.2.2 Concept of the Knowledge, Skills, and Attitudes (KSA) 49
    3.2.3 Setting Knowledge Skills and Attitudes for Safety Area 51
        3.2.3.1 Digital Safety and Security Underpinning Theory 51
        3.2.3.2 Digital Health and Well-Being Underpinning Theory 52
3.3 Methodology 55
    3.3.1 Research Problem and Design 55
        3.3.1.1 Phases of the Research 55
        3.3.1.2 Research Tools 56
        3.3.1.3 Research Analysis 58
3.4 Results and Discussions 59
3.5 Conclusions 71
Acknowledgments 72
Notes 72
References 73

3.1 Contextualization

With the United Nations Sustainable Development Goals (UNSDGs) taking key prominence in educational design, sustainability needs to be embedded within Higher Education curricula, on the radar of Higher Education policymakers, a priority for senior teams leading Higher Education Institutions and embraced throughout our institutions. The recent body of work updating the European DigComp Framework 2.1 saw researchers, policymakers, and the European directorate reframe and update the competence framework for all European citizens. This work directly influences the debate on how to strategically align Higher Institution efforts to create these universal principles for education.

    This chapter focuses on the outputs generated on digital safety, security health, and well-being as part of the European DigComp 2.2 updated framework, as these pertain particularly to the educational context. Understanding the fast-changing context through the lens of economic, social, environmental, technological, and legal and analyzing potential opportunities and threats are a key requirement for EU citizens (Wysokińska-Senkus, 2020). Far greater depth of knowledge about safety and security risks, with commiserate measures to mitigate against them are no longer optional for 21st-century learners. Digital competence is one of the eight key competences for lifelong learning that are necessary to engage and participate in society, and essential to citizens for personal fulfillment, a healthy and sustainable lifestyle, employability, active citizenship, and social inclusion (European Commission, 2019). According to Trindade (2018, 2020), digital competence is transversal to the other seventh key competences[1], and is aligned to progress in the domains of the other competencies. Digital competence involves the deep critical, responsible, and confident use of, and engagement with, digital technologies for different kinds of daily activities such as learning, work, and for participation in society (Vuorikari, Kluzer & Punie, 2022). Their key concepts encompass five areas of action:

i. information and data literacy;
ii. communication and collaboration, media literacy;
iii. digital content creation (including programming);
iv. safety (including digital well-being and competences related to cybersecurity); intellectual property-related questions;
v. problem-solving and critical thinking.

Trindade (2020) defines the confident, critical, and responsible use of digital technology as inherent to characteristics (skills, knowledge, attitudes) acquired or need to be acquired by an individual in the areas of security, communication and collaboration, digital content creation, information and data literacy, and problem-solving and critical thinking, to perform different activities with a specific level of performance in which the competence is applied. This definition presented by Trindade (2020) is grounded in the work developed by El Asame and Wakrim (2018) and in the DigComp 2.1 Framework (Carretero et al., 2017; Lucas & Moreira, 2017).

Aiming to continue the work done a decade ago (Ferrari, 2012), the European Commission, led by the Joint Research Centre (JRC), started the revision of the 4th dimension of the EU Digital Competence Framework, related to the Knowledge, Skills, and Attitudes (KSA) of each twenty-one digital competences of the DigComp 2.2 Framework (Vuorikari, Kluzer & Punie, 2022). The study sought to understand: What KSA do citizens need to engage with the digital environment in a confident, critical, and responsible way for participation in society in the safety area of the DigComp framework?

To respond to the challenge posed, qualitative research was conducted, using a Design-Based Research (DBR) approach (Mckenney & Reeves, 2014; Plomp, 2013).

The aim of this chapter is to:

- Report upon the new Knowledge Skill and Attitudes (KSA) encompassed in the revised European DigComp 2.2 Framework for safety, security, and well-being competencies;
- To apply these broad principles of KSA to Sustainable Global Higher Education;
- To describe the underpinning evidence base, the processes, and methodology designed by a group of experts working as part of the wider Community of Practice (CoP);
- To make recommendations for future areas of research and activity for the safety, security, and well-being KSA.

Good safety and digital health and well-being come from the Higher Education students having access to KSA that will enable them to consider and compare with other solutions, including non-digital options, and balancing potential threats, wherein DigComp Framework 2.2 (Vuorikari, Kluzer & Punie, 2022) illustrates how to deal with numerous opportunities for different daily interactions. Once the contextualization of the study is made, the theoretical framework is presented.

3.2 Theoretical Framework

3.2.1 The European Digital Framework and the United Nations Sustainable Goals (UNSDGs)

The interruption to schooling through the recent pandemic, with students across the globe unable to access study due to lack of connectivity, skills, and capacity to use digital tools (Al-Tammemi et al., 2020). At the same time, there is a skills shortage due to the lack of a digitally skilled workforce, in the EU and worldwide. Chong et al, in their 2020 Asia-Pacific Economic Cooperation (APEC) report noted that 69% of all job postings in 2019 were in occupations requiring digital skills across New Zealand, Australia, Singapore, the United States, and Canada. Framed as skills for a knowledge economy (González-Salamanca et al., 2020) and equipping citizens to face the new challenges of increasing complexity and uncertainty, growing individualization and social diversity, the literature review (APEC, 2020; Dede, 2010; González-Salamanca et al., 2020) found a gap between skills learned at school, and those required to function at work and in society. The conclusions showed that a broader range of skills is required to learn, communicate, collaborate, and solve problems in digital environments; and further, that students needed to take responsibility for their own ongoing digital skill acquisition based upon personal experience and action, a clear link through to the lifelong learning sustainable agenda. In this regard, Higher Education institutions need to link the UNDSGs and safety, security, and well-being KSA, to prepare students to take responsibility for their own ongoing digital skill acquisition. In this section, the chapter describes how the DigComp 2.2 framework is aligned with the UNDSGs.

3.2.1.1 DigComp Framework and Sustainable Education

The DigComp 2.2 Framework aligns with the broader educational goals, set out under the auspices of the UNSDGs. Adopted by the United Nations in 2015, set a universal call to action to end poverty, protect the planet and ensure that by 2030 all people enjoy peace and prosperity (UN 2015). Goal four is Quality Education, to "ensure inclusive and equitable quality education and promote lifelong learning all" (General Assembly, 2015, p. 14).

In fact, the work undertaken by the authors on the European Framework (Vuorikari, Kluzer & Punie, 2022) was underpinned by the values of the UNSDGs for education, and with the commitment to promote lifelong learning. With the broader remit of digital safety, security, and well-being, a vision statement was co-created to underpin the work done:

> Changes in digital life will land us in a quandary where two seemingly opposite things can be true simultaneously: digital tools will help us fight disease, increase productivity and assign menial and repetitive jobs to robots and algorithms. Yet these same digital tools alter our sense of self and our relationship to others. They may make us feel isolated, insecure, or lonely because we spend more hours in screen time rather than facetime.
> (Anderson, Rainie & Luchsinger, 2018, p. 2)

There are many inequalities in access to technology tools, and the health implications that studying online can create, including the impact of social isolation on young people who report in a United Kingdom Higher Education student survey for the charity "Student Minds" that during the pandemic increasing numbers of learner's report experiencing mental health challenges (Grubic et al., 2020). Authors such as Holley et al. (2020) advocate that underneath those challenges in the digital world, types of threats, such as i) trolling and online bullying; ii) increased peer pressure for perfect online social media life and appearance; iii) access and isolation.

The World Bank, in their "Closing the Digital Divide" conference (2020) outline key factors and concluded that digital divide goes beyond the issue of access to technology, that separates those with the skills to benefit from the use of technology from those without. In this regard, there needs to be equal concern for preserving the free choice of citizens in general and Higher Education students in particular, in seeking to engage consciously, as well as for those who are unable to take part as they would like, using online and digital technologies, and are prevented from doing so by physical, societal, or economic reasons. Following this understanding, the chapter suggests that the KSA related to the safety area of the DigComp Framework 2.2 needs to consider the promotion of critical thinking and the ability to assess the long-term risks and benefits of alternative technological paths for a hyper-vigilant to ensure more easily conscious decisions while using different types of technology (Anderson & Rainie, 2018).

3.2.2 Concept of the Knowledge, Skills, and Attitudes (KSA)

This section presents the definition adopted of essential KSA to set a group of KSA based on the underpinning theory described in the section below. The definition presented was proposed by Vuorikari, Kluzer, and Punie (2022). Essential knowledge is defined as the ability to understand how digital technologies can support communication, creativity, and innovation, and be aware of their opportunities, limitations, effects, and risks, as well as the general principles, mechanisms, and logic underlying evolving digital technologies and know the basic function and use of different devices, software, and networks (Vuorikari, Kluzer & Punie, 2022). Based on this definition, individuals can take a critical approach to the validity, reliability, and impact of information and data made available by digital means and be aware of the legal and ethical principles involved in engaging with digital technologies. The Implications of decisions made by themselves and for others (decisions that appear (and are) completely reasonable and justified, can be hurtful for other people involved, depending on abilities, religious beliefs, social conventions, personal preferences).

The essential skills are related to the capability to use digital technologies to support their active citizenship and social inclusion, collaboration with others, and creativity toward personal, social, or commercial goals (Vuorikari, Kluzer & Punie, 2022). The concept of skills includes either the ability to use, access, filter, evaluate, create, program, and share digital content. Individuals should be able to manage and protect information, content, data, and digital identities, as well as recognize and effectively engage with software, devices, artificial intelligence, or robots (Vuorikari, Kluzer & Punie, 2022). Finally, essential attitudes are understood as the engagement with digital technologies and content with a reflective and critical, yet curious, open-minded, and forward-looking attitude to their evolution. It also requires an ethical, safe, and responsible approach to the use of these tools (Vuorikari, Kluzer & Punie, 2022).

The KSA of the safety area developed by the group of experts were related to the following digital competences: 4.1 – protecting devices; 4.2 – protecting personal data and privacy; and 4.3 – protecting health and well-being.

- Protecting devices (4.1) focuses on "to protect devices and digital content, and to understand risks and threats in digital environments, knowing about safety and security measures and to have a due regard to reliability and privacy" (Vuorikari, Kluzer & Punie, 2022, p. 35).
- Protecting personal data and privacy (4.2) is related to the ability to

    protect personal data and privacy in digital environments, understanding how to use and share personally identifiable information while being able to protect oneself and others from damages, and understanding that digital services use a "Privacy policy" to inform how personal data is used.
    (Vuorikari, Kluzer & Punie, 2022, p. 37)

- Protecting health and well-being (4.3) refers to being able to

    (..) avoid health risks and threats to physical and psychological well-being while using digital technologies, protecting oneself and others from possible dangers in digital environments (e.g. cyber bullying), and be aware of the benefits digital technologies for social well-being and social inclusion.

(Vuorikari, Kluzer & Punie, 2022, p. 39)

3.2.3 Setting Knowledge Skills and Attitudes for Safety Area

The background theory regarding KSA for the safety area of the DigComp 2.2 Framework (Vuorikari, Kluzer & Punie, 2022), followed some theories that explore the importance and relevance of digital safety and security (Lukas et al., 2016; Salim & Madnick, 2016; Tsai et al., 2016) as well as well-being (Bleckmann & Mößle 2014; Bitzer & Schwendemann, 2020; Cheung, 2018; Leung & Lee, 2011; Norman & Skinner, 2006; Pangrazio & Selwyn, 2019; Tamar, 2017; Van der Vaart & Drossaert, 2017), grounding a critical thinking to operate consciously and with a confident engagement with digital technologies on daily basis. In this sense, the chapter presents first the theory related to safety and security KSA, and then to the theory that supports the well-being KSA.

3.2.3.1 Digital Safety and Security Underpinning Theory

Digital safety is an important theme to consider when talking about Sustainable Higher Education, concerning the threats related to identity theft, malware or viruses, security of financial information, and phishing attacks (Lukas et al., 2016; Salim & Madnick, 2016; Shillair et al., 2015; Tsai et al., 2016), that may harm the academic community, professional and personal lives. Higher Education Institutions need to establish digital safety measures to avoid that the academic community faces and is involved with cybercriminal and cyberattack actions, protecting learners, academic staff, academic administrators, and the whole higher institution. The first action is to ensure that students and academic staff acquire the essential KSA to put in practice in different kinds of daily personal and academic experiences. Tsai et al. (2016) present a motivation theory perspective regarding the necessity to understand online safety behavior. The authors explore a theoretical framework for understanding Internet users' security protection informed by past research, named Protection Motivation Theory (PMT). The PMT suggests that safety behavior is motivated by threat and coping appraisals, which are determined by perceived vulnerability susceptibility to risks, as well as rewards associated with unsafe behaviors. The PMT is organized into three categories: i) coping self-efficacy (the belief that individuals can successfully carry out protective behaviors); ii) response efficacy (belief in the effectiveness of the protections); and iii) response costs (the costs of using security protections) linked with safe or adaptive behaviors (Tsai et al., 2016).

Another suggested framework pointed out by Salim and Madnick (2016) is based on a model for accident analysis used in the Systems Safety field, called System-Theoretic Accident Model and Processes (STAMP), adapted to be cybersafe. The STAMP framework is organized into three categories, namely: i) safety constraints (critical, missing, or lack of enforcement of relevant constraints leads to elevated safety risks, which may cause loss event(s)); ii) hierarchical safety control structures (where a higher level imposes constraints over the level immediately below organized hierarchically as missing constraints, inadequate safety control commands, commands incorrectly executed at a lower level, or inadequate communication to constraint enforcement), and iii) process model (goal; action condition; observability condition; and model condition) as core concepts.

For Lukas et al. (2016), the theory of safety and security is drawn following three sources: i) security studies (analyze the security reality answering: whose security; security of which values? security against what?); ii) risk theory (evaluates which threats (or negative acts) affect the reference object, and which ones have more or less significant impact, identifying the worst possible impact of threats, preparing measures to counteract those threats and prevent their effects); iii) crisis theory and causality (unexpected and large negative situation; unmanaged control).

These theories (Lukas et al., 2016; Salim & Madnick, 2016; Tsai et al., 2016) were the background, among literature related to digital safety and security (Arboledas-Brihuega, 2019; Hall & Watson, 2016; Khalique, 2016; Shillair et al., 2015; Trindade, Balula & Miranda, 2018; Trindade, 2020; Yang & Lee, 2019) to set the KSA offering a methodological approach to understanding and identifying threats, analyzing risks and propose the choice method of risk management, and identifying either the safety and security breaches consequences and how to overcome it.

3.2.3.2 Digital Health and Well-Being Underpinning Theory

The development of digital well-being frameworks offers insights into the wider, more holistic approaches to be essential to the needs of the European citizen. The Jisc Digital Competence Framework (Danso, Bailey & Beetham, 2013) of the United Kingdom and the EU DigComp 2.1 Framework (Carretero et al., 2017) had already added in, and recognized, the importance of "digital health and well-being". The UK Jisc student experience report (Newman et al., 2018) showed only 54% of students surveyed considered technology embedded in their courses suitable to equip them for their future careers.

A highly contested area, a dualism exists between the offerings of hi-tech, digital self-sufficiency for the individual engaging with health services, with self-access to all the internet has to offer. Pointing to self-help online guidance and apps, is, however insufficient, given that the most marginalized citizens already struggle to access robust internet connections. It also neglects the potential direct and indirect negative effects of self-surveillance measures (Tamar, 2017) in line with the concept of critical data literacy (Pangrazio & Selwyn, 2019). Frameworks need to be designed for hybrid delivery and to meet individual needs. In setting out the agenda for the citizens of the European Union, the work needs to embrace diversity and inclusivity and be framed to meet the needs of all.

In terms of access to digital health, end users can either use digital media to find information on health issues, or they can use them for online contact with experts from the medical and therapeutic profession for remote diagnosis or online treatment or use entirely digital tools (online health applications). The skill set needed is then seen as like that of classical health literacy (access, understand, appraise, apply). Existing early models like the Lily model of eHealth Literacy (Norman & Skinner, 2006), but also wider models like Digital Health Literacy (Van der Vaart & Drossaert, 2017) are in line with this tradition. However, increasing issues are reported with online addiction to gaming; gambling, social media, and pornography the "dark web"; leading to requirements for an increase in KSA for the European Union citizen with regard to the risks, as well as benefits of the digital. Of note is the research by Leung and Lee (2011), and Cheung (2018) who concluded that the more technically skilled an individual is, the more time is spent online, and the more likely they are to become digitally addicted. Thus, societal boundaries are far more nuanced and diverse than previously envisaged.

At the Higher Education institutional level, McDougall et al. (2018) argue that human-centered approaches, prioritizing staff, and students' immediate and lifelong well-being are key to success in developing policies for student well-being, rather than the mere use of digital tools.

Innovative work at the University of Hertfordshire, led by Gilbert (2018, 2020), shows assessing and allocating credit to students for demonstrating compassionate micro skills in group work has been shown to improve student well-being and academic performance; and Biggins, Holley, and Zezekova (2020) in their three-year study call for more nuanced and planned strategies to promote and enhance well-being in Higher Education Institutions. Of particular concern is the excessive use of screens; this has become a major health concern. Urrila et al. (2017) widely agreed to have published the first authentic and evidence-based study of the effects of sleep problems, attention problems, loss of empathy, and school/academic failure.

A model was developed for framing "Digital balance literacy" considering where the "pivot points" are for supporting well-being in the digital era (Bleckmann et al., 2021; Trindade et al., 2021). These can map onto Lifelong Learning transition points. The experts group conceptualized their findings in the model of Figure 3.1. The model draws up two traditions, the first tradition is grounded in pediatrics and developmental (neuro)-science and draws upon research about the impact of the media, and the problematic aspects of screen usage, especially on children and adolescents. This is well documented and problem dimensions have been subdivided into excessive time, age-inadequate content and dysfunctional mood regulation as a predecessor to addictive use (Bleckmann & Mößle, 2014).

The other research tradition focuses on ways in which digital media can contribute to health and well-being in different ways. End users can either use digital media to find information on health issues, or they can use them for online contact with experts from the medical and therapeutic profession for remote diagnosis or online treatment or use entirely digital tools (online health applications). The skill set needed is then seen as like that of classical health literacy (access, understand, appraise, apply). The model presented in Figure 3.1 seeks to draw together both traditions.

54 ■ *Technologies for Sustainable Global Higher Education*

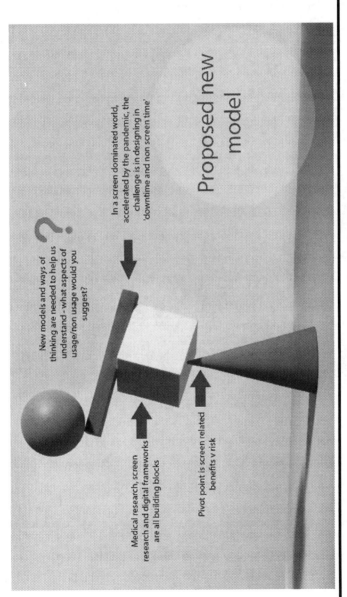

Figure 3.1 A revised digital balance literacy model: Bleckmann, Holley, and Bitzer (2021).

Note: The digital balance literacy model embraces the parameters of medical science, screen research, and digital frameworks. The pivot point offers a focal point enabling practitioners to consider screen-related benefits and risks. Higher Education Institutions can adapt the model to reflect their own theories of learning and develop policies to safeguard student safety, security, and well-being to mitigate risks to their students.

3.3 Methodology
3.3.1 Research Problem and Design
Taking the continuity of the work started in 2012 (Ferrari, 2012; Vuorikari, Kluzer & Punie, 2022), this section presents the methodology followed to collect a group of 37 KSA related to safety, security, and well-being presented on the DigComp 2.2 Framework revision (Vuorikari, Kluzer & Punie, 2022).

The research question that undertook the whole study was: what KSA do citizens need to engage with the digital environment in a confident, critical, and responsible way for learning, at work, and for participation in society in the safety area of the European DigComp 2.2 revision framework?

The research followed a designed-based research (DBR) protocol, which combines theory with practice, representing the voices of all stakeholders, and is designed to respond to complex educational questions. This is appropriate for environments that integrate digital technology (Mckenney & Reeves, 2014; Plomp, 2013) to investigate which skills, knowledge, and attitudes citizens, which also apply to students in Higher Education, as these are essential KSA to acquire.

For Plomp (2013), the DBR is organized into four cycles that fit the present study, namely: i) analyze existing practical problems; ii) develop innovative solutions based on existing design principles; iii) create iterative cycles of tests for the improvement of the solutions in practice; iv) reflect on the principles of improvement of the implemented solutions. According to McKenney and Reeves (2014), the structuring elements of DBR are i) analysis (where the phenomenon to be studied is explored); ii) design (construction of intervention measures for the analyzed context); iii) and evaluation (reflection on the implemented measures, to mature the solutions found, and create a theoretical field of understanding of the respective theme).

3.3.1.1 Phases of the Research

The DigComp revision model was organized into eight phases: initiation; collection of examples; review and vetting of examples; creation of dimension four for DigComp 2.2; International workshop; review and validation of new examples; completion of DigComp 2.2; and finally, its publication (Vuorikari, Kluzer & Punie, 2022). In the first phase, initiation (started in December 2020), the European Commission and JRC have introduced the work to be done, and the different working groups addressed to emerging topics and themes in the digital world, among others[2], safety and security and well-being. The next phases consist of the application of a DBR approach following the Plomp protocol (Plomp, 2013).

The **analysis of existing practical problems** was conducted in phases one and two, where different tasks were undertaken: i) identification of the new digital competence requirements for citizens which stem in the digital world, based on literature review and brainstorming and focus group sessions; ii) propose and select requirements for safety, security, and well-being, linked to the different competences of Framework 2.1; iii) organization of three strands of discussion:

- E-Health/well-being;
- Opportunities and limits to digital protection;
- How to build safety and security step by step in the development of users (cf. younger students, active workers, and elderly people).

The **development of innovative solutions based on existing design principles** took place in phases three and four: i) conducting a literature review about the themes that inform the scope of safety, security, and well-being; ii) applying underpinning literature and values triangulated back through to the DigComp 2.1 Framework; iii) initial suggestions for relevant KSA, statements related to the requirements previously identified, along with suggestions about where they might fit into the safety area of DigComp Framework 2.1 (digital competence 4.1 – protecting devices; 4.2 – protecting personal data and privacy; and 4.3 – protecting health and well-being).

The creation of iterative **cycles of tests for the improvement of the solutions in practices** was accomplished in phases five and six, where i) an iterative peer review/reflective cycle of work was undertaken, using online questionnaires, and organizing brainstorming meetings, and focus group discussions, involving more than 373 stakeholders/experts and more than 31 experts in the field of safety, security, and well-being, across Europe, as well as the expertise, consultation, and validation of experts, stakeholders, and civil society).

In these phases, the group of experts collect more than 100 statements (n = 133) for the safety area (51 statements (KSA) related to the digital competence "protecting devices" and its components; 41 statements (KSA) related to "protecting personal data and privacy", and 41 statements related to "protecting health and well-being"). Considering the definition of KSA presented in the theoretical framework, a knowledge statement starts with "knows/aware/understands that… or aware of". The skill statement begins with "knows how/can apply…, etc.". Finally, an attitude sentence starts with "inclined to/assumes responsibility/wary of/confident in… etc.).

It is concluded that **the principles of improvement of the implemented solutions** developed by the JRC in phases seven and eight, came up with a proposed list of KSA, some of which were directly applied and incorporated into the DigComp 2.2 version. All the communication and collaboration for the achievement of KSA for safety, security, and well-being was organized in the ALL-Digital Basecamp platform (Figure 3.2).

3.3.1.2 Research Tools

For data collection, direct techniques and indirect documentation techniques were used (Tuckman, 2012). The direct data collection techniques integrate three questionnaire surveys (used and applied to validate the KSA for each of the three digital

DigComp Framework Revision and Their Relevance ■ 57

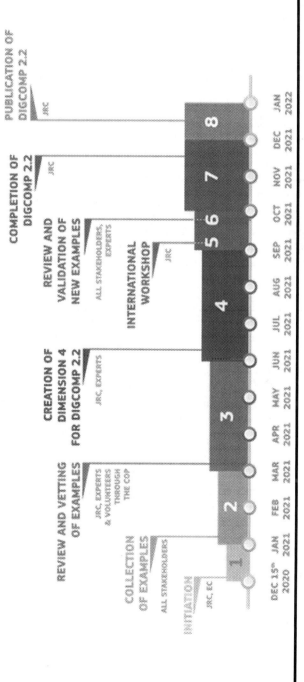

Figure 3.2 The process to finalize the DigComp 2.2 update (Vuorikari, Kluzer & Punie, 2022, p. 72).

Table 3.1 Process of Selection of KSA for DigComp 2.2 Update

Digital Competence	no. KSA Proposed by Experts (phases 3 and 4)	no. KSA Selected by JRC for Survey Validation (phases 5 and 6)	no. of KSA Selected through Public Validation to DigComp 2.2 (phases 7 and 8)
4.1 – Protecting devices	51	20	14
4.2 – Protecting personal data and privacy	41	20	9
4.3 – Protecting health and well-being	41	21	14
Total	133	61	37

Note: The example of the final statements of DigComp revision indicated in the third column is available on the DigComp 2.2 revision (Vuorikari, Kluzer & Punie, 2022, pp. 35–40).

competence of safety areas (4.1 – protecting devices; 4.2 – protecting personal data and privacy; and 4.3 – protecting health and well-being).

The first part of the survey collects data related to the characterization of the respondent. The second part of the survey measures the clarity of the KSA statement and the level of relevance of the statement with a Likert scale of five points. Each survey includes only 20 statements chosen by the JRC, among all statements collected by the experts through phases three and four (see Table 3.1). Before the online public validation through the surveys on phases five and six, on phases seven and eight only a few were selected to be included in the Digcomp 2.2 update (see Table 3.1).

The survey also collected additional comments about the DigComp 2.2 update, which were useful to rephrase some proposed statements. The survey was filled online by different types of stakeholders, from different countries and organizations across Europe. Despite a limited response, further useful information was gathered.

Regarding indirect documentation techniques, it includes documentary research (selection and analysis of sources and types of documents related to the concepts of safety, security, and well-being) and bibliographic research (bibliographic types and sources also inherent to safety, security analysis), which was analyzed and discussed through the lens of KSA required for all citizens.

3.3.1.3 Research Analysis

Based on the DBR approach, the analysis of the data collected occurs as the data were collected throughout each phase of the study (Plomp, 2013). In this sense, in the analysis and interpretation of the data collected in the questionnaire surveys in phases five and six of the DigComp 2.2 revision (international workshop and review and validation of new examples), the Microsoft Office Excel 365 software was used.

The analyses of those statements to be included in the surveys, and then in the framework, were conducted by the JRC. The JRC chose the framework update upon 9 and 14 ones that were voted the most relevant, analyzing the comments given by the stakeholders, and implementing changes. Second, the JRC checks if the final set has the right properties for a given statement on KSA to include in the framework update. In the next section, the chapter focuses on the discussion of the results achieved update (Vuorikari, Kluzer & Punie, 2022).

3.4 Results and Discussions

The new European DigComp 2.2 well-being Knowledge Skills and Attitudes bring a refreshed and welcome focus on some wider aspects of the digital imperatives of the modern world, namely screen time and balance, and an emphasis on communication, collaboration, managing digital identities, as well as protecting health and well-being (Trindade et al., 2021). Increasing the well-being, resilience, and potential for lifelong learning of students is now a core responsibility for institutions. The ways in which it can develop institutional compassion to promote and enhance the student experience are rapidly gaining traction within the sector.

The European DigComp 2.2 safety security knowledge skills and attitudes bring also a demand that protecting others starts with protecting oneself (Shillair et al., 2015), grounding in different safety and security theories: PMT; STAMP; theory of safety and security (Lukas et al., 2016, Salim & Madnick, 2016; Tsai et al., 2016).

Safety and security statements related to protecting devices and protecting personal data and privacy suggests that safety behavior is motivated by threat and coping appraisals, perceiving vulnerability susceptibility to risks, and the consequences associated with unsafe behaviors (Lukas et al., 2016, Salim & Madnick, 2016; Shillair et al., 2015; Tsai et al., 2016).

The literature related to digital safety and security (Arboledas-Brihuega, 2019; Hall & Watson, 2016; Khalique, 2016; Shillair et al., 2015; Trindade, Balula & Miranda, 2018; Yang & Lee, 2019) offered insights and critical concepts such as encryption; identity theft; risks in digital environments; two-factor authentication; software protection; security measure, and so many others presented in the DigComp 2.2 Framework, to understand and identify threats, analyze risks, and propose the choice method of risk management, and how to overcome them.

The stakeholder's public validation of the KSA collected by the group of experts, excluded some KSA considered, nevertheless by the experts, as important statements that Higher Education institutions should consider in their academic courses, by considering some recommendations that weren't included, evaluated as quite or somewhat relevant by the different type of stakeholders (see Tables 3.2–3.4).

Table 3.2 Examples of Final KSA for Digital Competence 4.1 – Protecting Devices Presented in the Survey Validation and Were Reframed or Excluded from the DigComp Framework 2.2

Type	Nr. Statement	Dimension 4 Statement	Decision Included	Decision Not Included	Decision Included with Arrangements
Knowledge	1	Knows about measures to protect devices (password, fingerprints, encryption) and prevent others (a thief) from having instant access to all data.	X		
	2	Knows that using different strong passwords for different online services is a way to mitigate the negative effects of an account being compromised (hacked).	X		
	3	Aware of the risk of identity theft on the internet, someone commits fraud or other crimes using another person's personal data (digital identity, username) without their permission.			X
	4	Aware of "social engineering" that uses psychological manipulation to obtain confidential information (passwords, pin-codes) from victims or convince them to take a harmful action (execute malicious software).		X	
	5	Understands that IoT applications can be vulnerable to cyberattacks as they require the exchange of data via wireless networks.		X	
	6	Knows that cybercriminals might have several motivations to conduct their unlawful activity (motivated by financial gain, protest, information gathering for spying).		X	

	7	Knows how to make backups and recover digital information and other content (photos, contacts) from a backup.		X
	8	Knows about the importance of keeping the operating system and applications (browser) up to date to fix security vulnerabilities and protect against malicious software (malware).	X	
	9	Knows that a firewall blocks certain kinds of network traffic aiming to prevent a number of different security risks (spam, denial of service, remote logins).	X	
Skills	1	Knows how to adopt proper cyber-hygiene regarding passwords (selecting strong ones difficult to guess) and managing them securely (password manager).	X	
	2	Knows how to activate two-factor authentication for important services.	X	
	3	Acquires digital tools that do not process unnecessarily personal data, check the type of data, and feature an app access on one's mobile phone.		X
	4	Able to encrypt sensitive data stored on personal devices or in a cloud storage.	X	
	5	Can identify the affordances of different data hosting/storing services, file versioning features of cloud storage to revert to previous files in case of corruption or deletion, to compare file versions to one another).		X

(Continued)

Table 3.2 (Continued)

Type	Dimension 4		Decision		
	Nr. Statement	Statement	Included	Not Included	Included with Arrangements
	6	Knows how to install and activate protection software and services (antivirus, anti-malware, firewall) to keep digital content and personal data safe.	X		
	7	Can respond to a security breach (an incident that results in unauthorized access to digital data, applications, networks, or devices), a personal data breach (leakage of their login and passwords), a malware attack (containing viruses), or a malware attack (ransomware).			X
Attitudes	1	Vigilant not to leave computers or mobile devices unattended, for example in public places (in a restaurant, train, car).			X
	2	Weighs the risks and benefits of using biometric identification techniques (fingerprint, face images) as they can affect safety in unintended ways (biometric information can be leaked or hacked and therefore become compromised).			X
	3	Vigilant toward practices to protect devices and digital content as security risks are always evolving.		X	
	4	Keen to consider some self-protective behaviors such as not using open Wi-Fi networks to make financial transactions or online banking.	X		

Note: The table presents the statements included, reframed, and excluded from DigComp 2.2 revision. To see the final statements, consult the Framework DigComp 2.2 update ((Vuorikari, Kluzer & Punie, 2022, p. 36).

Table 3.3 Examples of Final KSA for Digital Competence 4.2 – Protecting Personal Data and Privacy Presented in the Survey Validation and Were Reframed or Excluded from the DigComp Framework 2.2

Type	Nr. Statement	Dimension 4 Statement	Decision Included	Decision Not Included	Decision Included with Arrangements
Knowledge	1	Aware that secure electronic identification is a key feature to enable the safe sharing of personal data with third parties when conducting public sector and private transactions.	X		
	2	Understands the difference between simple, advanced, and qualified electronic signatures (ref to eIDAS).		X	
	3	Aware of possible negative consequences to one's online privacy, personal abuse (negative comments, cyberbullying, trolling or accessing disturbing content), theft of personal data (accounts being hacked), fraud (not receiving goods purchased online or these not being as described), and scams (ransomware, romance/dating, financial scams where victims are tricked into sending money to criminals posing as others).		X	
	4	Aware that a security or privacy incident can result in loss of control, compromise, unauthorized disclosure, acquisition, or access to personal data, in physical or electronic form.		X	

(Continued)

Table 3.3 (Continued)

Type	Nr. Statement	Dimension 4 Statement	Decision Included	Decision Not Included	Decision Included with Arrangements
	5	Knows that, in terms of the EU's GDPR, even voice interactions with a virtual assistant are personal data and can expose users to certain data protection, privacy, and security risks.		X	
	6	Knows that processing of personal data encompasses the collection, recording, organization, storage, and modifications of the data. When an AI system links different pieces of apparently anonymous information together, it can lead to de-anonymization, the identification of a particular person.			X
	7	Recognize that voice assistants, chatbots, smart devices, and other AI technologies that rely on users' biometric and other personal data might process such data more than is necessary (it is considered disproportionate and violates the principle of proportionality specified by GDPR).		X	
	8	Knows that reading a "privacy policy" of an app or service explains what personal data it collects and whether data is shared with third parties possibly including information about the device used (brand of the phone) and geolocation of the user.			X
	9	Knows how to identify suspicious email messages that try to obtain sensitive information (personal data, banking identification) or might contain malware.			X

Skills	1	Knows how to modify privacy settings to keep safe from unwanted contacts (spam texts, emails).	X		
	2	Knows how to apply basic security measures in online payments (never send a scan of credit cards or give the pin code of a debit/payment/credit card).			X
	3	Knows how to use electronic identification for services provided by public authorities or public services, filling in your tax form, applying for social benefits, requesting certificates, and by business sector (banks, transport services, eID validation of an account, on a digital marketplace).			X
	4	Uses digital certificates acquired from certifying authorities (digital certificates for authentication and digital signing stored on national identity cards).			X
	5	If informed by data controllers that there has been a data breach affecting users, act accordingly to take actions to mitigate the impact (change all passwords immediately, not just the one known to be compromised).		X	
	6	Can help mitigate the risks of personal data breaches by expressing concerns to relevant authorities relating to the usage of AI tools that collect data, especially if there is a suspicion that there is a violation of the GDPR or when the company does not make the information available.		X	

(Continued)

Table 3.3 (Continued)

Type	Nr. Statement	Dimension 4 Statement	Included	Not Included	Included with Arrangements
Attitudes	1	Emphasizes the importance of taking a conscious decision whether to share information about private life publicly, considering the risks involved (especially for children) while keeping control of the personal data.		X	
	2	Weighs the benefits and risks before activating a virtual assistant (Siri, Alexa, Cortana, Google Assistant) or smart IoT devices as they can expose personal daily routines.			X
	3	Weighs the benefits and risks before engaging with software that uses biometric data (voice, face images), checking that it complies with GDPR.		X	
	4	Weighs the benefits and risks before allowing third parties to process personal data, recognizes that voice assistants that are connected to smart home devices can give access to the data to third parties (companies, governments, cybercriminals).		X	
	5	Confident in carrying out online transactions after taking appropriate safety and security measures.			Emerged through survey analyses

Note: The table presents the statements included, reframed, and excluded from DigComp 2.2 revision of the protecting personal data and privacy competence. To see the final statements, consult the framework (Vuorikari, Kluzer & Punie, 2022, p. 38).

Table 3.4 Examples of Final KSA for Digital Competence 4.3 – Protecting Health and Well-Being Presented in the Survey Validation and Were Reframed or Excluded from the DigComp Framework 2.2

Type	\multicolumn{2}{c	}{Dimension 4}	\multicolumn{3}{c	}{Decision}
	Nr. Statement	Statement	Included	Not Included	Included with Arrangements
Knowledge	1	Aware of the importance of healthy personal digital balance regarding the use of digital technologies, including non-use as an option. Many different factors in digital life can impact personal health, well-being, and life satisfaction.			X
	2	Knows that some AI-driven applications on digital devices (sensors, wearables, smartphones) can support the adoption of healthy behaviors through monitoring and alerting about health conditions (physical, emotional, psychological). However, the decisions proposed could also have potential negative impacts on physical or mental health.			X
	3	Knows that for many digital health applications, there are no official licensing procedures like is the case in classical medicine.		X	
	4	Knows signs of digital addictions (loss of control, withdrawal symptoms, dysfunctional mood regulation) and that they can cause psychological and physical harm.			X
	5	Understands that remote online occupation (work or study) has benefits (flexibility, location independence) as well as risks (lack of in-person social contact, loss of clear boundaries between work and leisure).		X	

(Continued)

Table 3.4 (Continued) Examples of Final KSA for Digital Competence 4.3 – Protecting Health and Well-Being Presented in the Survey Validation and Were Reframed or Excluded from the DigComp Framework 2.2

Type	Dimension 4		Decision		
	Nr. Statement	Statement	Included	Not Included	Included with Arrangements
	6	Understands that cyberbullying is bullying with the use of digital technologies, a repeated behavior aimed at scaring, angering, or shaming those who are targeted.	X		
	7	Knows that the "online disinhibition effect" is the lack of restraint one feels when communicating online in comparison to communicating in person. This can lead to an increased tendency toward online flaming and inappropriate behaviors.	X		
	8	Knows that vulnerable groups (children), those with lower social skills and lack of in-person social support are at a higher risk of victimization in digital environments (cyberbullying, grooming).			X
	9	Aware that digital upskilling can create access to education and training as well as to job opportunities thus promoting social inclusion.		X	
	10	Aware that digital tools can create new opportunities for participation in society for vulnerable groups (older people, people with special needs), however, they can also contribute to the isolation or exclusion of those who do not use such digital tools.	X		

Skills	1	Able to apply for oneself and others a variety of digital usage monitoring and limitation strategies (delayed availability of devices for children, installing time limitation and filter software, rules, and agreements on screen-free times).			X
	2	Able to gather information about digital self-help health applications for improving physical and/or mental well-being (positive and negative effects) before deciding whether to use them or not.			X
	3	Knows how to recognize embedded user experience techniques designed to be manipulative and/or to weaken one's ability to be in control of decisions (make users spend more time on online activities, encourage consumerism).	X		
	4	Knows how to create a healthy digital space for remote work or study, correct position of chair, table, keyboard, mouse, monitor(s), and light; selection of good usability and accessibility options for a healthy interaction; keeping clear boundaries between work, non-digital breaks, and leisure.		X	
	5	Can apply and follow protection strategies to fight online victimization (block receiving further messages from sender(s), do not react/respond; forward or save messages only as evidence to legal procedures, deleting negative messages to avoid repeated viewing).	X		

(Continued)

Table 3.4 (Continued)

Type	Nr. Statement	Dimension 4 Statement	Decision Included	Decision Not Included	Decision Included with Arrangements
	6	Able to decide whether to deal with an online problem situation alone or to recruit professional or informal help.		X	
	7	Can select digital content and solutions that enhance usability and user engagement, chooses culturally relevant content in local languages, easy-to-access material for low-literate users, and applies captions for videos.		X	
Attitudes	1	Assumes responsibility for protecting personal and collective health and safety when evaluating the effects of medical products and services online as there are dangers in trusting and sharing false information on health.	X		
Attitudes	2	Inclined to focus on physical and mental well-being, and avoid negative impacts of digital media such as overuse, addiction, and compulsive behavior.	X		
Attitudes	3	Wary of the reliability of recommendations (are they by a reputable source in healthcare/well-being) and their intentions (do they really help the user vs. encourage to use the device more to be exposed to advertising).	X		
Attitudes	4	Being willing not to harm others online.		X	

Note: The table presents the statements included, reframed, and excluded from DigComp 2.2 revision for protecting health and well-being competence. To see the final statements, consult the framework (Vuorikari, Kluzer & Punie, 2022, p. 40).

The excluded statements related to protecting devices are crucial to informing Higher Education students in the knowledge field about "social engineering" that uses psychological manipulation to obtain confidential information, the vulnerability of IoT (Internet of Things) applications to cyberattacks as they require the exchange of data via wireless networks; the motivations behind cyber criminals' attacks; and the importance of digital information and other content recovery. In the skilled scope, affordances of different data hosting/storing services, still equally relevant, concerning the risks, and the consequences associated with unsafe behaviors (Lukas et al., 2016; Salim & Madnick, 2016; Shillair et al., 2015; Tsai et al., 2016).

The same is applied to all KSA statements of protecting personal data and privacy competence, not included in the DigComp Revision 2.2 (see Table 3.3).

Of the whole 20 KSA statements linked to protecting health and well-being, these were excluded: three knowledge statements; four skills statements, and one attitude statement (see Table 3.4). Nevertheless, the limit of sentences that can be included in the DigComp 2.2 update, and those that the public found quite or somewhat relevant, the experts also considered important the statements that didn't get much approval, considering the necessity to increase well-being and resilience of Higher Education students (McDougall et al., 2018; Gilbert, 2018, 2020).

3.5 Conclusions

The European DigComp Revision 2.2 plays a significant role in informing the citizens of Europe about the key areas where technologies are impacting their lives (Trindade et al., 2021). But information needs to be underpinned by evidence and education, and the experts of DigComp revision of safety, security, and well-being scope recommend that **Higher Institutions** consider the ways in which the revised framework can be embedded within their own policies and contexts. The key areas where this overlaps with the student experience are where young people start to explore, experiment, and seek out others in both online and offline contexts. Thus, the work and focus on lifelong learning, with the screen balance model recommended for educators, designers, and all tasked with the safety of young people flows through to **safeguarding and security, and digital health and well-being**. The group of expert conclusions considers how the European DigComp 2.2 can be framed for post-tertiary education.

The evolving concept of lifelong learning echoes calls from economies seeking to equip their graduates with skills for jobs that potentially do not yet exist. Employers forecast the speed and acceleration of the requirements for enhanced digital skills over the 2016–2030 period (Bughin, 2018). Nevertheless, the less participation of the stakeholders in the validation of the statements proposed by the JRC to include in the DigComp 2.2 (only 68 stakeholders participate globally in the three surveys launched), and also the necessity to significantly reduce the proposer KSA collected by the group of experts, the given statements presented in Framework 2.2 presents a kick start to rethink the KSA for safety, security, and well-being behaviors taking in account in a daily basis.

The demand of goal four (quality in education) of the UNSDGs advocates, among others, equal access for all men and women to affordable, quality technical, vocational, and Higher Education, including university. In this regard, issues related to digital safety, security, and well-being also require identifying the right KSA to be promoted in Higher Education institutions to ensure access to inclusive, quality, and equitable education, and promote lifelong learning opportunities for all.

Indeed, without undervaluing the other areas of competence in the DigComp 2.2 Framework, which are equally important and necessary, the experts believe that the area of safety presents itself as the foundation for ensuring that the other competences in the framework are fully achieved. Without a conscious understanding of the role of safety, security, and well-being in today's contexts, civil participation in society is compromised by the different threats and attacks that may arise from the adoption of inappropriate behavior in different contexts of the academic community.

Future research of the work presented could be related to the implementation and development of the KSA among Higher Education institutions learners and staff and analyze the impact of the KSA acquired by the Higher Education community to increase their adequate response to different challenges of nowadays digital evolution.

This study offers insights and illumination into hitherto hidden areas of policy creation, through making explicit the working practices and ongoing theory development undertaken by the safety, security, and well-being of the experts group. It suggests ways in which those responsible for the safety, security, and well-being of the academic staff can frame their work and makes a significant contribution to considerations those working in Higher Education Institutions need to be aware of for keeping their students, teachers, and the whole academic community safe and well in the world, becoming more and more digital. A proposed new model that identifies the pivot points between benefit and risk and can be utilized by Higher Education senior policy strategists, academics, European citizen groups as well as individuals in considering ongoing digital access, health, well-being, safety, security, and sustainability in implementing policy and practice.

Acknowledgments

We would like to acknowledge the JRC leadership, and our working group colleagues, as well as the Digital Community of Practice.

Notes

1 Literacy competence; multilingual competence; mathematical competence and competence in science; technology and engineering; personal, social and learning to learn competence; citizenship competence; entrepreneurship competence; cultural awareness and expression competence.

2 Information Literacy; data literacy; artificial intelligence; the Internet of Things; programming; privacy and personal data; consumer perspective/transaction services; creating multimedia/social media content; digital and the environment; cross-thematic content; digital accessibility.

References

Al-Tammemi, A. A. B., Akour, A., & Alfalah, L. (2020). Is it just about physical health? An online cross-sectional study exploring the psychological distress among university students in Jordan in the midst of COVID-19 pandemic. *Frontiers in Psychology*, 3083. https://doi.org/10.3389/fpsyg.2020.562213

Anderson, J. & Rainie, L. (2018). *The Future of Well-Being in a Tech-Saturated World*, Pew Research Center: Internet, Science & Tech. United States of America. Retrieved from https://policycommons.net/artifacts/617389/the-future-of-well-being-in-a-tech-saturated-world/1598187/ on 22 Jun 2023. CID: 20.500.12592/wswbkg.

Anderson, J., Rainie, L., & Luchsinger, A. (2018). Artificial intelligence and the future of humans. *Pew Research Center*, 10, 12.

Arboledas-Brihuega, D. (2019). A new character-level encryption algorithm: How to implement cryptography in an ICT classroom. *Journal of Technology and Science Education*, 9(3), 257–268.

Bitzer, E., & Schwendemann, H. (2020). The significance of health literacy for public health and health promotion. In Soboga-Nunes, L. A., Bittlingmayer, U. H., Okan, O., & Sahrai, D. (Eds), *New approaches to health literacy, linking different perspectives* (pp. 83–97). Springer. https://doi.org/10.1007/978-3-658-30909-1_5

Bleckmann, P., Holley, D., & Bitzer, E. (2021, September 7–9). *Digital balance literacy: A model for supporting well-being in the digital era*. [Conference Session]. Association for Learning Technology, Oxfordshire. Retrieved from https://www.youtube.com/watch?v=eyLJ_AzsBgU

Bleckmann, P., & Mößle, T. (2014). Position on problem dimensions and strategies for preventing problematic use of screen media. *SUCHT*, 60(4), 235–247.

Bughin, J., Hazan, E., Lund, S., Dahlström, P., Wiesinger, A., & Subramaniam, A. (2018). Skill shift: Automation and the future of the workforce. *McKinsey Global Institute*, 1, 3–84.

Carretero, S., Vuorikari, R., & Punie, Y. (2017). *The digital competence framework for citizens with eight proficiency levels and examples of use*. (Report No. EUR 28558 EN). https://doi.org/10.2760/38842

Cheung, Y. L. E. E. (2018). *Measurement of atmospheric neutrino oscillation parameters using three years of IceCube-DeepCore data*. Digital Repository at the University of Maryland.

Danso, M., Bailey, P., & Beetham, H. (2013). *Digital literacies: Joined-up approaches to digital literacy development to support student achievement and employability*. United Kingdom: Jisc.

Dede, C. (2010). Comparing frameworks for 21st century skills. *Rethinking How Students Learn*, 20(2010), 51–76.

El Asame, M., & Wakrim, M. (2018). Towards a competency model: A review of the literature and the competency standards. *Education and Information Technologies*, 23, 225–236. https://doi.org/10.1007/s10639-017-9596-z

European Commission, Directorate-General for Education, Youth, Sport and Culture. (2019). *Key competences for lifelong learning*. Publications Office.

Ferrari, A. (2013). *DIGCOMP: A framework for developing and understanding digital competence in Europe*. (Report No. EUR 26035 EN ISBN). https://doi.org/10.2788/52966

General Assembly (2015). Transforming our world: the 2030 Agenda for Sustainable Development.

González-Salamanca, J. C., Agudelo, O. L., & Salinas, J. (2020). Key competences, education for sustainable development and strategies for the development of 21st century skills. A systematic literature review. *Sustainability*, 12(24), 2–17.

Grubic, N., Badovinac, S., & Johri, A. M. (2020). Student mental health in the midst of the COVID-19 pandemic: A call for further research and immediate solutions. *International Journal of Social Psychiatry*, 66(5), 517–518.

Hall, G., & Watson, E. (2016). *Hacking: Computer hacking, security testing, penetration testing, and basic security*. CreateSpace Independent Publishing Platform.

Holley, D., Quinney, B. & Goldsmith, A. (2020). The mechanics of digital well-being in higher education: Beyond google garage. ALDinHE Conference 7–9 April [Online].

Khalique, A. (2016). A review on single sign on enabling technologies and protocols. *International Journal of Computer Applications*, 151(11), 18–25.

Lee, P. S., Leung, L., Lo, V., Xiong, C., & Wu, T. (2011). Internet communication versus face-to-face interaction in quality of life. *Social Indicators Research*, 100(3), 375–389.

Leung, L., & Lee, P. S. N. (2011). Impact of Internet literacy, Internet addiction symptoms, and Internet activities on academic performance. *Social Science Computer Review*, 30(4), 403–418. https://doi.org/10.1177/0894439311435217

Lucas, M., & Moreira, A. (2017). *Quadro europeu de competência digital para cidadãos com oito níveis de proficiência e exemplos de uso*. Aveiro: UA Editora.

Lukas, M., Rohn, H., Lettenmeier, M., Liedtke, C., & Wiesen, K. (2016). The nutritional footprint – integrated methodology using environmental and health indicators to indicate potential for absolute reduction of natural resource use in the field of food and nutrition. *Journal of Cleaner Production*, 132, 161–170. https://doi.org/10.1016/j.jclepro.2015.02.070

McDougall, J., Readman, M., & Wilkinson, P. (2018). The uses of (digital) literacy. *Learning, media and technology*, 1–17. https://doi.org/10.1080/17439884.2018.1462206

Mckenney, S., & Reeves, T. C. (2014). *Educational Design Research*. https://doi.org/10.1007/978-1-4614-3185-5_11

Newman, T., Beetham, H., & Knight, S. (2018). Digital experience insights survey 2018: Findings from students in UK further and higher education. *Jisc, Bristol*, England.

Norman, C. D. & Skinner, H. A. (2006). eHealth literacy: Essential skills for consumer health in a networked World. *Journal of Medical Internet Research*, 8(2), 1–10.

Pangrazio, L. & Selwyn, N. (2019). Personal data literacies: A critical literacies approach to enhancing understandings of personal digital data. *New Media & Society*, 21(2), 419–437.

Plomp, T. (2013). Educational design research: an introduction. In T. Plomp & N. Nienke (Eds.), *Educational design research: Part A: An introduction* (pp. 11–51). https://doi.org/10.1007/978-1-4614-3185-5_11

Salim, H. & Madnick, S. (2016). Cyber safety: A systems theory approach to managing cyber security Risks – applied to TJX cyber-attack. 1–16. http://web.mit.edu/smadnick/www/wp/2016-09.pdf

Shillair, R., Cotten, S. R., Tsai, S. H., Alhabash, S., LaRose, R., & Rifon, N. J. (2015). Online safety begins with you and me: Convincing Internet users to protect themselves. *Computers in Human Behavior*, 48, 199–207.

Tamar, S (2017). Self-Tracking for health and the quantified self: Re-articulating autonomy, solidarity, and authenticity in an age of personalized healthcare. *Philosophy & Technology*, 30(1), 93–121.

Trindade, A., Balula, A., & Miranda, G. (2018). Key processes for the construction of an Informal guide to develop digital competences: Support resettled refugees in active job search. In *INTED2018 Proceedings: 12th International Technology, Education and Development Conference*, Valencia, Spain, 2302–2309. https://doi.org/10.21125/inted.2018.0437

Trindade, A. R. (2020). *Desenvolvimento da competência digital com redes sociais online: Apoio a refugiados reinstalados na procura de emprego* (Doctor's Thesis, Universidade de Aveiro).

Trindade, A. R., Bleckmann, P., Holley, D., & Simunovic, D. E. (2021, May 18). *EU Digicomp framework review: WP 7 safety and well-being findings*. [Conference Session]. All Digital, Brussels. Retrieved from http://shorturl.at/vxN27

Tsai, H., Jiang, M., Alhabash, S., Larose, R., Rifon, N., & Cotten, S. (2016). Understanding online safety behaviors: A protection motivation theory perspective. *Computers & Security*, 59, 138–150.

Tuckman, B. W. (2012). *Manual de investigação em educação: Metodologia para conceber e realizar o processo de investigação científica*. Lisboa: Calouste Gulbenkian.

United Nations. (2015). Transforming our world: The 2030 agenda for sustainable development. Resolution adopted by the general assembly on 25 September 2015. Retrieved from https://sustainabledevelopment.un.org/post2015/transformingourworld

Urrila, A. S. et al. (2017). Sleep habits, academic performance, and the adolescent brain structure. *Scientific Reports*, 7(1), 1–9.

Van der Vaart, R. & Drossaert, C. (2017). Development of the digital health literacy instrument: Measuring a broad spectrum of health 1.0 and health 2.0 skills. *Journal of Medical Internet Research*, 19(1), 1–13.

Vuorikari, R., Kluzer, S., & Punie, Y., DigComp 2.2: The Digital Competence Framework for Citizens - With new examples of knowledge, skills and attitudes, EUR 31006 EN, Publications Office of the European Union, Luxembourg, 2022, ISBN 978-92-76-48882-8.

Wysokińska-Senkus, A. (2020). The concept of safety and security education in the context of sustainability. *Sustainability*, 12(5022), 2–16. https://doi.org/10.3390/su12125022

Yang, H. & Lee, H. (2019). Understanding user behavior of virtual personal assistant devices. *Information Systems and e-Business Management*, 17(1), 65–87.

Chapter 4

Digital Technologies as a Key Driver of Sustainable Global Higher Education

Said Jaboob, Mohammad Soliman,
Balaji Dhanasekaran, and Samskrati Gulvady
University of Technology and Applied Sciences, Salalah, Oman

Contents

4.1 Introduction	78
4.2 Sustainable Global Higher Education	80
4.2.1 United Nations' Role in Sustainable Global Higher Education	82
4.3 Digital Technologies in Higher Education	83
4.3.1 Digital Technologies Used in Learning Management	84
4.3.2 Digital Technologies Used in Teaching	85
4.3.3 Digital Technologies Used in Labs	88
4.3.4 Digital Technologies Used in Assessments	89
4.3.5 Digital Technologies Used in Group Activities	90
4.3.6 Digital Technologies Used in Academic Advising	91
4.4 Conclusions	91
References	92

DOI: 10.1201/9781003424543-5

4.1 Introduction

Digital technologies have become an integral part of today's organizations – be they industrial or educational. A literature review prepared by the Scottish Government (2015) indicates that when digital tools are used effectively, they influence interactive, collaborative, critical thinking, and leadership skills. Companies consider such skills vital. Accessibility to digital tools and resources are not the only factors that shape the effective usage of digital technology. Other significant factors like skill development (e.g., hands-on training, relevant support) for the teaching faculty also need to be taken into consideration. Goulart et al. (2022) express a similar need of the hour as the technology-related job market is experiencing substantial transformations owing to the technological advancement pushing the industry to aspire for "skilled professionals". Hence it becomes imperative for the academia to provide the appropriate skills (i.e. technological) and prepare future employees to make them market-proficient. According to Cabero-Almenara (2022), the coronavirus contagion has made a colossal shift in the domain of education, calling for updating and the addition of digital technologies, especially for differently abled students. Coldwell-Neilson (2020) discusses the prominence of the digital native youth, being digitally literate – where knowledge extends beyond technology usage; it is the proficiency to perform judiciously and efficiently in a digitally enriched milieu. Therefore, digital literacy is a "mindset and attitude, not just a skill set" (p. 18). Frankiewicz and Chamorro-Premuzic (2020) reiterate that as people need to acclimatize themselves to the futuristic digital reformation, the concern about human resources is higher than about technology.

Global sustainability is hugely influenced by higher education institutions (HEIs). According to Žalėnienė and Pereira (2021), HEIs are the key agents to educate prospective leaders thereby contributing to an affirmative enactment of the Sustainable Development Goals (SDGs) put forth by the United Nations (UN). Achieving the UN's aspirational SDGs demands varied efforts from across the sectors, that include HEIs. In this vein, Utama et al. (2018) propose five strategies to the HEIs to augment the targeted SDGs, by improving a) the quality of higher education; b) higher education equity; c) sanitation and environment; d) research and innovation; and e) global partnership. The report of United Nations University (Vaughter 2018) reiterates that decision-makers within governmental ministries as well as within the HEIs must engage themselves in streamlining and coordinating communication that incorporate comprehensively holistic concerns related to sustainable progress. Therefore, it recommends the following: a) creation of direct communication channels with the governmental bodies; b) emphasis on educators' competency building to assimilate sustainable development in their chosen areas; and c) confirm skill development of graduates in order to fathom sustainable development from a multi-disciplinary panoramic and holistic perspective. Filho et al. (2019) recognize that "education" is a distinct goal (SDG 4) which solicits active participation from universities, while others relate directly to teaching and learning.

Over the last decades, higher education management has paid more attention to sustainability. As a result, new educational programs, research institutes, academic journals, and scientific production evolved in higher education, all with an emphasis on sustainability (Figueiró and Raufflet 2015; Wang et al. 2013). In doing so, HEIs are expected to create an environment that is conducive to learning and encourages innovation and cultural diversity, promote the institution's specified basic and essential values, and provide adequate career development programs for their internal stakeholders including students and employees (Soliman et al. 2021a). Indeed, these transformations could be substantially achieved by the effective usage of digital technologies which are extensively adopted in teaching and learning-related activities, including classes, discussions, and assessment methods (e.g., laboratories, projects, group-based work, individual-associated work, exercises, and presentations) that do impact a student's academic progress and achievement in an HEI (Costa et al. 2022).

In this vein, it is clear that with the COVID-19 pandemic's breakout, the majority of countries have adopted a number of proactive measures to curb the virus's spread (Hassan and Soliman 2021) in all sectors including the higher education sector. As a result, HEIs were being asked to deal effectively with these circumstances, which are leading to a rapid shift to online teaching or emergency remote-linked teaching (DeCoito and Estaiteyeh 2022). Following these procedures, teachers and students in HEIs have shifted their interaction from face-to-face to online contexts, such as teleworking/distance teaching and other academic-related activities (Soliman et al. 2021b). To this end, the crucial role of digital technologies has greatly grown in HEIs, as a key component of the success and efficacy of the teaching and learning process, as well as the associated duties and activities carried out within those institutions. Based on the foregoing, a vital question has been raised, which is: *How to benefit from digital technologies in achieving sustainability of higher education?*

Considering the aforementioned discussion, the aims of the current research are to explain how digital technologies could be used as an effective tool to ensure sustainable global higher education. To be more specific, this work is to highlight the adoption of digital technologies in teaching- and learning-connected activities (i.e., learning management, teaching-linked activities, labs, assessment methods, group-based activities, and academic advising) at the UTAS-Salalah, a branch of UTAS, one of the biggest universities in the Gulf Cooperation Council (GCC) countries, and in Oman in particular.

The remainder of this chapter will be structured as follows. In the next section, sustainable global higher education will be provided by focusing on the role of the UNs in sustainable global higher education. The third section will discuss digital technologies in HE by demonstrating the digital technologies adoption and usage in teaching and learning-related activities at the UTAS-Salalah, Oman; including the usage of digital technologies in learning management, teaching-associated activities, labs, students' assessments, group activities, and academic advising. The last section will depict the conclusions of this book chapter.

4.2 Sustainable Global Higher Education

In their study, Krstić et al. (2020) elucidate that sustainable development comprises economic activities that are coherent with natural resource conservation along with protecting and improving the ecosystem, which is achievable not only by executing novel technological resolutions, political regulations, or financial instruments – rather it calls for a transformation in our thoughts and actions. Such transformations are dependent on quality education and learning at various levels and social contexts. Thus, the goal of education that converges on sustainable development enhances access to primary, secondary, and higher education, while facilitating learners to alleviate their behavior, skills, and knowledge that will be relevant in the present as well the future.

Mohamed et al. (2022) recognize that the development of humans involves a multifactorial amalgamation of societal, financial, and electoral aspects to enhance innovation and individual abilities. Apart from health upheaval, the COVID-19 pandemic brought with it manifold transformation in the education landscape too. Hence there is a pressing demand to further enrich the digital sustainable development in higher education teaching. This brings magnanimous challenges to the HEIs that need to be confronted in order to be the harbinger in adopting and amplifying the digital technological transformation to reinforce sustainable development (Sá and Serpa 2020). The global pandemic caused a huge shift from onsite to virtual teaching–learning, however, being a digital native proved beneficial in annihilating the challenges caused (Aristovnik et al. 2020). This substantiates the significance of being technologically literate to foster sustainable development in the spectrum of HEIs. Veidemane (2022) stresses the increasing importance of identifying indicators to measure institutional contribution in an effective manner (e.g., Education for Sustainable Development) as HEIs endeavor to indoctrinate sustainable development principles. It is essential to adopt effective approaches to sustain education while activating distinct, harmonizing, and assimilative actions to counter such crises. According to Krstić et al. (2020), sustainable development is not confined to a "need", but rather has become a "necessity" brought about by the pandemic crisis. It is noteworthy to discuss the role of social media usage in sustainably managing higher education, especially during global health crises (Al-Youbi et al. 2020). As shown in Figure 4.1, their study assessed the various strategies to sustain education (at King Abdulaziz University, Saudi Arabia) and proposed an organizational outline that integrates the following pillars, namely: governance; resilience; utilization; decision-making capability; and institutional strategy (p. 17) for calculative implementation of social media.

The development and transformation taking place in the sphere of higher education can be supported by Graves' model of systemic development (1974). The Graves' Model is a unique instrument to develop magnificent abilities among individuals, groups, institutions, or countries. It further elucidates the transformations

Digital Technologies: Driver of Sustainable Higher Education ■ 81

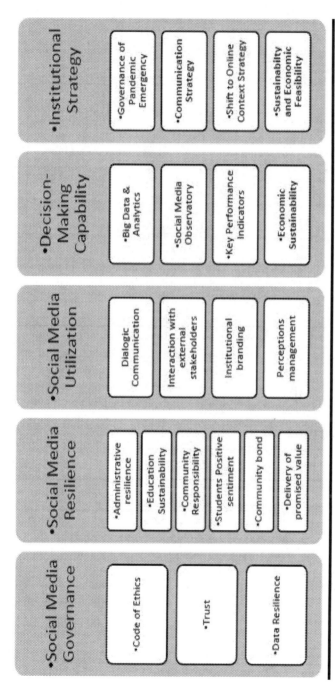

Figure 4.1 The KAU pandemic framework of leveraging social media in sustainable crisis management of HEIs.

Source: Al-Youbi et al. 2020.

taking place in relation to values, understanding, and behavior in humankind's cultural history, and the opportunities to predict future developments, with a positive backing. This model is concerned with the developing progressive competence of individuals on various levels. Giesenbauer and Müller-Christ (2020, p. 21) offer two ways based on Graves' Model to handle complexity and meet issues associated with sustainable development: a) Promote the overall systemic development of a specific HEI by gradually involving different stakeholders and emphasizing co-creative collaboration, and b) Take part in inter-organizational networks to get ideas for addressing difficult problems. Abad-Segura et al. (2020) indicated that keywords like "sustainability", "sustainable development", "higher education", "innovation", and "technology" were trending in global scientific research throughout the period of 1986–2019 as a result of the changes brought about by new digital technologies.

4.2.1 United Nations' Role in Sustainable Global Higher Education

Goal 4 of the UNSDGs calls for guaranteeing inclusive and equitable quality education and promoting opportunities for lifelong learning for everyone. In accordance with UN Declaration number 25 (2015), all educational levels, including early childhood, primary, secondary, tertiary, and technical and vocational training, must be inclusive and equitable. In addition, everyone should have access to opportunities for lifelong learning that would enable them to gain the knowledge and skills necessary to take advantage of opportunities and to participate fully in society, regardless of their sex, age, race, or ethnicity, as well as persons with disabilities, migrants, indigenous peoples, children, and youth, especially those in vulnerable situations. In order to enable countries to benefit from the demographic dividend, the declaration further states the attempt to provide children and youth with a caring environment for the extensive development of their rights and talents.

In the United Nations' "Higher Education Sustainability Initiative", the role of higher education in successful holistic recuperation and marching forward to the 2030 Agenda for Sustainable Development was highlighted (UN 2022). It was observed that if the modus operandi of teaching and learning is dynamic, cooperative, and ethical, it is bound to be effective while considering the responsibility of faculty as "managers" to construct and reconstruct students' knowledge. This would be encouraged via universal citizenship and obligation.

It is observed that skill deficit causes a barrier to the efficient usage of Information Communication Technology (ICT) use. A UN report (2022) states that during 2017–2020, more than 70% of individuals in only 10% of countries could carry out one of the basic activities like emailing with an attachment. Furthermore, over 40% of people in only 15% of countries had common skills like preparing a presentation using a relevant software. This illustrates that in spite of advancements, discrepancies in digital know-how are still surviving.

The SDGs must be supported by the worldwide network of higher education, according to the British Council Report (2021). Higher education prepares future leaders and professionals who will be in high demand to tackle regional and global problems. By preparing teachers, conducting research, and offering direction in the field of school teaching, HEIs are crucial for the entire educational system. In addition to providing data and guidance on policy, higher education also helps policymakers come up with creative solutions to larger societal problems. In order to address the sustainable growth and development agenda, which is frequently framed with the 17 Sustainable Development Goals (SDGs) of the UN, higher education is essential. (p. 34).

Thus, it becomes quintessential for the HEIs to recognize and identify their roles in driving the processes toward a sustainable present and future to achieve the goals put forth for sustainable global higher education. Along with the HEIs, the commitment of all concerned patrons will be a value addition to the sustainable initiatives.

Sustainability practices in higher education sphere demand thoughtful intervention due to their primary phase. Xiong and Mok (2020) reflect that decision-makers in HEIs are contemplating various pertinent approaches for assimilating sustainability in their curriculum, everyday practices, and policies. They observed that in such a scenario, social or environmental accounting or sustainability accounting is a novel management tool that is being adopted by various organizations including higher education. HEIs perceive sustainable development from two directions: a) promoting education for sustainable development; and b) introducing dynamic policies to accomplish this objective (Brusca et al. 2018). Therefore, sustainability education intends to nurture potential experts, leaders, and teachers to sustainably develop our future societies, by awakening this knowledge among the community by engaging them in various activities. HEIs also practice in-campus activities to accomplish sustainability goals like developing "green" or eco-friendly campuses (Xiong and Mok 2020). Vilalta (2018) stresses the role of HEIs as "catalysts of change on a local, regional and international scale" for developing public policy and its mechanisms, namely: technology, applied science, and social innovation). In this vein, Grau (2018) envisions a university as an "inescapable social force for good" that explores the pressing needs of our local community and the challenges facing the global society. He considers this as a major challenge for global universities, where they can endeavor to become a conscientiousness "global university".

4.3 Digital Technologies in Higher Education

Digital technologies have started their impact on the educational realm for more than five epochs, i.e., since the electronic era started. The supremacy of digital technologies increased when the Internet began to be part of people's lives. The stakeholders of higher education have perceived this since the genesis of e-learning.

Digital technologies imprinted its usage as a supplementary tool in face-to-face teaching also. For example, the lectures have started using digital tools like OHP in face-to-face teaching. Digital tools have almost replaced traditional face-to-face teaching tools like blackboards, chalks, etc., with smart boards, projectors, etc., for more than two decades. With the evolution of MOOCs, online degrees have started utilizing digital technologies in all precincts of teaching and learning. Digital technologies were supplementary tools for face-to-face teaching till 2019. Dhanasekaran and Malathi (2022) specified that the pandemic has changed the facade of teaching and learning completely and has become part and parcel of classroom teaching also. In this section, we have discussed a few of the popular digital technologies used in various traits of teaching and learning in higher education.

4.3.1 Digital Technologies Used in Learning Management

The ICT (Information and Communication Technology) or DTC (Digital Technology in the Classroom) are the broader areas of Learning management tools. Initially, it was used as a tool for sharing the teaching materials online with the students instead of using CD-ROM or DVD for distributing the materials. Cambridgeinternatrional.org (2017) specified in their research article that the technology has changed a lot and it evolved as Virtual Learning Environment (VLE) over the years. The University of Technology and Applied Sciences (UTAS) (CAS campuses) are using Blackboard as VLE. All the teaching and academic activities are integrated into this tool. It is used by the teachers throughout the semester even during the normal classroom teaching. The other campuses of UTAS (CoT campuses) are using Moodle as VLE. The teaching fraternity is using these web-based technologies for course materials sharing, announcements, forums for discussions, conducting quizzes, marks announcements, assignment handing over tools and plagiarism checking, etc. Based on Dhanasekaran et al. (2019) the above-mentioned technologies became very essential and in Oman, all the Higher education institutes are having VLE tools as a key tool for teaching and learning. The blackboard software in UTAS is managed by the Learning Resource Center (LRC). The LRC creates courses with the lecturer and students' detail at the beginning of each semester. The lecturers and students can log in to the Blackboard with their credentials to access the course page. The lecturers keep all the course materials of various types (text, video, audio, web link) in the Blackboard. The students can either download the content or they can access it online anywhere anytime. The lecturers intensively use this tool for making announcements, intimating tasks of that week, discussions through forums, etc. Assessments of many types like quizzes, assignments, tests, surveys, self-assessments, etc., can be conducted using Blackboard. Blackboard has the capability of checking plagiarism and marking the assessment fully or partially. The teachers can announce the results in a secure way through the grade center. Figure 4.2 is showing the blackboard content page which displays the variety of materials that are shared with the students in UTAS.

Digital Technologies: Driver of Sustainable Higher Education ■ 85

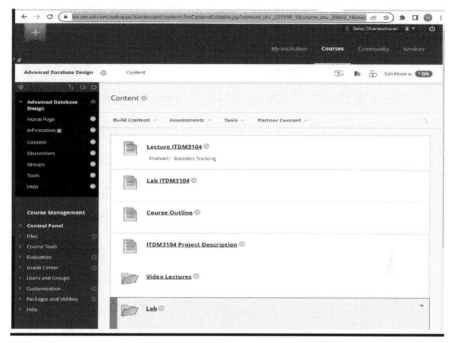

Figure 4.2 Screenshot of a content page of Blackboard in UTAS – Salalah.

The UTAS always encourages the teaching fraternity to use digital technologies which are more effective and convenient for their teaching. There are many lecturers using Google Classroom as an alternative tool for Blackboard or used along with the Blackboard. Google Classroom is more convenient for the students since they are familiar with the Google applications. Since the capability of Google classroom is less compared to the Blackboard, the layout and options are simple and user-friendly. Figure 4.3 is the screenshot of the Google Classroom used in UTAS, IT department.

A few other popular learning management systems are listed below:

1. Mindflash
2. Rippling
3. MasterStudy WordPress LMS
4. SkyPrep
5. Schoology
6. TalentLMS, etc. (softwaretestinghelp.com, 2022)

4.3.2 Digital Technologies Used in Teaching

The classroom teaching part in higher education was the one impacted first by digital technologies. The lecturers started using OHPs, projectors, slide projectors, etc., in

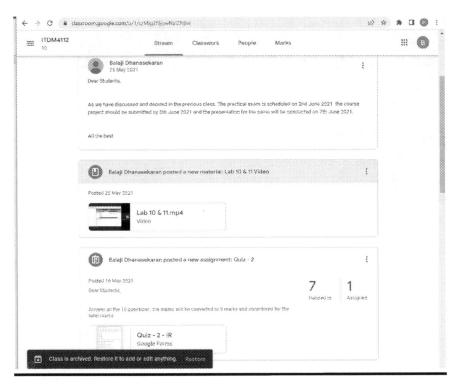

Figure 4.3 Google classroom.

the mid-1970s. The digital technologies adopted by the distance learning program made it a key tool for teaching and learning. The video recordings of the lectures were made available to the students online or through digital media. The library of the HEI became digitalized in the 1980s. Nowadays, classrooms are filled with many digital tools like smart boards, projectors, BYOD (Bring Your Own Device), Personal Learning Networks (WhatsApp, Twitter, Facebook, Instagram groups), and LMSs. The LMS are playing the role of an online content-sharing tool. This issue was discussed in detail in the previous section. The more visual the materials are, the more interactive and dynamic they will be for use in the learning process in higher education. Hence, the lecturers usually put more effort into making their materials more attractive and presentable. Meeting software like Google Meet, Skype, Zoom, WebEx, and other online meeting apps played a major role in delivering the content during the pandemic. These meeting apps are also having options like video recording, jam board as a whiteboard, screen sharing options, attendance recording options, chatting facility, and many other facilities. These options made the classes more interactive and interesting. The lecturers used the digital pad for explaining the concepts by writing on it.

The universities offering courses in MOOC are having dedicated teams for preparing the video lectures. The research paper of Dhanasekaran et al. (2015) specified

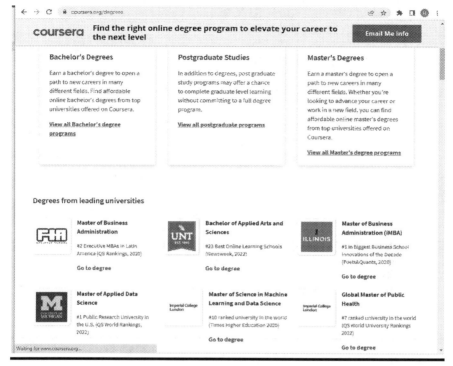

Figure 4.4 Coursera.com offered degree page.

that these video lectures are interactive and also embedded with the assessments (quizzes). The famous MOOCs like Coursera, Udacity, Udemy, etc., offer bachelor's and master's degrees through top universities around the world. The short-term courses of these MOOCs are popular and gives a chance to the academicians to share their specialized knowledge through these mediums. The volunteering translation groups of these MOOCs make the materials available in various languages and this attracts students from around the world. Figure 4.4 is the screenshot of Coursera with a list of a few degrees offered by the universities. The teaching fraternity uses a few software like Loom, Screencase-O-Matic, QuickTime, etc., for preparing their lecture videos. A few of the lecturers in UTAS are using "Camtasia" software to record the screens during their lectures and prepare video lectures for their students. UTAS has Promethean smart board in the meeting/seminar hall which benefits the lecturers to give interactive classes for the students. The Promethean smart board has the facility to connect with students' smartphones to check students' performance in the class and also helps students to participate in group activities through this smart board.

These smart boards and LMS come with Artificial intelligence capability and give the students and staff a personalized learning experience. The LMSs are also coming with a mobile app version. The mobile app versions help the students to manage their studies with reminders and setting milestones in their learning process.

4.3.3 Digital Technologies Used in Labs

The learning process of lectures and labs is entirely different. The key challenge faced by most lecturers during the pandemic was "how to deliver the lab sessions for the students?". The key challenge is software availability for the students at their home or outside the campus. Monitoring the students' practical work and debugging the errors that happen in the students' terminals is another major challenge faced by the lecturers. The IT lecturers of the UTAS are using remote screen-controlling software like "Teamviewer", "Anydesk", etc. The UTAS labs have "LAN School" software for the students' screen control during the lab sessions. Hence the lecturers were familiar with using these screen-controlling software and quickly adopted it during the pandemic time.

The lecturers made a swift decision to move from the usage of usual software to the Free Open Source Software. Dafalla et al. (2015) mentioned that the lecturers preferred to use simulators instead of using the hardware components in the lab as his research finding. Figures 4.5 and 4.6 are screenshots of the Packet Tracer used by the UTAS students.

Lakshminarayanan et al. (2016) highlighted that the IT lecturers are using online compilers and Oracle repository options for the Database and programming courses lab sessions. The teaching community and students have benefited a lot from the free software provided by major software giants like Oracle. The augmented reality and Digital twin technologies made the learning of any hardware component more realistic is the statement given by Lakshminarayanan et al. (2013).

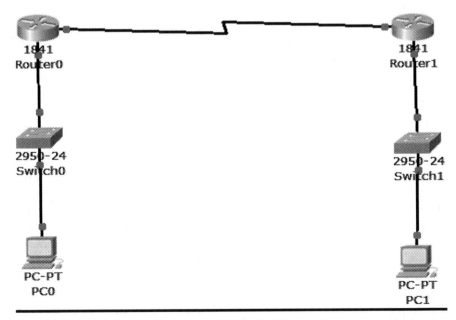

Figure 4.5 LAN network design by using Packet Tracer.

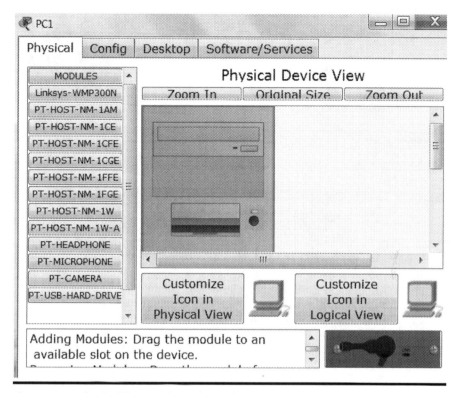

Figure 4.6 Physical layout view of a PC by using Packet Tracer.

There are many other researches going on in bringing real-time experience through these technologies for the students. The cost of using these technologies may come less over the years, even though it is not affordable to the students for their personal learning experience and even for the small institutions at present.

4.3.4 Digital Technologies Used in Assessments

Assessments are the core component and are inevitable in the process of teaching and learning. This helps to assess the student's understanding of the subject. There are many types of assessments like quizzes, assignments, projects, descriptive exams, etc., used by the teaching fraternity. Figure 4.7 shows the assessment cycle of the UTAS.

All the LMS come along with the assessment component. We have already mentioned this in the LMS section. Apart from the formal assessments, lecturers use a few informal assessment techniques to draw the attention of the students during class and to know the understanding level of the topics they are dealing with presently. Such assessments can also be conducted with the LMS assessment component. But there are no marks allotted for these assessments and to avoid confusion of

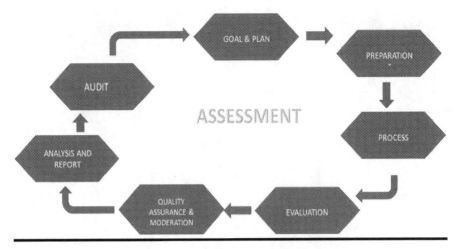

Figure 4.7 Assessment role in teaching and learning.

having many assessments in one place, usually lecturers prefer to use other tools for conducting these informal assessments. In the UTAS, most of the lecturers are using Google Forms and Kahoot for conducting such assessments. There are many other tools available in the market with a minimal cost or almost free. A few such tools are:

1. Socrative
2. Google Forms
3. Mentimeter
4. Pool Everywhere
5. And Kahoot

All the above-mentioned tools help teachers to conduct quizzes with many types of questions like multiple choice questions, fill in the blank, descriptive, questions with pictures and audio, questions with multiple answer options, etc. These tools give various analytical options on the exam results.

4.3.5 Digital Technologies Used in Group Activities

All the above sections related to the digital technologies used in the classrooms are supporting the group activities. Social media is playing a major role in influencing individuals and society. The education domain also takes full advantage of all the group activities and as a group communication tool officially. In UTAS, teachers have WhatsApp groups for their courses to communicate with the students and for general discussions. Lecture-related videos are shared through Facebook, Instagram, Twitter, etc., by the teachers. Students are also feeling more comfortable using these social media tools than the LMS for group activities and group communications.

4.3.6 Digital Technologies Used in Academic Advising

The HEIs are using digital technologies not only for teaching and learning but also for advising the students by mentors. The UTAS uses the Students Information System (SIS) for all registration and other students related administrative activities. The lecturers are using this system extensively for the purpose of advising. Developing a specialized system is also underway in UTAS. In Oman, all the HEIs are having their own academic advising systems. These systems help students in the following ways

1. To register for courses for the current semester
2. To know the remaining courses
3. To know and print their transcript
4. To change the program within the institution
5. To apply for the diploma program
6. To apply for the grievances
7. To print their timetable
8. To change their information in the institution
9. To know their progress in the current semester (attendance etc.,)

4.4 Conclusions

Digital technologies are into every component of teaching and learning. The above sections have highlighted the usage and influence of digital technologies in an HEI. There are many other ways digital technologies are used in the broad and deep in educational field. A few general benefits of digital technologies are listed below:

1. Helping students to learn anywhere and anytime.
2. Helping students to learn in their own phase and students-centred learning experience.
3. Collaborating and communicating among the stakeholders (e.g., management, teachers, and students) are easy and fast.
4. Helping to improve students' performance.
5. Archiving helps to reduce the repeating efforts.
6. Making the learning experience fun.
7. Reducing the knowledge loss in teaching- and learning-connected processes.

With regard to the UTAS, digital technologies are widely applied in teaching and learning at the UTAS. All staff and students at the UTAS are using these technologies in teaching (such as online classes), labs, assessments (such as exams, quizzes, individual case studies, etc.), group-based activities (such as group assignment, presentations, group discussions, etc.), graduation project, and academic advising related activities.

The present research provides various theoretical and managerial contributions and implications. To begin with, this work adds to the extant body of knowledge related to digital technologies in the higher-education-associated context. This chapter also contributes to the existing literature on the role of digital technologies as a main driver of sustainable HE. In addition, the current study provides solid insights and practical guidelines and outstanding evidence on the effective adoption of digital technologies in HEIs by focusing on the application of such technologies in the activities which are related to teaching and learning at one of the biggest universities in the GCC countries and in Oman in particular, namely the UTAS. Providing these practical evidence does provide the management of higher education and concerned stakeholders with clear backgrounds and valuable insights on the efficiency of the process of teaching and learning activities, leading to higher levels of academic achievements on the one hand, and sustainable HE on the other.

References

Abad-Segura, E., González-Zamar, M. D., Infante-Moro, J. C., & Ruipérez García, G. 2020. Sustainable management of digital transformation in higher education: Global research trends. *Sustainability*, 12(5): 2107.

Al-Youbi, A. O., Al-Hayani, A., Bardesi, H. J., Basheri, M., Lytras, M. D., & Aljohani, N. R. 2020. The King Abdulaziz University (KAU) pandemic framework: A methodological approach to leverage social media for the sustainable management of higher education in crisis. *Sustainability*, 12(11): 4367.

Aristovnik, A., Keržič, D., Ravšelj, D., Tomaževič, N., & Umek, L. 2020. Impacts of the COVID-19 pandemic on life of higher education students: A global perspective. *Sustainability*, 12(20): 8438.

British Council Report. 2021. Role of international higher education partnerships in contributing to the sustainable development goals. https://www.britishcouncil.org/education/he-science/knowledge-centre/partnerships-collaboration/international-higher-education-partnerships-and-sdgs

Brusca, I., Labrador, M., & Larran, M. 2018. The challenge of sustainability and integrated reporting at universities: A case study. *Journal of Cleaner Production*, 188: 347–354.

Cabero-Almenara, J., Guillén-Gámez, F. D., Ruiz-Palmero, J., & Palacios-Rodríguez, A. 2022. Teachers' digital competence to assist students with functional diversity: Identification of factors through logistic regression methods. *British Journal of Educational Technology*, 53(1): 41–57.

Coldwell-Neilson, J. 2020. Unlocking the code to digital literacy. Department of Education, Skills and Employment. https://ltr.edu.au/resources/FS16-0269_Coldwell-Neilson_Report_2020.pdf: 18.

Costa, J. M., Araújo, S., Soliman, M., & Sousa, M. J. 2022. Assessment Methods Determining the Higher Education Students' Academic Success. In: Primo, T. T., Gomes, A. S., Moreira, F., Collazos, C. (eds.) Advanced Virtual Environments and Education. WAVE 2021. *Communications in Computer and Information* Science, vol 1425. Springer, Cham. https://doi.org/10.1007/978-3-031-07018-1_7

Dafalla, Z. I., Dhanasekaran, B., & Al-Shanfari, L. 2015. Enhancing the Understanding of Computer Networking Courses through Software Tools. The 3rd International Conference on Educational Technology -2015, OSET, Muscat, Oman, 25–26 March 2015.

DeCoito, I., & Estaiteyeh, M. (2022). Online teaching during the COVID-19 pandemic: Exploring science/STEM teachers' curriculum and assessment practices in Canada. *Disciplinary and Interdisciplinary Science Education Research*, 4(1): 1–18. https://doi.org/10.1186/s43031-022-00048-z

Dhanasekaran, B., Fatma Al-Mahri, F., & Fatnassi, T. 2015. Social Impact of MOOC's in Oman Higher Education. The 3rd International Conference on Educational Technology -2015, OSET, Muscat, Oman, 25–26 March 2015.

Dhanasekaran, B., Madanan, M., Sayed, B. T., & Balaji, M. 2019. Proposing Smart Classroom for The Efficient Optimized Utilization of Resources. In CAS-Salalah, The Fourth Industrial Revolution Symposium - FIR2019, College of Applied Sciences - Ibri, Oman. 15–16 April 2019.

Dhanasekaran, B., & Malathi, R. 2022. Adaptive teaching and learning technologies and the impact during pandemic in UTAS: A perspective. *Journal of Applied Sciences, Technology and Innovation (JASTi)*, 1(1): 118–136. https://sur.cas.edu.om/ckfinder/userfiles/files/JASTi-Vol_1-Iss_1-Jan22(1).pdf

Figueiró, P. S., & Raufflet, E. 2015. Sustainability in higher education: A systematic review with focus on management education. *Journal of Cleaner Production*, 106: 22–33. https://doi.org/10.1016/j.jclepro.2015.04.118

Filho, Walter L., Vargas, Valeria R., Salvia, Amanda L., Brandli, Luciana L., Pallant, Eric, Klavins, Maris, Ray, Subhasis, Moggi, Sara, Maruna, Marija, Conticelli, Elisa, Ayanore, Martin A., Sen, Salil, Paço, Arminda, Michalopoulou, Eleni, Saikim, Fiffy H., Koh, Hock L., Frankenberger, Fernanda, Kanchanamukda, Wasan, Antônio da Cunha, Dênis, Akib, Noor A. M., Clarke, Amelia, Wall, Tony, Vaccari, Mentore, Radovic, Vesela, & Gupta, Bhumika 2019. The role of higher education institutions in sustainability initiatives at the local level. *Journal of Cleaner Production*, 233: 1004–1015.

Frankiewicz, B., & Chamorro-Premuzic, T. 2020. Digital transformation is about talent, not technology. *Harvard Business Review*, 6(3). https://hbr.org/2020/05/digital-transformation-is-about-talent-not-technology

Giesenbauer, B., & Müller-Christ, G. 2020. University 4.0: Promoting the transformation of higher education institutions toward sustainable development. *Sustainability*, 12(8): 3371.

Goulart, V. G., Liboni, L. B., & Cezarino, L. O. 2022. Balancing skills in the digital transformation era: The future of jobs and the role of higher education. *Industry and Higher Education*, 36(2): 118–127.

Grau, X. 2018. The "Glocal" University. https://www.guninetwork.org/articles/glocal-university

Hassan, S. B., & Soliman, M. 2021. COVID-19 and repeat visitation: Assessing the role of destination social responsibility, destination reputation, holidaymakers' trust and fear arousal. *Journal of Destination Marketing & Management*, 19: 100495. https://doi.org/10.1016/j.jdmm.2020.100495

https://sdgs.un.org/2030agenda

Krstić, M., Filipe, J. A., & Chavaglia, J. 2020. Higher education as a determinant of the competitiveness and sustainable development of an economy. *Sustainability*, 12(16): 6607.

Lakshminarayanan, R., Dhanasekaran, B., & Ephre, B. G. 2016. A study on features and limitations of on-line C compilers. *International Journal of Computer Applications*, 125(9). https://doi.org/10.5120/ijca2015905892

Lakshminarayanan, R., Dhanasekaran, B., Kumar, B., & Balaji, M. 2013. Augmented reality in ICT for minimum knowledge loss. *(IJCSIS) International Journal of Computer Science and Information Security*, 11(4): 34–38. https://doi.org/10.48550/arXiv.1305.2500

Mohamed, B. H., Disli, M., Al-Sada, M. B. S., & Koç, M. 2022. Investigation on human development needs, challenges, and drivers for transition to sustainable development: The case of qatar. *Sustainability*, 14(6): 3705.

Sá, M. J., & Serpa, S. 2020. The COVID-19 pandemic as an opportunity to foster the sustainable development of teaching in higher education. *Sustainability*, 12(20): 8525.

Soliman, M., Di Virgilio, F., Figueiredo, R., & Sousa, M. J. 2021a. The impact of workplace spirituality on lecturers' attitudes in tourism and hospitality higher education institutions. *Tourism Management Perspectives*, 38: 100826. https://doi.org/10.1016/j.tmp.2021.100826

Soliman, M., Ivanov, S., & Webster, C. 2021b. The psychological impacts of COVID-19 outbreak on research productivity: A comparative study of tourism and non-tourism scholars. *Journal of Tourism and Development* 35: 23–52. https://doi.org/10.34624/rtd.v0i35.24616

UN. 2022. The Higher Education Sustainability Initiative discusses the transformation of higher education as a result of the COVID-19 pandemic. https://sdgs.un.org/news/higher-education-sustainability-initiative-discusses-transformation-higher-education-result.

UN Declaration. 2015. Transforming our world: the 2030 Agenda for Sustainable Development. https://sdgs.un.org/2030agenda

Utama, Y. J., Ambariyanto, A., Zainuri, M., Darsono, D., Setyono, B., & Putro, S. P. 2018. Sustainable development goals as the basis of university management towards global competitiveness. *Journal of Physics: Conference Series* 1025 (1), 012094. IOP Publishing.

Vaughter, P. 2018. Beacons, not towers: How higher education can help achieve the sustainable development goals. UNUIAS Policy Brief. No. 13.

Veidemane, A. 2022. Education for sustainable development in higher education rankings: Challenges and opportunities for developing internationally comparable indicators. *Sustainability*, 14(9): 5102.

Vilalta, J. M. 2018. Sustainable Development Goals: from science to action. https://www.guninetwork.org/articles/sustainable-development-goals-science-action

Wang, Y., Wang, R., Shi, H., Huisingh, D., Hansson, L., & Hong, J. 2013. Green universities and environmental higher education for sustainable development in China and other emerging countries. *Journal of Cleaner Production*, 61: 1–138.

Xiong, W., & Mok, K. H. 2020. Sustainability practices of higher education institutions in Hong Kong: a case study of a sustainable campus consortium. *Sustainability*, 12(2): 452.

Žalėnienė, I., & Pereira, P. 2021. Higher education for sustainability: A global perspective. *Geography and Sustainability*, 2(2): 99–106.

Chapter 5

Higher Education: Networks and Technology – The Complex World of Sustainability

Lourdes Caraça
Instituto Politécnico de Santarém, Santarém, Portugal

Contents

5.1 The Role of Social Networks in the Learning Process 96
5.2 The Complex World of Dependencies 98
5.3 Higher Education Institutions and Sustainability 100
5.4 Final Thoughts 102
References 103

The popularization of the Internet and the new digital technologies has shifted the way we relate to each other, transforming both economies and societies.

Progressively, technology has gained space and form while also bringing benefits to our work environments, public health, and life, and it has even changed the way we learn and study.

Over the last few years, a few higher education institutions have looked into adapting to digitalization and all it has to offer, promoting the acquisition of new values, different educational and investigation models, and developing digital platforms that help with managing education.

This transition has simultaneously been made highly noticeable and put to the test after more restrictive measures were introduced thanks to the Coronavirus pandemic.

Even while not being directly compromised by the creation of sustainable methods for higher education, stakeholders were nonetheless pushed into a new stage, one that has various new requirements for their institutions. It is a stage where the worth of information and communication digital technologies (or ICTs) was shown, mostly in their capacity to gather and keep an educational network in operation, and, as a result, fulfilling the immediate objectives of sustainability of the entire educational system.

With the onset of presenting some reflections and proposals, we will look into approaching and connecting the role of social networks in the learning process; the concept of dependence, namely online dependencies, highlighting the problems that can arise from the use of information and communication technologies and the organizational and educational benefits that promote the sustainability of the higher educational system, as well as the transdisciplinary contribute to life and the planet's global sustainability.

5.1 The Role of Social Networks in the Learning Process

The concept of a social network got its boost in the 1930s with Jacob Moreno's sociometry. It had its origins in sociology, social psychology, and anthropology – not the Internet or globalization and it is commonly divulged.

Information and communication digital networks are seen by our traditional educational model as a support of the education process and not a real tool for learning.

Silva (2009) states that pedagogy is based on a dynamic between interactivity and co-authorship which always requires the death of the lecturer; the narcissistical keeper of the power.

The true development of learning with autonomy establishes a two-way dialogue where the collaborative and interactive methodological strategy of the learning networks concerns more than the access to lecturers and schoolbooks. It concerns the access to the stimuli these digital networks provide as global networks, the access to entertainment and information, and surrounding cultural values.

In order for there to exist educational effectiveness, it is necessary to create a relational structure without a defined core; a relational pedagogical structure purely based on a rhizomatic relation: one that is permanently open.

It is important to mention that learning networks have always existed, there it be in the familiar education process or in a community. These do not rely on digital technologies for their existence. Nonetheless, there is no doubt that the Internet is an enabler in how it helps increase people's contact with various sources of information.

If we look into this concept of a network that congregates aspects of the neurosciences, cognitive science, network, and chaos theories, we can easily understand that the better the quality of a network and its connections, the better exchanges of knowledge and learning will be (Siemens, 2010).

Moreover, the detention of knowledge is collective and dynamic, and collective intelligence is more than purely cognitive: "no one knows everything, everyone knows something, all knowledge is in Humanity" (Levy, 2000, p. 29).

It does seem that the virtue of dialogue is not in the intensive use of ICTs but in the pedagogical stance taken by the lecturer.

Only the lecturer has the authority to forego the conventional approach, in which the professor takes the lead and structures formative stimuli instead of establishing pathways on the digital network with their students. In this manner, they will permit the free flow of interactions and information throughout all educational communication channels.

However, this is not the only challenge put before higher education institutions. Digital education needs to be tuned to various phenomena that are nothing but simple, namely:

- The increased power of disinformation, commonly known as fake news – for which higher education and its lecturers need to be properly qualified to mediate, stepping up as trusting teachers who possess arguments of relevant scientific sources.
- The growth of the reach of social networks and current digital and technological structures are the perfect fertilizer for the occurrence of cyberbullying.

In the specific case of cyberbullying, as the human being is inherently social, we know well how these phenomena can negatively impact individuals, specifically regarding their individual satisfaction and inclusion in a certain group or community.

- The influential strength of digital maps that take advantage of our interests and expectations, through algorithms that work as a structural element for a new framework for relationships, and for which there exists a very low caliber of digital literacy.

In this specific aspect, young people are seen as the most gullible given their need for approval. Likes on social media are conjugated in a perfect storm with the influence they can create. This can be more or less dangerous given the maturity of each individual.

- The way in which information and communication digital networks provoke a dependency always adds extra concerns. Sean Parker, the first president of

Facebook, stated that the platform was designed in such a way as to take advantage of people's psychological vulnerabilities. In this sense, it is known the production of dopamine in our brain soars with each like and interaction. These are shown in real-time, promoting a reinforcement of the behavior that is addicting. We should add that this hormone is also at play in other dependencies such as drugs or gambling.

5.2 The Complex World of Dependencies

Since the beginning of Humanity, societies have battled with dependency issues, such as psychoactive substances that modified the state of consciousness. In traditional societies, however, this use was part of rituals and contributed to the cohesion of the society itself. Nevertheless, from the beginning of the 19th century onward, usage grew, its ritualized context was lost, and our society started looking at these substances in a different way (Castro, 2004). As an example, opium went from a remedy to fight pain, to an enemy to destroy.

Beyond the fact that context stopped controlling the use of psychotropic substances, science could now isolate and study the chemical compounds involved in these substances and identify their strong addicting power.

In turn, and when discussing the Internet and digital content, frequently with the aid of artificial intelligence, the vulnerabilities of humans have been explored as a way to capture their interest while online. As a result, a pattern of problematic use of the Internet can occur, a pattern that can turn into an online dependency (Patrão and Fernandes, 2019).

This risk of dependency is associated with what content is produced, content that is continuously in search of the perfect algorithm in order to capture the attention of individuals, Although this problem is transversal to various generations, we do know teenagers and young adults are at a bigger risk thanks to their use of the Internet during their daily routines whether it be at the academical level or purely for entertainment and desocialization purposes (Patrão and Fernandes, 2019).

These harmful effects and behaviors are very identical to the ones observed in other dependencies and in all biopsychosocial perspectives. The first warning is the inability to control its use. In fact, the problem surges when the online preferences of teenagers become what is most important to them. The individual will dedicate most of their time connected to the Internet and become careless of themselves (i.e. their feeding, hygiene, and sleeping habits), their relationships, and daily routines (i.e. face-to-face socialization with friends, family, and peers, taking time for leisure activities) and often times will isolate. In this sense, Young (2009) emphasizes the damages and losses of this specific population when it comes to their biopsychosocial skills.

Once inside the circuit, changes in the individual's long- and short-term memories occur, as the chemical and neuronal effects produced are similar to the ones that are found in users of cocaine.

As a matter of fact, one of the key factors that create this dependency on the Internet and other technologies is its characteristic of allowing for faster communication without any type of restrictions. On the other hand, and taking into consideration a proper psychological understanding, without the development of this capacity of waiting for the completion of a task, a lot of essential skills are left undeveloped, skills which are necessary for the control of different states of frustration. These skills are essential as their management precedes the inception of the creative thinking implied in the practical solving of problems.

Consequently, if these skills are not developed this can bring serious implications for the individual and their preparation for the adversities of everyday complications. Emotionally, there will also be an impact on the mechanisms that control and regulate our behavior, making it very likely that the individual will act on impulse since decision-making processes will struggle in being supported by rationality.

As we can see, such characteristics are essential for our everyday life and are also a big part of the academic DNA that highly permeates the learning and motivational processes involved in higher education.

These implications can be vastly disruptive, both in the application and selection of strategies that are placed on behalf of the concentration and focus of the students. For example, connected devices can also mean permanent distractions that halt intellectual involvement during learning, research, and studying. These mainly capture the attention of the individual toward other settings, becoming distractions to the learning process.

As we have previously seen, the same types of equipment can also create tremendous opportunities in the learning system. What is needed is that the individual possesses a proper conscience of the processes which are involved, is allowed to identify moments where these devices are favorable or unfavorable, and can, as a result, exercise control over their own behavior and usage of said devices.

Although higher education institutions and their lecturers still need to recognize the benefits of these technologies for the sustainability and learning system of the educational system, it is also necessary to be alert to the fact some of their students can be a part of risk groups. Some of these groups can include students who are curious and keen to explore while simultaneously presenting a smaller degree of control and lesser use of their metacognition, and those who have more difficulties in social settings and present a degree of social inhibition. For these students, digital channels can be the best or only form for them to relate socially to others as they make it easier to express thoughts, feelings, and emotions.

In spite of this, we truly believe that the benefits of using information and communication technologies outweigh the less positive implications, mainly because of the understanding of how massively used these tools are in our everyday lives and their strong social acceptance. It seems that, for most people, ICTs do not seem to have anything inherently problematic as a lot of the more unwanted phenomena are mostly explained by the individual/psychological, cultural, and biological characteristics of each person.

However, if the programming and online content production industry continues to be adamant in yielding purely to economical interests and appropriating knowledge produced by the neurological and behavioral sciences, soon we will watch their products be tailored to the vulnerabilities of the human being. Much like Taylorism, people will think sequence to sequence, click to click and their future interactions and learning processes will be completely incognito.

Therefore, the risk seems to reside in the lack of precautions that the economic interests pursue.

For this reason, and for there to be more benefits, especially in the higher education system, it is imperative that educational institutions incorporate these concerns and do not overlook the vulnerabilities associated with the use of digital technologies and the Internet as the principal means of the learning process.

5.3 Higher Education Institutions and Sustainability

Unfortunately, climate change has reached global exposure mostly thanks to the escalation of the perceived changes, changes in which their intensity overflows in rhythm and extension throughout the planet.

Currently, and as some of the damage inflicted on the global equilibrium is well documented, a concern often surfaces: Where were the universities? Did they alert and keep track of the damage happening to our planet?

Even if they did not do it, it has now come the time to acknowledge that these institutions need to set an example, teach and produce knowledge and share it.

Although the educational system does not necessarily need to completely abandon the traditional model, which includes face-to-face instruction, we recognize the need to respond to the arguments that are made in support of climate change, the reduction of catastrophe risks, reduced consumption, and sustainable production.

The use of digital and communication technologies, specifically when mentioning e-education platforms, brought the right momentum which, as a consequence, allowed for the internationalization of higher education. These tools have reduced the necessity for physical presence in institutions, reduced the costs for the entire system, and, at the same time, increased the equality of access for all students.

All this became possible, thanks to the diminishing geographical relevancy, allowing for more stakeholders to contribute and enjoy the knowledge acquired equally.

The same ends up happening with the opening of specialization and updating possibilities throughout one's career, making access to professional, personal, and academic conciliation easier. This also fosters access to new paths in a professional career.

It then seems that if we remove the importance of physical presence, we can promote more just, equal, and universal access to higher education.

Caraça (2022) mentions that in our path toward global sustainability, it increasingly seems that we augment the value for society if we involve all components, especially when we are working toward having these contribute positively to the life and health of a population.

We believe that in a phenomenon with this reach, institutions of higher education and their lecturers should also play a role: they must be ready to act concerning risks and vulnerabilities and always offer alternative routes to the traditional models.

In fact, with the help of the ICTs, we can look forward to the success of a sustainable model for various systems, mainly if the lecturer can appreciate the autonomous search for knowledge in their students. Consequently, the elimination of face-to-face contact between students and teachers always creates an increase in the availability of the lecturer to establish mentorships. These always benefit from proper consulting and flexibility in the agenda. It is at this moment that another inquiry arises: Will the academic community be prepared for such a change?

If they are truly motivated for this process (and even if they are not), it is necessary to mobilize the educational community to initiate these changes. They shall be more than simple reactions and abrupt adjustments.

The Academy should also be involved, prioritizing a coordinated aid in favor of the creation of global objectives for sustainable development and thereafter in the creation and monitoring of sustainability indicators. In this manner, we can make sure we are (all) on the right path.

We believe higher education institutions possess the right energy because we are moved by transdisciplinary knowledge and we can divulge in the noblest of missions – protecting our "home", by creating Critical Thinking Centers. The center's global vision would be to prioritize and coordinate local actions, finding transdisciplinary solutions which are based on deep analysis that guarantees the ethical utility and the promotion of literacy around the topic at hand.

In these Critical Thinking Centers, coordinated local actions should take place, ones that can, in multilevel, bring education to a higher degree of sustainability by developing various abilities in all social players:

a. involving students in useful social activities;
b. elaborate and put in practice skill-developing programs that take into consideration the mental well-being of the educational community;
c. involving lecturers and students, management, and administrative support teams in the continuous development and testing of apps, platforms, and equipment;
d. mobilizing stakeholders who are external to the community for active participation in the development of competitive educational offerings, as well as content that corresponds to the regional, national, and/or international necessities of the institution. As a result of this, institutions will always have remote accessibility offerings for all the services they provide to whoever wants to make use of them and for all their internal stakeholders.

Given the complexity of such problems, it is important to emphasize that if we, instead of adopting a transdisciplinary modus operandi, work separately, our solutions can have a diminished or even unexistent impact.

Without organizational innovation, digital and technological innovation can not become effective given that it can not even develop itself properly due to the existence of blockages connected to traditional organizational models and educational forms, some of which have already been mentioned above. If this happens, there is no way we can fully take advantage of the ICTs in order to modernize our educational systems.

Therefore, it is our understanding, that we need to engage the entire educational community and society itself in this project. In this context, higher education institutions are in charge of planning their educational procedures, continuous professional upgrades, the development of innovative solutions, and the creation and monitoring of social policies. These should all be coherent and adapted to the specificities of our societies so the sustainable and productive objective we have for our knowledge-based economy can be achieved.

The academic community that observes and acts on the way we interact with each other is also challenged to transform their own educational procedures in order to respect each person's individual freedom of choice. In the context of emotional skills, the community should pay attention to the individuals who might reveal to be struggling and in particular the mental health of their stakeholders.

5.4 Final Thoughts

Easy access to the Internet and digital technologies has revolutionalized people's way of life and allowed Humankind to try new ways to connect, including the manner in which we learn. Recently, the pandemic has justified its biggest test to date, even in areas where life had resisted its usage, allowing for generalized expansions of digital solutions that brought many benefits in multiple sectors: health, education, economics, institutional management, and in its frequent application to the everyday life of individuals.

However, this same expansion has also unraveled the unprotection of people, something the regulating system has tried to fight back against, mostly against low levels of literacy – specifically in the perception of the real value and importance of all data.

Even so, we share an optimistic view in regard to the decisive and positive action of digital transformation in the conquest of the challenges that come with global sustainability.

Higher education institutions will surely have a fundamental role in the production of answers, especially in the production of transdisciplinary knowledge, in which such solutions shall embody more than purely specified ones.

Concerned in the creation of answers for the problems caused by the downgrading of the presential role of relationships, higher education institutions will surely collaborate in helping the fight against digital isolation and other issues. As a result, they should firstly contribute to the development of strategies that protect those who are considered more vulnerable or predisposed to be – thanks to their immaturity or biopsychosocial disturbance or their behavioral literary deficit; and secondly, to the development of e-learning platforms, equipments and apps which are currently in use and that were not designed for a large amount of usage by the collegiate community.

Concomitantly, the ultimate challenge of educational institutions should be fulfilled: the promotion of an apprenticeship where its institutions and their lecturers must not postpone the fostering of a new educational methodology that will allow for the replacement of the traditional model.

The responsibility of steering the pedagogic abilities that our societies have at their disposal will always rely on higher education institutions. It is their duty to increase the value of the richness shared by the collective, developing, in turn, the technological and digital literacy of our society's human resources.

We conclude this chapter with the thoughts of renowned Brazilian pedagogue and philosopher Freire who alludes to the fact that we are constantly conversing with the world and with others and it is in this process that we create and recreate everything.

References

Caraça, L. (2022). As Cidades Inteligentes e a Saúde. BSN-Business Science Network. Smart Cities 1 edition. Maio de 2022.
Castro, M (2004). Do prazer à dependência. *Revista Toxicodependências*, 10 (3), 49–56.
Levy, P. (2000). *A inteligência coletiva: por uma antropologia do ciberespaço*. São Paulo: Loyola.
Patrão, I. & Fernandes, P. A. (2019). Dependências online: estudo sobre a perceção da supervisão parental numa amostra de pais de crianças e jovens. In Monteiro, V., Mata, L., Martins, M., Morgado, J., Silva, J., Silva, A., & Gomes, M. (eds.). *Educar hoje: Diálogos entre psicologia, educação e currículo* (133–140). Lisboa: Edições ISPA.
Siemens, G. (2010). Conociendo el conocimiento. Traducción de Emilio Quintana, David Vidal, Lola Torres y Victoria A. Castrillejo [Grupo Nodos Ele].
Silva, M. (2009). Formação de professores para a docência online. X congresso internacional galego português de psicopedagogia, Universidade do Minho, pp. 25–45. Braga, Portugal.
Young, K. (2009). Internet addiction: diagnosis and treatment considerations. *Journal Contemp. Psychother*, 39, 241–246. doi: 10.1007/s10879-009-9120-x.

Chapter 6

Artificial Intelligence and Blockchain in Higher Education Institutions: A Bibliometric Review

Andreia de Bem Machado, Gertrudes Aparecida Dandolini, and João Artur de Souza
Federal University of Santa Catarina, Florianópolis, Brazil

Marco Tulio Braga de Moraes
Universidade Federal de Santa Catarina, Florianópolis, Brazil

Maria José Sousa
ISCTE – University Institute of Lisbon, Lisbon, Portugal

Contents

6.1	Introduction	106
6.2	Methodology – Bibliometric Review	107
6.3	Methodological Path	107
6.4	Results of Bibliometrics	108
6.5	Final Conclusion	119
References		120

6.1 Introduction

Today's world is constantly changing and innovation has become a necessary life skill. In this context, it is realized that the numerous socio-ecological problems experienced in the digital age have provided different challenges for society, which require innovative solutions in all dimensions of society. In this sense, artificial intelligence is an interdisciplinary subject that is dedicated to the research and development of technologies and techniques used to simulate, extend, and expand human intelligence (Zhong et al., 2018). In another step, and with technological advancement, trust in the relationships between parties needs to evolve, and in this regard, blockchain technology is the ability to make the relationships between parties more secure, reliable, and with fewer intermediaries (Zhang et al., 2021). Possibly humanity is facing a new socio-technical paradigm, which will exert unprecedented influence on global society and create opportunities for transformation in many sectors of the traditional economy. Both technologies have the potential to provide innovation in the teaching–learning process (Zawacki-Richter et al., 2019).

Recently, researchers, technologists, and entrepreneurs have been devoting attention to the topic of blockchain. The interest is mainly due to the establishment of trust for recording and sharing information in distributed systems (Zhong et al., 2018). The innovative technology has other attractive benefits such as decentralization, security, and data integrity. Despite the new possibilities that the technology has been providing to various layers of society, little has been explored regarding the practices involving blockchain and educational activities. In this context, in consideration of the analytical purposes of this research, preliminary scientific investigations (Alammary et al., 2019) address topics such as the creation of applications, the analysis of the benefits of blockchain for educational institutions and other parties involved, as well as highlighting the challenges to the use of blockchain in education.

The concept of artificial intelligence originated from the Dartmouth Society in 1956 (Dodigovic, 2007) and has been applied to an increasing number of aspects of our lives since then, including the educational context. The purpose of artificial intelligence is to build intelligent artifacts and machines, or at least ones that behave as if they were intelligent. As an essential branch of computer science, artificial intelligence technology is dedicated to the research and development of technical sciences used to simulate, extend, and expand human intelligence. In recent years, thanks to the tremendous advances made in machine processing and machine learning, and the exponential growth of data, artificial intelligence has ushered in an explosive period. Due to its advantages in analysis, prediction, judgment, and decision-making, artificial intelligence can fundamentally empower industries such as security, finance, retail, transportation, and education, among others.

Thus, these two technologies (Zhang et al., 2021) have common requirements for data analysis, security, and trust and can cooperate with each other. For example, artificial intelligence depends on three key elements: algorithms, computing power, and data. Blockchain, on the other hand, can break down the data island and realize the flow of algorithms, computing power, and data resources, based on its characteristics, including decentralization, immutability, and anonymization. In addition, blockchain can ensure the credibility of the original data, as well as the audit credibility and traceability of artificial intelligence. As cutting-edge technologies (Zhang et al., 2021), blockchain and artificial intelligence have attracted increasing attention due to the irreplaceable role they play in technological innovation and industrial transformation in different settings, especially in the educational field.

Thus, the objective of this research is to map in light of the bibliometric review of how blockchain technology and artificial intelligence can be applied to higher education. To achieve this goal, a bibliometric review was conducted.

This research is divided into four parts: the first is this introduction, the second addresses the methodology adopted, the third discusses the results, and finally, the authors' final considerations.

6.2 Methodology – Bibliometric Review

In order to increase knowledge, and measure and analyze the publications in the scientific literature on trust in how Blockchain technology can assist in environmental sustainability, the bibliometric analysis was performed, starting with a search in the Web of Science (WoS) database by Clarivate Analytics. The study was developed using a strategy consisting of three phases: execution plan, data collection, and bibliometrics. To analyze the bibliometric data, the Bibliometrix software was used because it is the most compatible with the WoS database. The Bibliometrix package (Bibliometrix - home, 2022) is an RStudio "library" that provides a set of tools for quantitative research and is recommended for performing bibliometric analyses (Aria and Cuccurullo, 2017). These data provide the organization of relevant information in a bibliometric analysis, such as temporal distribution; main authors, institutions, and countries; type of publication in the area; main keywords, and the most referenced papers. Scientific mapping allows investigating and drawing a global picture of scientific knowledge from a statistical perspective. It uses mainly the three knowledge structures to present the structural and dynamic aspects of scientific research.

6.3 Methodological Path

The study carried out to answer the problem of this research is classified as exploratory-descriptive, with the intention of describing the theme and increasing the familiarity of the researchers with the fact. The literature search method used was a systematic search in an online database, followed by a bibliometric analysis of the results. Bibliometrics is a methodology from the information sciences that uses mathematical and statistical methods to map documents from bibliographic records stored in databases (Linnenluecke, 2017). Bibliometrics allows relevant findings such as production number per region; temporality of publications; organization of research by knowledge area; literature count related to the citation of the study;

identification of the impact factor of a scientific publication, among others that contribute to the systematization of the research results and the minimization of the occurrence of bias when analyzing a given topic.

For the bibliometric analysis, the study was organized into three distinct stages: planning, collection, and results. These stages occurred in a convergent manner to answer the guiding question of the study, namely: How can blockchain technology and artificial intelligence be applied to higher education?

Planning began in September and ended in May 2022, when the research was carried out. In the scope of planning, some criteria were defined, such as limiting the search to electronic databases, and not contemplating physical catalogs in libraries, due to the number of documents to be considered sufficient in the database chosen for this research. In this phase, the WoS was established as relevant to the research domain, due to the importance of this database in the academic environment and to its interdisciplinary character, the focus of research in this area, and also due to the fact that it is one of the largest databases of abstracts and bibliographic references of peer-reviewed scientific literature and its constant updating (Woszezenki et al., 2013). Considering the research problem, it was defined, still in the planning phase, the search terms, namely "artificial intelligence" and "education" and "blockchain" and "higher education".

It is considered that the variations of the expressions used for the search are presented, in a larger context, within the same proposal, since a concept depends on the context to which it is related. And, finally, when planning the search, it was defined to use the terms defined in the title, abstract, and keyword fields, without temporal, language, or any other restriction that could limit the result. In addition, the inclusion criterion adopted was article as the type of document.

From the planning of the research, the data collection was carried out on May 30, 2022, and retrieved a total of 31 indexed works, which included records from 2019, the first publication, until 2022.

6.4 Results of Bibliometrics

As a result of this data collection, it was found that the 31 papers retrieved in the search were written by 112 authors from 22 different countries. A total of 158 keywords were used. Table 6.1 shows the results of this collection in a general bibliometric analysis.

The eligible articles in the WoS database were published from 2019 to 2022. In 2019, there were two publications, in 2020, nine published papers, in 2021, 15 publications, and in 2022, five published papers, as shown in Figure 6.1.

In the 31 works, there is a varied list of authors, institutions, and countries that stand out in research on blockchain, artificial intelligence, and higher education. When analyzing the 20 countries with the highest number of citations in the area, it can be seen that China stands out with 137 citations, 55% of the total citations.

Table 6.1 Bibliometric Data

Bibliometric Data	
Description	Results
MAIN INFORMATION ABOUT DATA	
Timespan	2019–2022
Sources (journals, books, etc.)	25
Documents	31
Average years from publication	1.03
Average citations per document	8.097
Average citations per year per doc	3.763
References	1,141
DOCUMENT TYPES	
Article	31
DOCUMENT CONTENTS	
Keywords Plus (ID)	49
Authors keywords (DE)	158
AUTHORS	
Authors	112
Author appearances	129
Authors of single-authored documents	3
Authors of multi-authored documents	109
AUTHORS COLLABORATION	
Single-authored documents	3
Documents per author	0.277
Authors per document	3.61
Co-authors per document	4.16
Collaboration Index	3.89

Source: Prepared by the authors (2022).

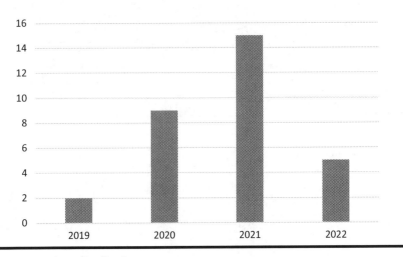

Figure 6.1 Time distribution.

Source: Prepared by the authors (2022).

In the second place, the United Kingdom stands out with 26 citations, 10% of the total citations, as shown in Figure 6.2.

Figure 6.3 presents the intensity of publications by country and, in Europe and Asia, the relationship established between them, through citations between published works.

The authors with the largest production on the subject are Lejun Zhang, with five documents, and Huiling Chen and Weizheng Wang with four publications each, as shown in Figure 6.4.

The most cited authors worldwide were Oran Doherty, Roisin Woods, and Simon Stephens, with only one citation in the area, as illustrated in Figure 6.5.

The productivity and relevance of the main authors' production over time are represented in Figure 6.6, where the size of the dot represents the number of publications; and the intensity of the color, the number of citations of the annual publications. It is observed that the productivity and relevance of publications over time are dynamic.

The documents analyzed were published in 25 different journals, and among the total of 31 studies, four (15%) were published in only one journal: Sustainability, as shown in Table 6.2, which presents the 20 scientific sources with the most publications on blockchain, artificial intelligence, and higher education.

Among the 20 sources listed in the table, CMC-Computers Materials & Continua; Georesursy; and Industry And Higher Education rank second with two papers each.

Figure 6.7 presents an innovative three-field graph in the columns of which, from left to right, the most relevant interactions between author keywords, authors, and countries are shown. It can be observed that keywords about blockchain, artificial intelligence, and higher education were published by Haibo Yi from China.

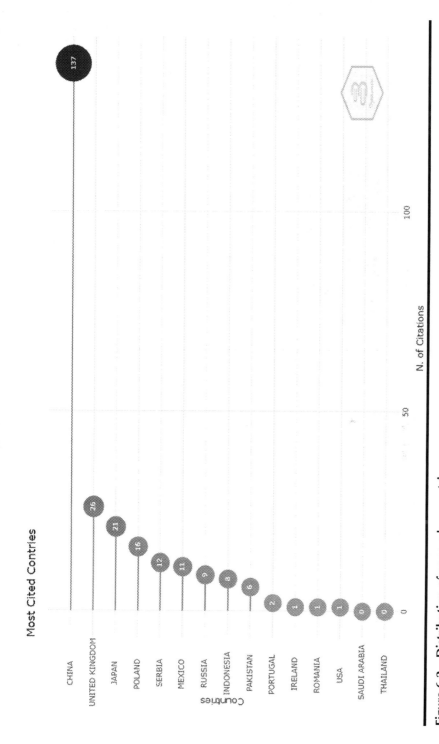

Figure 6.2 Distribution of papers by countries.
Source: Prepared by the authors (2022).

112 ■ *Technologies for Sustainable Global Higher Education*

Figure 6.3 Spatial distribution and relationships of publications on blockchain, artificial intelligence, and higher education.

Source: Prepared by the authors (2022).

AI and Blockchain in Higher Education ■ 113

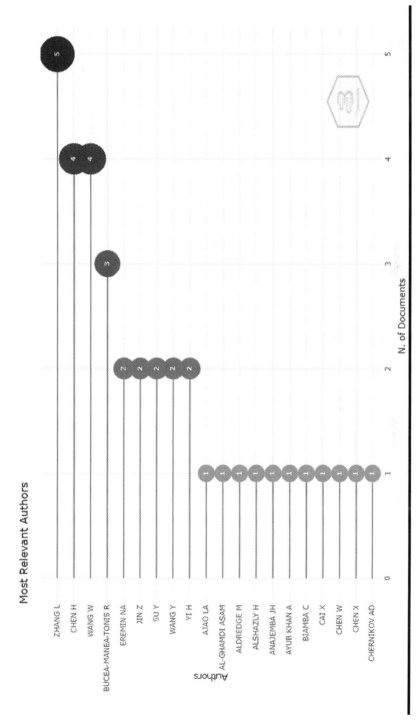

Figure 6.4 Authors with the highest number of publications on the subject of the search.
Source: Prepared by the authors (2022).

114 ■ *Technologies for Sustainable Global Higher Education*

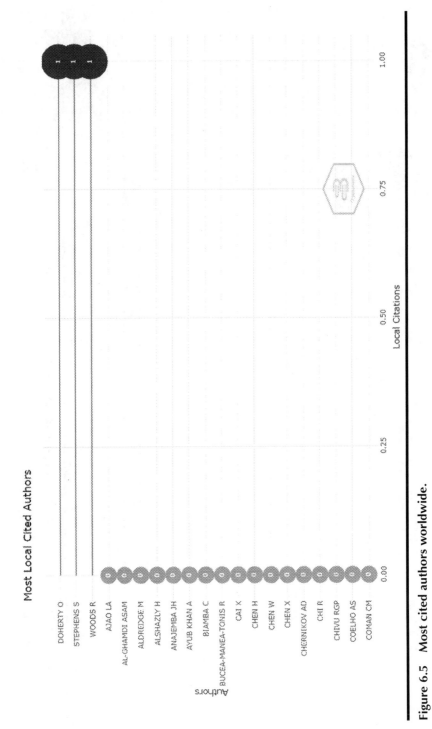

Figure 6.5 Most cited authors worldwide.
Source: Prepared by the authors (2022).

AI and Blockchain in Higher Education ■ 115

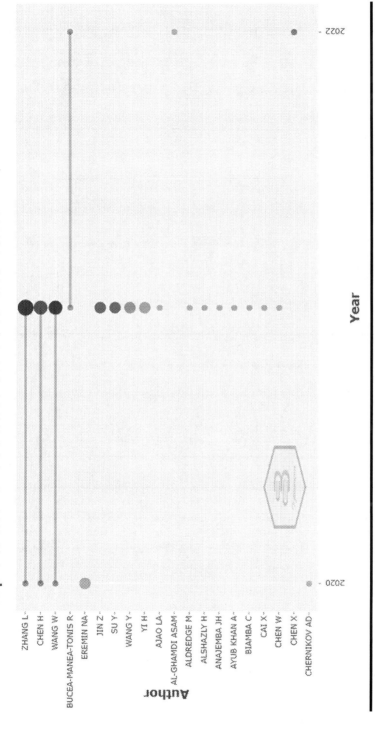

Figure 6.6 Productivity and relevance of publications by author.
Source: Prepared by the authors (2022).

Table 6.2 Scientific Sources with the Largest Number of Publications

Sources	Articles
Sustainability	4
CMC-Computers Materials & Continua	2
Georesursy	2
Industry And Higher Education	2
Applied Sciences-Basel	1
Computer Standards & Interfaces	1
Computers & Security	1
Electronics	1
Energies	1
Enterprise Information Systems	1
Entrepreneurial Business and Economics Review	1
European Journal of Investigation in Health Psychology and Education	1
IEEE Access	1
IEEE Internet of Things Journal	1
IEEE Transactions on Intelligent Transportation Systems	1
International Journal of Cyber Criminology	1
International Journal of Engineering Business Management	1
International Journal Of Interactive Design and Manufacturing - IJIDEM	1
Journal of Higher Education Policy and Management	1
Peer-To-Peer Networking and Applications	1

Source: Prepared by the authors (2022).

From the general survey, it was possible to further analyze the hierarchy of the sub-branches of the research in the area of blockchain, artificial intelligence, and higher education. The set of rectangles presented in the TreeMap shows that the words that stand out are blockchain with 16 occurrences, and higher education and internet of things with four occurrences each. Figure 6.8 shows, in a proportional way, the hierarchy of the sub-branches of the research.

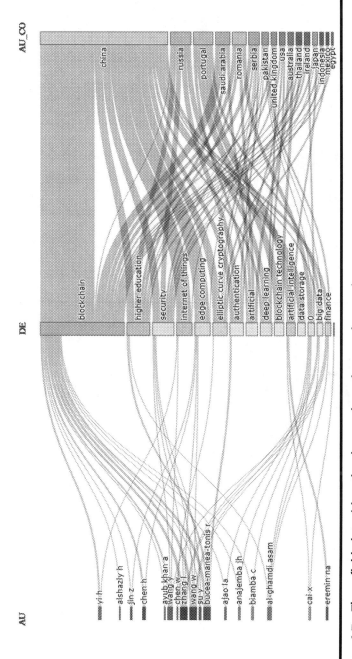

Figure 6.7 Three-field plot with author keywords, authors, and countries.
Source: Prepared by the authors (2022).

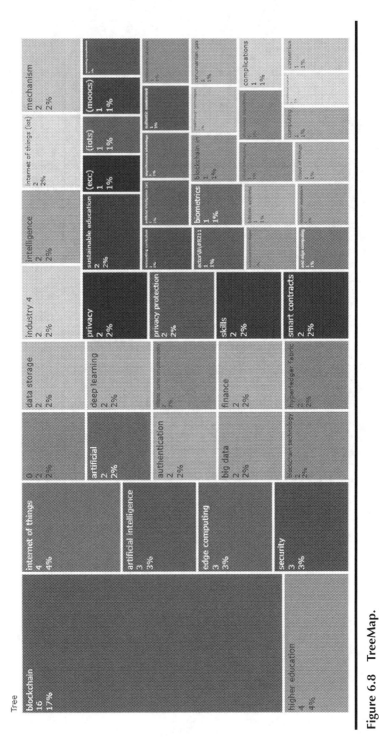

Figure 6.8 TreeMap.
Source: Prepared by the authors (2022).

Figure 6.9 Tag cloud.

Source: Prepared by the authors (2022).

Using the bibliometric analysis in the group of papers retrieved, it can be seen that in the base of 158 keywords indicated by the authors, blockchain, with 16 occurrences, and higher education and internet of things, with four occurrences each, stood out, as shown in Figure 6.9.

The "Internet of Things" is also highlighted, from which it can be concluded that this is an area of application of Blockchain technology and AI in higher education extensively explored in the literature.

6.5 Final Conclusion

The main objective of this research was to map, in light of the bibliometric review, how blockchain technology and artificial intelligence can be applied to higher education. This study aims to answer two research questions: (1) What is blockchain? (2) How can blockchain technology and artificial intelligence be applied to higher education? To answer the first research question, the 31 identified articles were reviewed and the applications of blockchain technology and artificial intelligence to higher education were identified.

The analyzed articles were published from 2019 to 2022. In the 31 works, there is a varied list of authors, institutions, and countries that stand out in research on blockchain, artificial intelligence, and higher education. When analyzing the 20 countries with the highest number of citations in the area, it can be seen that China stands out with 137 citations. The author with the highest production in the theme on the subject is Lejun Zhang with five documents. The journal that has more publications in the area is Sustainability. The article that stood out with 44 citations was

"Resource allocation and trust computing for blockchain-enabled edge computing system", by authors Lejun Zhang Yanfei Zou, Weizheng Wang, Zilong Jin, Yansen Su, and Huiling Chen.

Although this study answered the two research questions, there are some limitations that should be considered. First, the documents reviewed were limited to articles published in WoS-indexed journals. Although the WoS is the largest database, future studies may also include Scopus, EBSCO, and ProQuest databases. Second, conference papers and book chapters were excluded from this study but may be included in future reviews. Finally, the criteria for inclusion and exclusion of articles were based on subjective judgments.

For future works, the objective is to carry out an empirical research to verify the applicability of blockchain technology and artificial intelligence to the main higher education institutions in Europe.

References

Alammary, A., Alhazmi, S., Almasri, M., & Gillani, S. (2019). Blockchain-based applications in education: A systematic review. *Applied Sciences (Basel, Switzerland)*, 9(12), 2400. doi:10.3390/app9122400

Aria, M., & Cuccurullo, C. (2017). Bibliometrix: An R-tool for comprehensive science mapping analysis. *Journal of Informetrics*, 11(4), 959–975. doi:10.1016/j.joi.2017.08.007

Bibliometrix - home. (2022). Retrieved June 26, 2022, de Bibliometrix.org website: https://www.bibliometrix.org/home/

Dodigovic, M. (2007). Artificial intelligence and second language learning: An efficient approach to error remediation. *Language Awareness*, 16(2), 99–113. doi:10.2167/la416.0

Linnenluecke, M. K. (2017). Resilience in business and management research: A review of influential publications and a research agenda: Resilience in business and management research. *International Journal of Management Reviews*, 19(1), 4–30. doi:10.1111/ijmr.12076

Woszezenki, C. R., Besen, F., Santos, J. L., & Steil, A. V. (2013). Desaprendizagem organizacional: Uma Revisão Bibliométrica E Analítica Da Literatura. *Perspectivas Em Gestão &Amp; Conhecimento*, 3, 128–147. Recuperado de https://periodicos.ufpb.br/ojs2/index.php/pgc/article/view/16217

Zawacki-Richter, O., Marín, V. I., Bond, M., & Gouverneur, F. (2019). Systematic review of research on artificial intelligence applications in higher education – where are the educators? *International Journal of Educational Technology in Higher Education*, 16(1). doi:10.1186/s41239-019-0171-0

Zhang, L., Peng, M., Wang, W., Jin, Z., Su, Y., & Chen, H. (2021). Secure and efficient data storage and sharing scheme for blockchain-based mobile-edge computing. *Transactions on Emerging Telecommunications Technologies*, 32(10). doi:10.1002/ett.4315

Zhong, Jiemin et al. (2018). A blockchain model for word-learning systems. In: *2018 5th International Conference on Behavioral, Economic, and Socio-Cultural Computing (BESC)*. IEEE. pp. 130–131.

Chapter 7

Educational Strategies in Smart and Sustainable Cities for Education in the Post-Covid Era

Andreia de Bem Machado
Federal University of Santa Catarina, Florianópolis, Brazil

João Rodrigues dos Santos
IADE/Universidade Europeia, Lisboa, Portugal

António Sacavém
Universidade Europeia, Lisboa, Portugal

Marc François Richter
Universidade Estadual do Rio Grande do Sul, Porto Alegre, Brazil

Maria José Sousa
ISCTE – University Institute of Lisbon, Lisbon, Portugal

Contents

7.1	Introduction	122
7.2	Smart and Sustainable Cities	123
7.3	Educational Strategy	124

DOI: 10.1201/9781003424543-8

7.4 Methodological Approach 125
7.5 Results 126
7.6 Final Considerations 136
References 140

7.1 Introduction

The major centers of human and economic activity are cities. Cities can produce synergies that will benefit the development and quality of life of their residents. However, when they develop in size and complexity, cities cause a wide range of difficulties that can be challenging to address. The smart city is a relatively recent paradigm that has emerged to solve problems in modern cities and improve the quality of life by using information and communication technologies (Taamallah et al., 2018). The smart and sustainable city concept emerged to address these difficulties and explore new opportunities since a smart city's ultimate objective is to deliver a new method to urban administration in which all components are dealt with the interconnectivity that occurs in everyday city life (Monzon, 2015). Many studies have been conducted on smart and sustainable cities to clarify definitions, activities, and other measures. Lately, the focus of these studies has shifted from infrastructure-oriented technology to a citizen-oriented approach, inviting specific fringes of society to rethink the way it imagines future cities (Liu et al., 2017). Moving our focus from a predominant technological vision to other priorities was accelerated by the Covid-19 pandemic. Nevertheless, the coronavirus epidemic has only added to the urgency, by exacerbating existing inequities and posing enormous trials to how we live, work, and educate future generations. Several cities are now implementing the smart and sustainable city idea to improve society's quality of life, particularly in the sphere of education. The lessons learned from this outbreak hint at better-coordinated government- and public-sector responses, and new degrees of urban digital connectivity (Costa & Peixoto, 2020), particularly in health services and education (Kunzmann, 2020). Education fosters creativity and innovation, which are essential for a city's long-term viability and prosperity. In the organization of a smart and sustainable city, there are two factors that are critical, namely, educational technology and educational system (Nur et al., 2018). Both are relevant components of educational strategies which may facilitate the unlocking of creativity. Furthermore, according to Liu et al. (2017), there is a link between city creativity and the living experience of citizens, which is directly connected to city learning settings and strategies. Therefore, pinpointing the educational strategies of smart and sustainable cities in the Covid-19 era is a crucial movement to deepen the current understanding of the phenomenon and to support the decision-making process.

To this end, a bibliometric analysis was performed with the aim to identify a wide-range list of authors, institutions, and countries that stand out in the research on educational strategies in smart and sustainable cities for education in the post-Covid era.

The chapter is organized into six sections: first, the introduction; the second section focuses on smart and sustainable cities; the third section addresses educational strategies; in the fourth section, the methodology is exposed; the results appear in the fifth section; and the sixth section includes the final considerations.

7.2 Smart and Sustainable Cities

Smart or not, the concept of "city" already presents different approaches from country to country, making direct comparisons difficult. The criteria for classifying an area as urban are generally based on characteristics such as population, population density, types of employment, infrastructure, and the presence of education or health services (Allam & Newman, 2018). In fact, the notion of "city" has been historically attributed to the population concentration in an environment of interaction and material and immaterial exchanges. Such a process, if well planned, allows generating high productivity, competitiveness, and innovation in the urban environment and consequently to its citizens. However, these elements alone do not necessarily make a city "smart" (Bettencourt & West, 2010).

The concept of smart cities has been gaining popularity over the last few years, although there is no consensus on its meaning in the literature. The term "Smart City" first appeared in 1992, in the book titled *The Technopolis Phenomenon: Smart Cities, Fast Systems, Global Networks* (Gibson et al., 1992), which sought to conceptualize the phenomenon of urban development dependent on technology, innovation, and globalization from an economic perspective (Rizzon et al., 2017).

Over the years, the expression "Smart Cities" became the symbol of the application of ICTs in urban development and innovation, attracting the attention of researchers from universities, governments, and companies. However, it was in the second half of the 2000s that the concept gained amplitude in the scientific debate with Giffinger et al. (2007).

Currently, there are many definitions for the concept "Smart City". However, the main approaches can be classified into two main streams. The first presents a technocentric approach, focusing on ICTs as the main factor for the intelligence of cities (Mora et al., 2017). The second stream adopts a holistic citizen-centric approach that seeks to combine human and social capital with natural and economic resources, through ICT-based solutions, for the improvement of the quality of life in cities. This holistic perspective is supported by the research report "Smart Cities: Ranking of European Medium-sized Cities" published by Giffinger et al. (2007), the most influential reference on the topic between 1992 and 2012.

The use of ICTs to provide an improved quality of life for its citizens, at an affordable cost and optimizing the use of our planet's resources, is important. Technology, therefore, is only a means to enable a larger goal to be achieved and not the main focus of the discussion on smart and sustainable communities (Pathak & Pandey, 2021). Smart and sustainable cities should be cities that no longer treat their citizens as just beneficiaries of services or even as customers, but rather as co-creators of the mechanisms for improving the quality of life in that community. In other words, the governance of a smart human city must be participatory, which, by definition, contributes to promoting cohesion, that is, to optimizing the territorial and human resources available in the city.

This humanized smart city model was coined version 3.0 of the evolution of this type of city (Shamsuzzoha et al., 2021). The initial version consisted of companies that own the technology offering some smart city service to governments, convincing them that it would be good to buy their product to offer such a service to their citizens. Version 2.0 refers to a situation in which governments decide, on behalf of citizens, how the resources applied in smart cities should be invested to solve existing problems.

Some of the most important technologies to support platforms for the development of a smart and sustainable city are 1) sensor technology and its connections in a network (the Internet of Things – IoT), as, probably, the most important; 2) radio communication technology with low delay and high capacity; 3) robotics and civil applications of drones; 4) transport logistics; 5) data aggregation and analysis, so that governments and communities can benefit from the amount of data validated and obtained from their sensors; 6) security in the processing and transmission of citizens' data, because it is impossible for a public service to be successful without citizens having confidence in it; 7) energy efficiency in general.

The guarantee of these factors in urban spaces has generated intense debate recently, as they currently have a great influence on urban poverty, income inequalities, and access to policies and social and economic opportunities.

Finally, another important issue is linked to the area of education: ensuring access to culture and offering quality education are the main aspects to measure Human Capital. It is clear that planning and managing the number of universities, schools, museums, and other places that contribute to education and culture is something essential in Smart Cities (De Bem Machado & Richter, 2021). In other words, cities must focus on strengthening the circular economy, investing more in education, lowering school dropout, which is strongly related to the issue of security in cities, and seeking balance in all sectors of society based on these measures (de Bem Machado et al., 2021).

7.3 Educational Strategy

Sustainable cities' educational strategies for education in the Covid-19 era were developed through mobile learning, smartphones, and computers that facilitated changes in teaching models across all subjects. With the application of technology, teaching is no longer limited by time, space, psychological state, or geopolitical boundaries. This way, people can learn anywhere and form lifelong learning habits. (Xu, 2019). Many universities have built their own online teaching platforms in recent years, using the resources of the Internet and digitization to offer students an interactive and personalized learning channel that is not limited to the time and space of learning (Cornali & Cavaletto, 2021). Once again, such learning can be supported by mobile technologies, and apps for tablets and smartphones (Sousa & Rocha, 2020).

Technologies applied in the digital world such as gamification (Асташова et al., 2020), MOOCs (massive open online courses) (Lehmann, 2019) and SPOCs (Fu, 2019), among others, demonstrate that students learn new knowledge through instructional videos that include auditory and visual content (Lehmann, 2019). In this way, the limited time in the classroom can be used primarily for teaching activities that employ two-way interaction or communication, such as practice, problem-solving, and discussion, to enhance learning effects and realize the idea of student-centered education (Shen et al., 2017). Plus, with digital materials, students can learn repeatedly anytime, anywhere.

7.4 Methodological Approach

With the aim of increasing knowledge and measuring and analyzing trust in relation to publications of a scientific nature related to the theme "educational strategies of sustainable cities for education in the Covid-19 era", a bibliometric analysis was performed, starting with a search in the Web of Science (WoS) database of Clarivate Analytics. The study was developed using a strategy consisting of three phases: execution plan, data collection, and bibliometry. To analyze the bibliometric data, the Bibliometrix software was used because it is the most compatible with the Web of Science database. The R Bibliometrix package, called Biblioshiny, has the most extensive and appropriate set of techniques among the tools surveyed for bibliometric analysis (Moral-Muñoz et al., 2020). These data provide the organization of relevant information in a bibliometric analysis, such as temporal distribution; main authors, institutions, and countries; type of publication in the area; main keywords and the most referenced papers. Scientific mapping makes it possible to investigate and draw a global picture of scientific knowledge from a statistical perspective. It mainly uses the three knowledge structures to present the structural and dynamic aspects of scientific research.

Bibliometrics is a methodology that originated from the information sciences that uses mathematical and statistical methods to map documents from bibliographic records stored in databases (Linnenluecke, 2017). Bibliometry allows relevant findings such as the number of production per region; temporality of publications; organization of research by area of knowledge; count of literature related to the citation of the study; identification of the impact factor of a scientific publication among others that contribute to the systematization of the research result and the minimization of the occurrence of biases when analyzing a particular theme.

Planning began in the month of September and ended in May 2022, when the research was conducted. In this phase, some criteria were defined such as the limitation of the search to electronic databases, and not contemplating physical catalogs in libraries, due to the number of documents deemed sufficient in the research bases in the database chosen in the present research. In the scope of planning, the WoS database was stipulated as relevant to the research domain due to the relevance of this database in academia and its interdisciplinary character focus of research in this area, and also for the fact that it is one of the largest databases of abstracts and bibliographic references of peer-reviewed scientific literature and it's constantly updating. Considering the research problem, the search terms, namely "education" and "covid-19" and "sustainable cities", were defined during the planning phase.

The variations of the expressions used for the search are considered, within a larger context, because a concept depends on the context to which it is related.

Finally, in the planning of the search, the use of the terms defined in the fields "title", "abstract" and "keyword" was defined, without parameterizing restrictions of time, language or any other that could limit the result.

Considering the research problem, the search terms were defined, still in the planning phase. First, the following descriptor was chosen: What are the educational strategies of sustainable cities for education in the Covid-19 era? To refine the search according to the research problem, another search was carried out with the terms "education" and "covid-19" and "sustainable cities", which resulted in 27 documents.

7.5 Results

As a result of this search, it was identified that the 27 scientific articles were written by 97 authors, and linked to 121 institutions from 33 different countries. Also, a total of 143 keywords were used. Table 7.1. shows the results of this data collection in a general bibliometric analysis.

The referred papers found in the Web of Science database were published in the period from 2021 to 2022. In the year 2021, there were 24 publications, while in 2022, there were 3 published documents.

The 27 papers comprise a varied list of authors, institutions, and countries that stand out in the research on "educational strategies in smart and sustainable cities for education in the post-Covid era". When analyzing the 20 countries with the highest number of citations in the research area it can be seen that China stands out with an average of 96 (= 28%) of total citations, a total of 96 citations. In the second place, Turkey stands out with 56 (16%) of total citations, and Servia with a total of 47 (13%), as shown in Figure 7.1.

Figure 7.2, presents the publication intensity per country and the relationship established between them, through citations between published papers.

Another analysis carried out involved the identification of authors and their research production. The authors who have more production in the subject in analysis are Li, Shuangjin; Pan, Yue; Zhang, Limao and Wang, Xi Wang, each of them with two publications in the area, according to Figure 7.3.

Table 7.1 Bibliometric Data

Description	Results
MAIN INFORMATION ABOUT DATA	
Timespan	2021:2022
Sources (Journals, Books, etc)	4
Documents	27
Average years from publication	0.815
Average citations per document	12.67
Average citations per year per doc	6.407
References	1705
DOCUMENT TYPES	
Article	27
DOCUMENT CONTENTS	
Keywords Plus (ID)	103
Author's Keywords (DE)	143
AUTHORS	
Authors	97
Author Appearances	101
Authors of single-authored documents	2
Authors of multi-authored documents	95
AUTHORS COLLABORATION	
Single-authored documents	2
Documents per Author	0.278
Authors per Document	3.59
Co-Authors per Documents	3.74
Collaboration Index	3.8

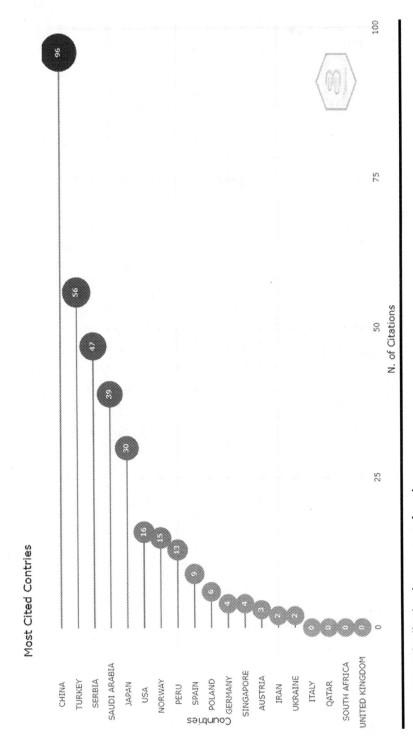

Figure 7.1 Distribution by country of works.
The authors (2022).

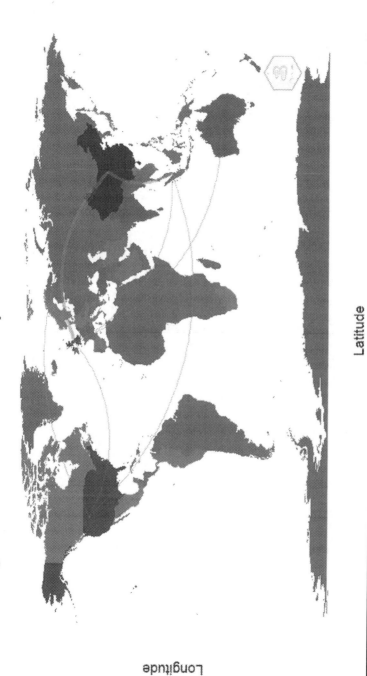

Figure 7.2 Spatial distribution and relationships of the publications.
The authors (2022).

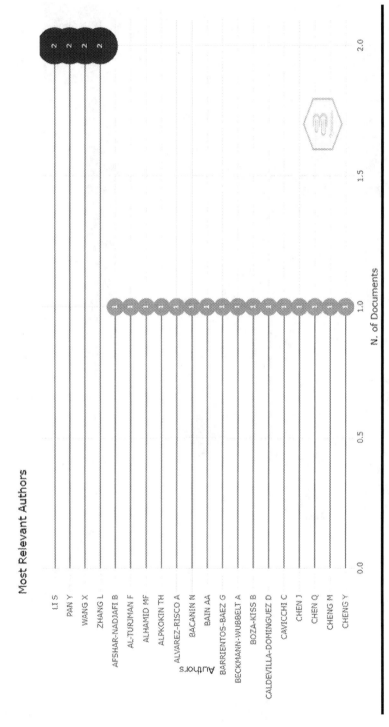

Figure 7.3 Authors with the highest number of publications in the search topic.
The authors (2022).

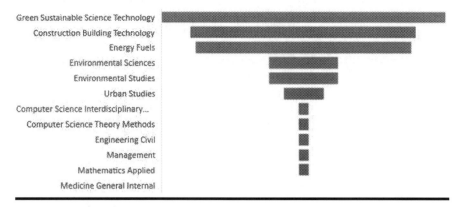

Figure 7.4 Research areas.

The authors (2022).

The top ten research areas publishing on this topic educational strategies in smart and sustainable cities for education in the post-Covid era are Green Sustainable Science Technology, Construction Building Technology, Energy Fuels, Environmental Sciences, Environmental Studies, Urban Studies, Computer Science Interdisciplinary Applications, Computer Science Theory Methods, Engineering Civil, Management, Applied Mathematics, Medicine General Internal, as shown in Figure 7.4.

With 87% of the publications, the areas of Green Sustainable Science Technology and Building Technology stand out with 69% of the publications, followed by Energy Fuels with 66%.

The documents analyzed were published in four different journals, and among the total of 27, 20 articles (74%) were published in only one journal *Sustainable Cities and Society*, according to Figure 7.5.

The second most relevant source, among the four explained in Figure 7.5, is *Frontiers In Sustainable Cities* with four documents. In the sequence there is, with two publications, the magazine titled "Sustainability".

From the general survey, it was also possible to analyze the hierarchy of the sub-branches of research in the area of educational strategies in smart and sustainable cities for education in the post-Covid era. The set of rectangles represented in the TreeMap, where the words that stand out are "cities" and "health" with three occurrences. Figure 7.6 shows, in a proportional way, the hierarchy of the sub-branches of the present search.

From the bibliometric analysis, based on the workgroup recovered, on the basis of 143 keywords indicated by the authors, "cities" and "health" stood out with 3, according to Figure 7.7. The word "curriculum" also stands out, from which we conclude it is an application area, that is, the educational strategy adopted in smart and sustainable cities for education in the post-Covid era, explored by the literature.

The 20 most cited documents globally are listed in Figure 7.8.

132 ■ Technologies for Sustainable Global Higher Education

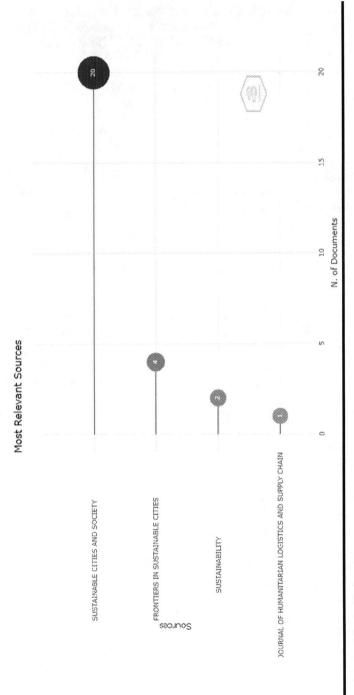

Figure 7.5 Most cited sources.
The authors (2022).

Educational Strategies in Smart and Sustainable Cities ■ 133

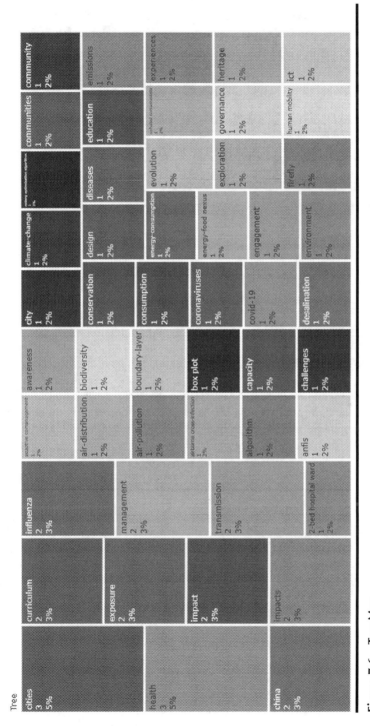

Figure 7.6 TreeMap.
The authors (2022).

Figure 7.7 Tag cloud.

The authors (2022).

The paper that gained prominence with 56 citations was "Impact of the COVID-19 pandemic on travel behaviour in Istanbul: A panel data analysis", by authors Shahin Shakibaei, Gerard C.de Jong, Pelin Alpkökin, and Taha H. Rashidi, and published in the year 2021. The paper investigates the impacts of the pandemic on travel behavior in Istanbul, Turkey, through a longitudinal panel study conducted in three phases during the early stages of the epidemic and pandemic.

After the bibliometric analysis of the 27 publications, all titles and abstracts were read in order to answer the research question: What are the educational strategies of sustainable cities for education in the Covid-19 era? Considering the 27 articles found, 4 answered the research question.

The first article that answers the question was "Expectations and Interests of University Students in COVID-19 Times about Sustainable Development Goals: Evidence from Colombia, Ecuador, Mexico, and Peru", by authors Aldo Alvarez-Risco, Shyla Del-Aguila-Arcentales, Marc A. Rosen, Veronica Garcia-Ibarra, Sandra Maycotte-Felkel, and Gabriel Mauricio Martinez-Toro, which assesses students' knowledge of the Sustainable Development Goals (SDGs), the relationship of students' professional careers to the SDGs, the importance of the SDGs for economic development after the Covid-19 pandemic, and the survey of student interest in SDG issues. The article answers the problem of the study as it makes explicit that the educational strategies of sustainable cities for education in the post-Covid-19 era are tied to (Alvarez-Risco et al., 2021):

 a. Teach the concepts of sustainable development.
 b. Promote research on sustainable development issues.
 c. Transform campuses toward sustainability.
 d. Support sustainability efforts in the community to which they belonged.
 e. Engage and share the results with international structures

Educational Strategies in Smart and Sustainable Cities ■ 135

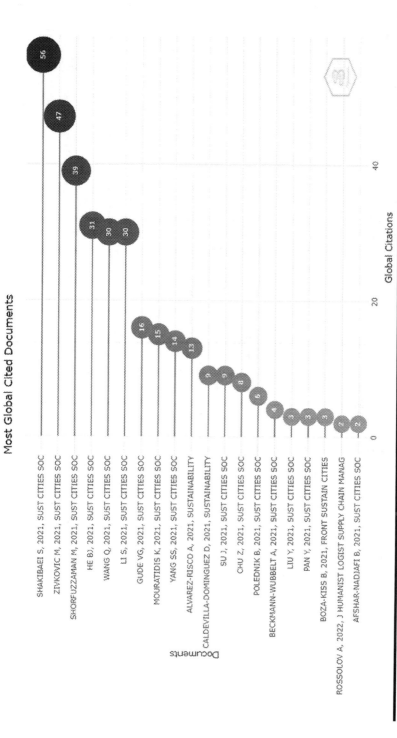

Figure 7.8 Most cited documents globally.
The authors (2022).

Another article is titled: "COVID-19 cases prediction by using hybrid machine learning and beetle antennae search approach" by authors Miodrag Zivkovic, Nebojsa Bacanin, Venkatachalam, K., Anand Nayyar, Aleksandar Djordjevic, Ivana Strumberger, and Fadi Al-Turjman (2021). Research spells out that the educational strategies of sustainable cities for education in the post-Covid-19 era are related to the hybrid model and machine learning through artificial intelligence (Zivkovic et al., 2021).

The article, titled: "COVID-19, internet, and mobility: The rise of telework, telehealth, e-learning, and e-shopping", by authors Kostas Mouratidis and Apostolos Papagiannakis, published in 2021, explains changes in the importance and frequency of engagement in online activities before and during Covid-19. Their results show that both the importance and frequency of engaging in telecommuting, teleconferencing, online learning (e-learning), telehealth, and online shopping (e-shopping) increased significantly during Covid-19 compared to pre-Covid-19. And that sustainable cities' educational strategies for education in the post-Covid-19 era are tied to the information and communication technologies used to carry out online activities (Mouratidis & Papagiannakis, 2021).

Finally, the article "Perceptions of the Acquisition of Sustainable Development Competences", by author Catarina Cavicchi (2021), indicates that the educational strategies of sustainable cities for education in the post-Covid-19 era are based on the use of a constructivist approach in the teaching–learning process, aiming at competency-based structures for sustainable development (SD) in higher education so that they can empower them to become agents of change.

7.6 Final Considerations

The crisis caused by the Covid-19 pandemic had a huge impact on the education system, which was forced to face emergency and contingency measures. These solutions were based, above all, on the use of technological resources and distance learning. While the virtues and inefficiencies of distance and traditional education have long been the subject of much discussion, online learning has suddenly become the only option because of the pandemic crisis (Oranburg, 2020).

Indeed, the mandatory use of technological resources has accelerated some dynamics of transformation in education systems, allowing, particularly, to apprehend some of the benefits that result from the use of Information and Communication Technologies (ICT) applied to the education sector. "Covid-19 has triggered many educators to start using new teaching methodologies including synchronous, interactive communications to continue delivering their curricula and educational programs". (Camilleri, 2021, p. 15)

Even so, there is still some fear among the academic community regarding the possibility that these changes, resulting from the period of the Covid-19 pandemic, will not last, with a significant impact, in the future. Kevin and Ravi (2020, p. 2) emphasize in this regard:

> And when the crisis passes, what will come of the online learning experience? We fear that the answer might be, nothing. Why? Because, in the minds of policymakers for national education, the physical institution symbolizes a history of teaching and research that cannot possibly be challenged.

And it is within the scope of the technological impact that Covid-19 has unleashed on educational systems that the concept of "smart city" gains relevance.

The essence of smart cities consists of the systematization of large volumes of data on urban areas, which are continuously collected, generated, and compiled (big data), with the objective of composing useful and strategically valid key performance indicators (metrics).

The technological and digital essence of smart cities becomes crucial for one of the main desiderata of the post-Covid era, which is, according to Cahapay (2020, p. 2), "rethinking the goals of education, preparing curricula so that they can respond effectively in times of disasters, diseases, and emergencies".

Regardless of the pandemic crisis, ICT and digital literacy are conceptually inseparable from the "smart city" concept. This logic is based on the high levels of efficiency in the management of (scars) resources that ICTs, by processing the key indicators collected at each moment, allow to achieve. This symbiosis between ICT and real-time data allows the development of transformative and effective actions by the different layers of society, with two objectives: to improve collective well-being, through the optimization of management processes; and to promote economic growth.

From an economic perspective, for example, Werner and Woessmann (2021, p. 51), in relation to the impact of learning losses resulting from Covid-19 on GDP growth, refer that "a learning loss equivalent to one-third of a school year for the current student cohort is estimated according to the historical growth relationships to be 1.5 percent lower GDP on average for the remainder of the century".

In the same context, Santos (2020, p. 49) reinforces that "low incomes are, as a rule, the result of low levels of education".

From this point of view, the smart city concept must necessarily be considered from an economic perspective. Due to its technological nature, it offers the necessary resources for the continuity of education, in the most formal sense of the term, even in times of crisis. Literacy, in its broadest sense, is an indispensable condition for understanding and using the new information systematically produced in a smart city. Only a conscious and cognitively developed citizen will be able to take advantage of the added value of a smart city and, at the same time, contribute to its development.

Following the previous paragraph, once again, ICTs are fundamental. Hilbert (2010), for example, in this context, states that "it is a well-established fact that Internet access is correlated with income and education [critical thinking]".

Critical thinking assumes preponderance in the "environment" of a smart city. Only by reflecting and pondering will an active citizenship be achieved; a citizenship oriented toward entrepreneurial, social, cultural, and inclusive projects that promote economic growth and guarantee a better quality of life for the entire community.

In this regard, it is important to highlight that the macroeconomic effect of education in promoting growth also depends on other key complementary factors, namely: policies, institutions, and infrastructure resources (including ICT). Even so, Hanushek & Woessmann (2007, p. 45), in their "The Role of Education Quality for Economic Growth" study, refer that "even in countries with a poor institutional environment", "still also find a significant positive growth effect [derived from] cognitive skills", which strongly suggests that education is the most important key factor for development.

When addressing the importance of education in citizenship, it is also democracy that is in the equation, since citizenship is a mandatory condition of democratic exercise. In a democratic and "smart" society, the act of learning and the development of cognitive capacity and critical thinking are the requirements that guarantee: a simultaneously conscious and proactive citizenship; and universal equality in access to tangible and intangible goods and services of a collective nature.

Interestingly, these requirements, which guarantee full citizenship, also played (play) a decisive role during the Covid-19 confinement periods.

According to UNESCO (United Nations Educational, Scientific and Cultural Organization), "education for global citizenship" is essential in promoting civic, social, and political involvement. Ultimately, it "prepares children and youth to deal with the challenges of today's increasingly interconnected and interdependent world" (Tang, 2014, p. 15). Continuous and dynamic learning is the key element in this regard. The focus should be on self-regulated learning, which allows adjusting knowledge to each specific situation. And from this point of view, the traditional pedagogical model is relatively inadequate. The pandemic crisis reinforced this evidence, by demanding the use of more active pedagogical strategies and methodologies, which share more responsibility in the teaching–learning process with those who are learning.

Sandoval et al. (2020, p. 15), in their work on "Legal Education During the Covid-19 Pandemic: Put Health, Safety and Equity First", came to the conclusion that "the Covid-19 pandemic calls for legal education to reevaluate its pedagogical model and values".

Once again, the UNESCO concept of "education for global citizenship", whose relevance is reinforced in the post-Covid period, has three basic conceptual dimensions, namely:

1. "Cognitive dimension", which consists of acquiring knowledge and critical thinking about global, regional, national, and local issues, as well as about the interrelationships and interdependencies of different countries and population groups.

2. "Socio-emotional dimension", which is based on the feeling of belonging to a community, which shares values, responsibilities, empathy, solidarity, and respect for differences and diversities.
3. "Behavioral dimension", which includes effective and responsible action, locally, nationally, and globally, for a more peaceful and sustainable world.

This "contemporary" approach to education for global citizenship is very much adjusted to the so-called "soft skils", or transversal competences, which, according to Bordenave and Pereira (2014), can be promoted through some specific educational strategies: Observing; To analyze; Theorize; Synthesize; Apply and transfer learning.

Obviously, even these "universal" educational strategies are currently based on a mandatory technological and digital dimension, which will even tend to be increasingly exponential.

In fact, according to Sinha (2020, p. 2), the disruption in the delivery of education caused by the pandemic crisis forced "policymakers to figure out how to drive engagement at scale while ensuring including e-learning solutions and tackling the digital divide".

Today, "digital" teaching is no longer viewed with such reluctance; or as "doubtful". Covid-19 has accelerated the transformation of educational "traditionalism" in relation to the use of ICT in the teaching–learning process, in its broadest sense.

In this regard, Parentela and Vargas (2021, p. 10), referring to the transition process from traditional face-to-face pedagogical strategies to virtual-online relationship strategies (synchronous or asynchronous) during the Covid-19 period, underline that "innovations not just in strategies but also in the technology aided so much in the said transition serving students and learners in general".

In conclusion, the use of ICT in the context of smart cities and post-Covid/future educational strategies is essential for three reasons:

1. Only with the use of ICT will it be possible to develop the level of critical thinking necessary to understand the immense and increasingly complex intricate layers of contemporary societies and continue to incorporate more information;
2. Only using ICT is it possible to process the information collected in real-time in a smart city and transform this information into more efficiency in the management of educational activities, adapting it to each specific situation, including pandemic crises such as Covid-19;
3. Only by understanding and using ICT will it be possible to acquire the "meta-knowledge" (especially digital literacy) necessary for self-regulated learning, which must necessarily occur, without interruption, throughout life. Otherwise, the Citizen no longer sees guaranteed the rights and duties that fully characterize him, becoming an info-excluded and, therefore, an unadapted.

References

Асташова, Н. А., Мельников, С. Л., Тонких, А. П., & Камынин, В. Л. (2020). Технологические ресурсы современного высшего образования. *Образование и наука, 22*(6), 74–101.

Allam, Z., & Newman, P. (2018). Redefining the smart city: Culture, metabolism, and governance. *Smart Cities, 1*(1), 4–25.

Alvarez-Risco, A., Del-Aguila-Arcentales, S., Rosen, M. A., García-Ibarra, V., Maycotte-Felkel, S., & Martínez-Toro, G. M. (2021). Expectations and interests of university students in COVID-19 times about sustainable development goals: Evidence from Colombia, Ecuador, Mexico, and Peru. *Sustainability, 13*(6), 3306.

Bettencourt, L., & West, G. (2010). A unified theory of urban living. *Nature, 467*(7318), 912–913. doi:10.1038/467912a

Bordenave, J. D., & Pereira, A. M. (2014). *Estratégias de ensino-aprendizagem* (32ª ed.). Petrópolis: Editora Vozes.

Cahapay, M. B. (2020). Rethinking education in the new normal post-COVID-19 era: A curriculum studies perspective. *Aquademia, 4*(2), 1–5.

Camilleri, M. A. (2021). Evaluating service quality and performance of higher education institutions: A systematic review and a post-COVID-19 outlook. *International Journal of Quality and Service Sciences, 13*(2), 268–281.

Cavicchi, C. (2021). Higher education and the sustainable knowledge society: Investigating students' perceptions of the acquisition of sustainable development competences. *Frontiers in Sustainable Cities, 3*, 51.

Cornali, F., & Cavaletto, G. M. (2021). Emerging platform education: What are the implications of education processes' digitization? In Editor is IGI-Global (Ed.), *Handbook of Research on Determining the Reliability of Online Assessment and Distance Learning* (pp. 359–378). IGI Global, Hershey, PA, Estados Unidos de América.

Costa, D. G., & Peixoto, J. P. J. (2020). COVID-19 pandemic: A review of smart cities initiatives to face new outbreaks. *IET Smart Cities, 2*(2), 64–73.

De Bem Machado, A., & Richter, M. F. (2021). As estratégias educacionais nas cidades inteligentes e sustentáveis para educação na era pós-covid. In A. De Bem Machado (Comp.), *Desafios da educação: Abordagens e tendências pedagógicas para futuro pós-covid* (pp. 66–77). Editora BAGAI, Brazil.

De Bem Machado, A., Rodrigues dos Santos, J., Richter, M. F., & Sousa, M. J. (2021). Smart cities: Building sustainable cities. In C. Chinmay (Ed.), *Green Technological Innovation for Sustainable Smart Societies* (pp. 1–19). Springer, Cham.

Fu, Y. (2019). "Maker education+ SPOC" teaching model for college political economics courses. *International Journal of Emerging Technologies in Learning, 14*(3), 139–150.

Gibson, D. V., Kozmetsky, G., & Smilor, R. W. (Eds.). (1992). *The technopolis phenomenon: Smart cities, fast systems, global networks.* Rowman & Littlefield.

Giffinger, R., Fertner, C., Kramar, H., & Meijers, E. (2007). City-ranking of European medium-sized cities. *Centre of Regional Science Vienna UT, 9*(1), 1–12.

Hanushek, E. A., & Woessmann, L. (2007). *The Role of Education Quality for Economic Growth.* The World Bank, Washington, D.C.

Hilbert, M. (2010). When is cheap, cheap enough to bridge the digital divide? Modeling income related structural challenges of technology diffusion in Latin America. *World Development, 38*(5), 756–770.

Kevin, Jones & Ravi, Sharma (2020). Reimagining a Future for Online Learning in the Post-COVID Era. First posted on medium.com.

Kunzmann, K. R. (2020). Smart cities after COVID-19: Ten narratives. *disP-The Planning Review*, *56*(2), 20–31.

Lehmann, A. (2019, April). Problem tagging and solution-based video recommendations in learning video environments. In *2019 IEEE Global Engineering Education Conference (EDUCON)* (pp. 365–373). IEEE.

Linnenluecke, M. K. (2017). Resilience in business and management research: A review of influential publications and a research agenda. *International Journal of Management Reviews*, *19*(1), 4–30.

Liu, D., Huang, R., & Wosinski, M. (2017). Development of smart cities: Educational perspective. In L. Dejian, H. Ronghuai, & W. Marek (Eds.), *Smart Learning in Smart Cities* (pp. 3–14). Springer, Singapore.

Monzon, A. (2015, May). Smart cities concept and challenges: Bases for the assessment of smart city projects. In *2015 International Conference on Smart Cities and Green ICT Systems (SMARTGREENS)* (pp. 1–11). IEEE.

Mora, L., Bolici, R., & Deakin, M. (2017). The first two decades of smart-city research: A bibliometric analysis. *Journal of Urban Technology*, *24*(1), 3–27.

Moral-Muñoz, J. A., Herrera-Viedma, E., Santisteban-Espejo, A., & Cobo, M. J. (2020). Software tools for conducting bibliometric analysis in science: An up-to-date review. *Profesional de la Información*, *29*(1), 11–18.

Mouratidis, K., & Papagiannakis, A. (2021). COVID-19, internet, and mobility: The rise of telework, telehealth, e-learning, and e-shopping. *Sustainable Cities and Society*, *74*, 103182.

Nur, M. N. A., Musaruddin, M., & Zulkaida, W. O. (2018). Concept of smart city for education: A case study in Kendari, Southeast Sulawesi. *KnE Social Sciences*, *1*, 1558–1565.

Oranburg, S. (2020). Distance Education in the Time of Coronavirus: Quick and Easy Strategies for Professors. *Legal Studies Research Paper Series*. Duquesne University School of Law Research Paper, 2020-02.

Parentela, G., & Vargas, D. (2021). Pandemic era (COVID-19) and higher education in the philippines against the world perspective: A literature survey analysis. *SSRN Electronic Journal*, *1*, 18.

Pathak, S., & Pandey, M. (2021, January). Smart cities: Review of characteristics, composition, challenges and technologies. In *2021 6th International Conference on Inventive Computation Technologies (ICICT)* (pp. 871–876). IEEE.

Rizzon, F., Bertelli, J., Matte, J., Graebin, R. E., & Macke, J. (2017). Smart city: um conceito em construção. *Revista Metropolitana de Sustentabilidade (ISSN 2318-3233)*, *7*(3), 123–142.

Sandoval, C. J., Cain, P. A., Diamond, S. F., Love, J. C., Smith, S. E., Nabipour, S., & Hammond, A. S. (2020). Legal education during the covid-19 pandemic: Put health, safety and equity first. *Santa Clara Law Review*, *61*, 367–466.

Santos, J. R. (2020). *Economia Indispensável*. Lisbon International Press, Lisboa.

Shamsuzzoha, A., Nieminen, J., Piya, S., & Rutledge, K. (2021). Smart city for sustainable environment: A comparison of participatory strategies from Helsinki, Singapore and London. *Cities*, *114*, 103194.

Shen, K. M., Wu, C. L., Lee, M. H. (2017). A study on Taiwanese undergraduates' conceptions of Internet-based learning. *International Journal on Digital Learning Technology*, *9*(3), 1–22.

Sinha, B. (2020). Post-COVID challenges and opportunities in the education sector. *SSRN Electronic Journal*, *1*, 12.

Sousa, M. J., & Rocha, Á. (2020). Learning analytics measuring impacts on organisational performance. *Journal of Grid Computing, 18*(3), 563–571.

Taamallah, A., Khemaja, M., & Faiz, S. (2018, October). Toward a framework for smart city strategies design. In *Proceedings of the 3rd International Conference on Smart City Applications* (pp. 1–7).

Tang, Q. (2014). *Global Citizenship Education: Preparing Learners for the Challenges of the 21st Century.* UNESCO, India.

Werner, K., & Woessmann, L. (2021). The legacy of COVID-19 in education. *Economic Policy*, eiad016.

Xu, D. (2019). Research on new English mobile teaching mode under the impact of mobile Internet age. *Open Journal of Social Sciences, 7*(5), 109–117.

Zivkovic, M., Bacanin, N., Venkatachalam, K., Nayyar, A., Djordjevic, A., Strumberger, I., & Al-Turjman, F. (2021). COVID-19 cases prediction by using hybrid machine learning and beetle antennae search approach. *Sustainable Cities and Society, 66*, 102669.

Chapter 8

Accounting Education: New Pedagogies and Digital Approaches Based on the Research Agenda

Hugo Palácios
University of the Algarve, Faro, Portugal

Maria José Sousa
Instituto Universitário de Lisboa, Lisbon, Portugal

Contents

8.1 Introduction	144
8.2 Accounting Education	145
8.2.1 Evolution	145
8.2.2 Trends	146
8.2.3 Digital Accounting	148
8.3 Materials and Methods	150
8.3.1 Data Collection and Research Strategy	150
8.3.2 Data Analysis and Visualization	150
8.4 Results	151
8.4.1 Conceptual Structure of Knowledge	163
8.4.2 Intellectual Structure of Knowledge	164
8.4.3 Social Structure of Knowledge	169

8.5	Discussion and Conclusions	171
8.6	Implications of the Research	176
	8.6.1 Theoretical Implications	176
	8.6.2 Practical Implications	177
	8.6.3 Limitations	177
References		177

8.1 Introduction

In 2018, the World Economic Forum report, "The future of jobs report 2018", was published, which predicted that high-speed mobile internet (5G); artificial intelligence; "big data" and cloud storage, influence the competitiveness and sustainability of companies significantly by 2021. With the confinement enacted in March 2020, as a result of the Covid-19 pandemic, companies were forced to enter this new digital age abruptly and quickly, as they felt the need to be able to produce and have remote work processes (telework), access to all kinds of data in real-time, and increase the efficiency and effectiveness of organizations. This digital transformation was vital and various types of collaborative platforms and tools began to play a key role in data transmission, making the various stakeholders of companies constantly connected anywhere in the country or the world and working simultaneously with the same files. This urgent need for digital transformation has also occurred in companies in the accounting sector. With the adaptation and use of new technologies, digital accounting began to be implemented in many accounting companies around the world, in order to be able to provide more agile services, through more efficient processes, transforming bureaucratic services, manuals, and intermediaries into new business models, providing value and presenting differentiating services to customers.

At the level of accounting education, there was also rapid adaptability to new practices and methodologies, changing the teaching and evaluation of a face-to-face format for non-face-to-face or "online". Despite the effectiveness of all actors in adapting to new technologies in order to overcome the specific crisis, there have been obstacles and difficulties to their efficiency, with possible integrity consequences, which may jeopardize the credibility and reputation of educational institutions.

This article aims to review and summarize the scientific production on accounting education, through bibliometric and visualization techniques, to analyze the evolution and trends of research [Objective 1, O1], the origin and evolution of scientific production (by countries [O2], authors [O3], institutions [O4], and collaboration [O5]), the dissemination of production by sources [O6] and the classification and analysis of the content of articles from the keywords and keywords-plus [07] and quotes [O8].

8.2 Accounting Education

The actuality of accounting is the past of accounting education. The future of societies is the present of universities. Today's teaching is the future of the next generations (Bialik et al., 2016). One of the great difficulties of the coming years is related to the capacity of polytechnic and university education, to be able to follow this whole process of change, renew its courses according to the requirements of this new digital age, and adapt the programs of the curricular units to the needs of the new labor markets. Schools and universities are not having the capacity in good time to prepare people for all this change and, in many cases, continue to neglect the adaptation of their programs to technological change.

Economist Erwann Tison, director of the French institute Sapiens, criticizes the education sector for not adapting curricula to new technological changes. According to him, this digital revolution will mirror a relationship between the destruction and construction of new professions. Many professions will disappear and most of them are being transformed by technology. It is necessary to find, collectively, solutions to be able to accompany these people in professional retraining. Education must establish strategies to urgently adapt to the new realities of the market, even if it becomes obsolete, and this will be a disaster for a large part of the population.

8.2.1 Evolution

For more than 20 years, there has been a need for significant changes in accounting education due to constant changes and changes in the environment (Albrecht & Sack, 2000). Boyce et al. (2001) conclude that existing technical-based learning styles are not suitable for acquiring generic students' skills and that accounting education should take responsibility for the development of these generic skills ("soft-skills", skills or attitudes) together with technical skills of the discipline, in order to enhance their employment prospects. This skills gap was perceived by employers and transmitted to the higher education sector that suggested the implementation of curricular changes and new teaching methods, much more interdisciplinary and analytical, in order to overcome these differences in expectation (Gammie et al., 2002).

At the level of accounting service providers, the literature began to look at a decrease in the percentage of invoicing associated exclusively with legal compliance with obligations and record keeping, coupled with technological developments, as this would empower almost all companies in the sector with the same resources. According to this view, differentiation and competitive advantages would become focused on business consulting services. In this context, Howieson (2003) concludes that, in addition to the technological skills of new professionals, the most important will be related to the capacity for analysis, innovation in problem-solving, communication, and interpersonal relationships, namely teamwork and leadership. For about a decade, many of the accounting education jobs studied and discussed the perceptions and expectations of students and employers for the development of these and other skills in future accounting professionals (Ballantine & McCourt Larres, 2009; De Lange et al., 2006; De Villiers, 2010; Hassall et al., 2005; Jackling & De Lange, 2009; Kavanagh & Drennan, 2008; Wells et al., 2009).

Boyce (2004) argues that the reform of accounting education needs a greater scope beyond the institutional needs and agendas of organs and professional orders. In 2012 it presents a new approach that incorporates social and critical perspectives, with an interest in ethical, social, and environmental responsibility, based on a conception that accounting and accountability are social processes with a lot of power (Boyce et al., 2012). With the support of the Institute of Management Accountants (IMA) and the Management Accounting Section (MAS) of the American Accounting Association (AAA), Lawson et al. (2014) published the competencies-based educational structure in which the objective is to link accounting technical knowledge to a skills map and thus create curricular models for the future.

8.2.2 Trends

The literature on accounting education (Apostolou et al., 2020; Apostolou et al., 2015; Apostolou et al., 2010; Apostolou et al., 2001) segregates publications according to five topics associated with traditional knowledge bases. Briefly, the articles are categorized into (1) curricular subjects and teaching approaches; (2) thematic areas; (3) technology; (4) students; and (5) faculty.

In the first category, with a more comprehensive spectrum, there is a tendency to study and discuss the integration of new curricular themes such as data analysis and "big data" (Richardson & Shan, 2019; Sledgianowski et al., 2017) or the XBRL language (Wulandari & Ali, 2019), as well as the possibility of adapting to "Work-Integrated Learning" (Stanley & Xu, 2019). At the level of competences, the need to develop non-technical skills is generally accepted by the literature (Douglas & Gammie, 2019; Howcroft, 2017), critical thinking (Cloete, 2018), communicational (Holmes et al., 2019; Shauki & Benzie, 2017), or writing (Liu et al., 2019), to meet the needs of employers (Tan & Laswad, 2018). About new approaches to teaching, Butler et al. (2019) advocate that experiential education improves the critical thinking of students and presents a structure to facilitate the implementation of experiential learning, which will require students to make, reflect, think, and apply. Other approaches have been proposed and studied, such as "storytelling" as a way to promote active learning (Freeman & Burkette, 2019; Taylor et al., 2018), "Team-based learning" (Christensen et al., 2019), "Choice-based learning" (Opdecam & Everaert, 2019), "Game-based learning" (Silva et al., 2019) and "Case-based teaching" (Tan, 2019).

Regarding the thematic areas, it is worth noting the studies on the development of new curricular units. The conceptual structure for the teaching of management accounting (Samuel, 2018), the structures on accounting ethics (Blanthorne, 2017; Shaub, 2017) or new approaches to "big data" (McKinney et al., 2017), trust

(Palácios et al. 2021b), and accounting information systems (Loo & Bots, 2018), are examples of new paths in accounting education.

One of the biggest barriers to the adoption and use of educational technologies is resistance to change, innovation, and the technological incapacity of teachers (Watty et al., 2016). Despite this, technology is an integral part of accounting education (Blankley et al., 2018) in such a way that development technologies should be included in curriculum plans (Kotb, Abdel-Kader, Allam, Halabi & Franklin, 2019). Increasingly, new branches of study arise, namely on the modes of teaching: face-to-face, hybrid, or "online" (McCarthy et al., 2019; Taplin et al., 2017), employers' perception of new online education models (Grossman & Johnson, 2016; Kohlmeyer et al., 2015; Mauldin et al., 2019), the perception of students to tutorials and conferences "online" (Coetzee et al., 2018) or about the use of YouTube videos (Jill et al., 2019). Worrying is, at the level of the assessment, the perception of teachers about academic dishonesty (Sayed & Lento, 2016). In fact, academic fraud is a real problem for which preventive and detection controls should be implemented (Bujaki, Lento & Sayed, 2019; Lento, Sayed & Bujaki, 2018). The existence of "ghostwriters" and the lack of effective controls in online evaluations, requires a discussion on authentication techniques, identity management, and surveillance methodologies (Fisher et al., 2016).

Accountants, orders, professional associations, and teachers represent the image of accounting for their clients, students, and society in general. It is important to establish a strategy that alters people's stereotyped perceptions of accounting (P. K. Wells, 2019). In this sense, it is important to understand the influence of students' attitudes in choosing this profession (Hammour, 2018), what are the determining factors in this decision (Hutchins & Roberts, 2019), and what their behavioral intentions are (Djatej et al., 2015). The characteristics of students and their skills have been studied, from various perspectives, from the most common ones such as resilience (Smith et al., 2019), personality (Holt et al., 2017), and decision-making (Blay & Fennema, 2017; Palácios et al., 2017), through emotional intelligence (Coady et al., 2018), creativity (Birkey & Hausserman, 2019) and ending in the joint effects between narcissism and psychopathy (Bailey, 2017, 2019).

Teachers have to adapt to the way new generations ("Millennial" and Generation Z) learn, and to that extent, the question is how adaptation should be made to better motivate and educate future accounting professionals. Teachers need skills that allow them to take risks, face challenges, have solutions to various problems, able to understand the interdisciplinary issues that allow them to create appropriate materials (Reid & Petocz, 2004). From this perspective, there are publications sharing teaching strategies (Wygal et al., 2017) and identifying effective and ineffective teaching practices in order to improve effectiveness and influence on teaching (Allen, 2019). It is true that on the part of teachers, there is a perception of deteriorating standard of accounting teaching and the quality of students, as well as evidence of frustration, disappointment, and institutional pressures to achieve approval rates and of students with a low level of basic skills (Steenkamp & Roberts, 2017).

In many institutions, budgetary pressures have significantly reduced the share of full-time teachers with the implications on stability (Boyle et al., 2015) and, consequently, in the definition of projects in the medium and long term.

8.2.3 Digital Accounting

The history of accounting is a discipline with content rich in changes, changes, and adaptations, both in terms of legal, economic, financial, and technological aspects. From paradigm to paradigm, these evolutions transported accounting as science to the concept of utility. Accounting is an information system that aims to communicate to interested users all the information useful for decision-making (Palácios et al., 2017). Accountants perform daily functions of organizing the accounting information of companies and institutions, covering various areas of management. In this way, the accountant gains a primary role as responsible for managing a large number of data and information of his clients and plays a fundamental role in trust (Kelton et al., 2008) and in ensuring confidentiality and protection thereof.

It is increasingly difficult to dissociate technology from the sustainability of the economy (Khuntia et al., 2018). If on the one hand, we can identify disadvantages in these technological changes, attributing to it the threat weight for the future of certain activities or professions (Forum, 2020; Ionescu & Andronie, 2019), on the other hand, is a great opportunity to redesign processes, increase profitability and discover new competitive advantages.

Regardless of the size, companies providing accounting services must ensure the availability, performance, and stability of IT systems, so that the activity is not disruptive, and, on the other hand, invest in technological innovation, to increase levels of competitiveness, in the face of the demands of the digital market (Dias, 2020).

Faced with the need to follow this evolution of the market, the business model of this sector is no longer focused on the accounting process to direct the focus to the client. This change in positioning changed the way the accounting professional carries out his activity, starting to have a more active role, as consultants with specialized experience and strategic and operational knowledge (Frolova et al., 2020). Manual work is getting smaller and smaller, but the accounting professional has gained a more analytical role, with the need for skills in data processing, interpretation of information, communication and written reporting and problem-solving skills, and decision-making support (Mesquita, 2021).

The more useful the information available in decision-making, the more likely it is to be assertive. Technology provides accounting with the ability to work on information in real-time by facilitating the process of making investment decisions and reducing costs or new business models. The ability to produce more in less time has changed the accounting cycle of companies, reduced the operational execution time, and increased the time available for data analysis. Accountability, financial reporting, and the structure of companies' information outputs have been changed to adapt to digital technologies. One of the central elements of digital accounting that underpins international financial reporting is the IFRS Taxonomy. The adaptation and implementation of this stun industry have implications for the practice and accounting standards (Troshani et al., 2018).

We define digital accounting as an information system based on digital technology, which aims to communicate, in an integrated and interactive "online", interactive way, to interested users, all the information useful for decision-making. Technological implementation has given rise to digital accounting where information is treated digitally, fundamental for companies, because it helps decision-making, more quickly, more usefully, and with fewer context costs. The concept of digital accounting is relatively new and is related to the recent Industrial Revolution 4.0 (Ardianto & Anridho, 2018). Although, there have been few studies in the literature globally since the work of Deshmukh (2006) that this field of research has increased its interest (Deniz, 2021). Brukhansky and Spilnyk (2021) explore the concept of digital accounting from its historical roots and discuss the formation of a new digital accounting paradigm.

The strategic planning of companies in this sector must invariably go through the adaptation to the use of these new technologies, with integrated systems, which offer in real-time, an overall view of companies, as a way to increase the quality of service, increase operational productivity and optimize execution times. Otherwise, they are likely to disappear (Azzari et al., 2020). From this point of view, adaptation to digital accounting must be seen as an opportunity to improve the agility and efficiency of services. This increase in flexibility allows the professional and the client direct access to information from anywhere, reducing the need for face-to-face meetings in meetings, creating value and customer satisfaction, and maintaining the quality of service.

Although technology has brought numerous benefits, some new problems are emerging. One of the most significant problems of today's systems is related to the security vulnerabilities and users' increased security and responsibility, and the confidentiality and reliability of digital accounting records (Mosweu & Ngoepe, 2021). In this sense, we find in the literature studies on the influence of "big data" (Bonsón & Bednárová, 2019) or Blockchain (Warren et al., 2015) in accounting, as well as Blockchain solutions in order to preserve trust and mitigate these challenges (Awuson-David et al., 2020). Another problem is related to the effect of the digital transformation of society and the consequent changes in work, namely the effect of artificial intelligence (AI) on accounting, focusing on the accounting profession, tasks, and skills. The results of Leitner-Hanetseder et al. (2021) have shown that tasks and skills will be subject to major changes over the next 10 years due to AI-based digital technologies. The accountant increasingly has to understand the effectiveness and efficiency of the use of information systems adopted by companies, having the obligation to always keep up to date with developments and novelties, adapting to the needs of companies.

The World Economic Forum "The Future of Jobs Report 2020" predicts that in this sector, more than 40% of the skills currently needed to perform these professions well will soon be redundant and that the accounting profession is the third most declining. "Cloud computing" (Tugui, 2015) "5G" "Big Data" (Balios, 2021), "Cybersecurity" (Demirkan et al., 2020), "Blockchain" (Maffei et al., 2021), and "Artificial Intelligence" (Whitman & Sobczak, 2018) will be the next digital challenges that will turn these professionals into financial and accounting data scientists. All actors in this sector need to adapt and learn new skills and knowledge and, as such, these should be included in the curriculum (Diane et al., 2020). The actuality of accounting is the past of accounting education. The future of societies is the present of universities. Today's teaching is the future of the next generations (Bialik et al., 2016).

8.3 Materials and Methods

In order to increase the level of knowledge, and measure and analyze the published scientific literature on accounting education, we performed a bibliometric analysis, having as a starting point research in the Web of Science (WoS) database of Clarivate Analytics.

Thus, the main research questions of bibliometric analysis are: RQ1: What were the main keywords of accounting education research? RQ2: How do an author's studies on accounting education influence research? RQ3: How do authors, institutions, and countries interact with each other in accounting education studies?

8.3.1 Data Collection and Research Strategy

The data used in this study were obtained in WoS, because it is one of the most complete sources of electronic information, of scientific and multidisciplinary character. Data collection took place on February 5, 2021, through a virtual private network (VPN) connection from the University of Algarve. We searched the term "accounting education" (TS = "accounting education") in WoS core collection indexers and, according to eligibility criteria, we chose articles in English. To ensure that metadata is complete and comparable, we did not limit the search for sources. Thus, it was intended to include all articles, even those that were not reviewed and qualified by a selected panel of recognized experts. We did not delimit the search period (time interval), so the search strategy included all publications dating back to 2020. All available results have been exported to text files, including citation information, bibliographic information, summaries, and keywords. To delete duplicate posts and manage the database, we chose endnote x8.2 software.

8.3.2 Data Analysis and Visualization

We chose the open-source statistical software R to operationalize bibliometric analysis and used Bibliometrix R 3.0.1 in the Biblioshiny version (Aria & Cuccurullo, 2017). To produce an overview of the data, descriptive statistics and bibliometric indicators were used, including annual publication growth, collaboration index (CI), and analysis of sources, authors, citations, keywords, keywords-plus, and productivity by country. The application and presentation of some of these indicators followed the analysis methodology reported in Sweileh et al. (2017) and replicated by Palácios et al. (2021a). We used visualization techniques to analyze the structures of knowledge: conceptual, intellectual, and social (Aria et al., 2020) through networks of collaboration of authors, international collaborations between institutions and countries, networks of "co-citation", and bibliographic references and networks of co-occurrence of keywords.

For network visualization, we opted for VOSviewer software (Van Eck & Waltman, 2010) in that it uses a unified structure for mapping and grouping (Waltman, Van Eck & Noyons, 2010) and has been used in more than 500 publications since 2006 (www.vosviewer.com/publications). According to Van Eck and Waltman (2010), VOSviewer is a tool for constructing and visualizing bibliometric networks focused on graphical representation and is useful for interpreting large bibliometric maps. These networks may include sources, authors, or institutions and can be constructed from citation, bibliographic coupling, co-citation, or co-authorship relationships. In the figures, the circles represent the items under analysis associated with their denomination. The wider the circle, the greater the weight of the item in the network. The distance between the items indicates the degree of relationship. The thicker the associated lines, the larger the connection. Location and color are ways to group items by clusters.

8.4 Results

From the search for the term "accounting education", in the titles, abstracts, keywords, and keywords-plus of the WoS database, we obtained a total of 779 publications. After applying the eligibility criteria, combined with the boolean operators, a total of 442 articles were obtained, according to Table 8.1.

We then imported the references to the EndNote X8.2 software. After the removal of the articles' "early access" and "proceeding paper" (n = 27), 415 articles remained.

Eligible articles were published between 1957 and 2020. The annual average was 11 articles published per year. Figure 8.1 shows that there are three delimited moments

Table 8.1   Number of Articles Found Per Search

Criteria	WoS
TS = ("accounting education")	779
Booleans	Indexes	Timespan = [1957;2020]	Type:	Review Pairs	English	442
Removal of "early access" and "proceeding paper" articles	415

Own elaboration | Software: Excel

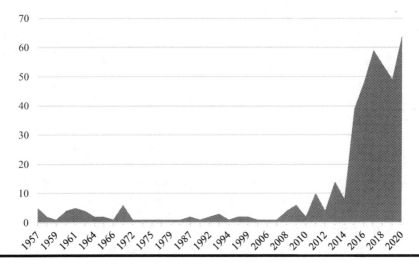

Figure 8.1 Annual scientific production.

Vertical axis – number of articles | Horizontal shaft – years | own elaboration | Software: Excel

in time. At first, between 1957 and 2010, articles published annually have a residual character with an average of 2 articles per year. During the first 53 years, we identified only 66 articles, representing 15.90%. In the period between 2011 and 2014, there was a slight increase in the number of articles published, with an increase in the annual average of 9 articles published per year. It is during this period that we identified the point from which the annual growth of scientific production intensified. Between 2015 and 2020, there is a sharp growth and there is an average of 52 articles published per year. In this period, there are 303 articles (75.42%) and the highest productivity is in 2020, with a total of 64 articles (15.42%), which demonstrates the timeliness of the theme. The average annual growth rate is 6.94% during the study period.

The 415 articles were published by 127 sources. According to Bradford's Law (Bradford, 1934; Brookes, 1969), we verified the existence of three clusters: the central zone is composed of five sources that published 145 articles (34.94%). An intermediate zone whose 20 sources published 137 articles (33.01%), and the smaller zone composed of 102 sources and 133 articles (32.05%). Of a total of 2,416 citations, as of February 6, 2021, the five sources in the central zone represent 861 citations (35.64%). In Table 8.2, we can observe the impact of the sources calculated through different measures.

In terms of the dynamics of publications of the sources with the most impact, we can see over the years, with cumulative effect (Figure 8.2), a sharp growth of the "Accounting Review" from the first publication in 1957 to 1970. From that year on, growth stabilized, with only 4 articles between 1971 and 2020. The first publication of "Critical perspectives on accounting" is from 2013, followed by "Accounting education", "Issues in accounting education" and "Meditari accountancy research",

Table 8.2 Impact of Sources: Top-15

Rank	Sources	Cluster	h_index	g_index	m_index	TC	NP	PY_start
1	Accounting education	Central Zone	9	13	1.28571429	315	62	2015
2	Accounting review	Central Zone	3	11	0.04615385	140	27	1957
3	Issues in accounting education	Central Zone	5	7	0.71428571	66	21	2015
4	Critical perspectives on accounting	Central Zone	9	15	1	252	18	2013
5	Meditari accountancy research	Central Zone	5	8	0.71428571	88	17	2015
6	Journal of accountancy	Intermediate Zone	3	6	0.04615385	41	15	1957
7	Journal of business ethics	Intermediate Zone	9	14	0.3	296	14	1992
8	Journal of education for business	Intermediate Zone	3	6	0.42857143	41	11	2015
9	South African journal of higher education	Intermediate Zone	2	2	0.5	6	11	2018
10	Accounting research journal	Intermediate Zone	2	2	0.4	8	8	2017
11	South African journal of accounting research	Intermediate Zone	3	4	0.5	25	8	2016
12	Accounting and finance	Intermediate Zone	4	7	0.28571429	71	7	2008
13	Accounting history	Intermediate Zone	2	3	0.28571429	15	7	2015
14	Asian review of accounting	Intermediate Zone	2	4	0.33333333	22	6	2016
15	Australian accounting review	Intermediate Zone	3	6	0.23076923	42	6	2009

TC – Total quotes | NP – Number of articles | PY_start – Year of 1st publication | own elaboration | Software: Excel

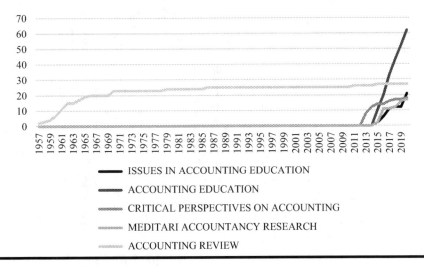

Figure 8.2 Production by sources.

Vertical axis – number of articles (cumulative) | Horizontal axis – years | own elaboration | Software: Excel

with the first articles in 2015. We highlight the upward curve of "Accounting education", representative of 62 articles in 6 years, with an annual average of 10 articles per year, being evident in the propensity of this source to publish on the subject. In 2020, the year of higher productivity, the articles of "Accounting education" (10 articles) and "Issues in accounting education" (9 articles) represent 29.69% of the total publications.

A total of 732 authors were identified, with an average of articles per author of 0.567 and 1.76 authors per article. The average number of co-authors per article was 2.16. A total of 120 authors published 138 articles (33.25%) of single authorship and a total of 277 publications (66.75%) were authored by multiple authors. We identified 612 authors collaborating in 277 articles, representing a collaboration index of 2.21 (Elango & Rajendran, 2012; Koseoglu, 2016, 2019). From the analysis of the authors' productivity through Lotka Law (Lokta, 1926) (Figure 8.3), we found 723 occasional authors, and of these, 609 authors published only 1 article. Only 9 authors (1.10%) can be considered nuclear with more than 4 published articles. The nuclear author who stands out most for the number of articles published (7 articles), the longevity of scientific production (28 years), the total number of citations (71), and the measure "h-index" (4) is Alan Sangster of the University of Aberdeen Business School (UK), whose most recent article is "Insights into accounting education in a COVID-19 world" (Sangster et al., 2020).

Affiliated with these 732 authors are 376 institutions of which stand out (Figure 8.4) the "Deakin University" in Geelong (Australia) with 28 associated articles and "Macquarie University" in Sydney (Australia) and "RMIT University" in Melbourne (Australia), both with 23 associated articles.

Accounting Education ■ 155

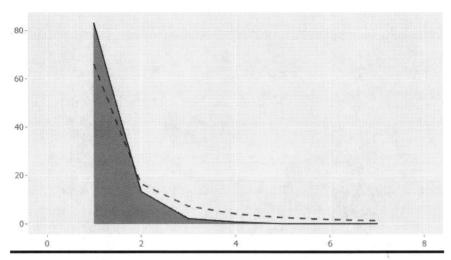

Figure 8.3   Frequency distribution of scientific productivity.

Vertical axis – % of authors | Horizontal axis – number of documents written | Theoretical distribution | own elaboration | Software: Biblioshiny

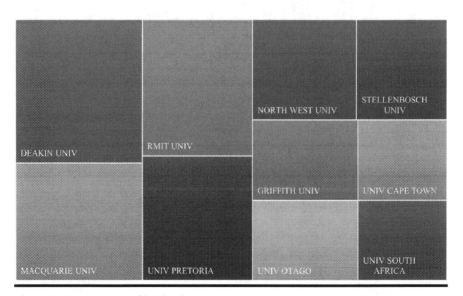

Figure 8.4   Treemap of institutions.

Own elaboration | Software: Excel

We have identified the contribution of 50 countries. At the level of scientific production by country, we verified the leadership of Australia, followed by the USA, South Africa, the UK, Canada, and China (Figure 8.5). Table 8.3 shows the countries with the most articles, with a minimum production of 4 articles

156 ■ *Technologies for Sustainable Global Higher Education*

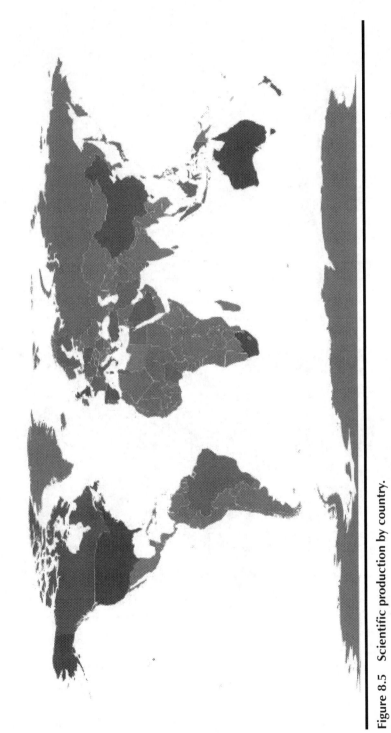

Figure 8.5 Scientific production by country.
Own elaboration | Software: Biblioshiny

Table 8.3 Articles of Single Authorship and Co-authorship

Country	Articles	Freq	SCP	MCP	MCP_Ratio
Australia	79	0.20955	71	8	0.1013
USA	69	0.18302	65	4	0.058
South Africa	46	0.12202	42	4	0.087
United Kingdom	29	0.07692	23	6	0.2069
Canada	17	0.04509	13	4	0.2353
China	15	0.03979	14	1	0.0667
New Zealand	15	0.03979	12	3	0.2
Spain	9	0.02387	7	2	0.2222
Indonesia	7	0.01857	5	2	0.2857
Kuwait	7	0.01857	4	3	0.4286
Italy	5	0.01326	3	2	0.4
Saudi Arabia	5	0.01326	3	2	0.4
Cyprus	4	0.01061	3	1	0.25
Malaysia	4	0.01061	3	1	0.25
Portugal	3	0.00796	2	1	0.3333

Own elaboration | Software: Excel

and compares countries by unique authored articles with multiauthor articles. It should be noted that at the level of collaboration, the three countries with the most scientific production have very low percentages of articles with multiple authors. Australia comes up with 79 articles and only 8 are from multiple authors (10.13%), and the USA and South Africa corroborate this trend with 5.8% and 8.7%. At the level of citations, Australia is the country with the highest number, with 761 citations (Figure 8.6), followed by 548 and 208 citations, representing 31.49%, 22.68%, and 8.61%, respectively, of the total of 2,416 citations. It should be noted that the United Arab Emirates has an average of 15 citations per article, well above the averages of Australia (9.67), the USA (7.94), and the United Kingdom (7.17). Portugal appears in the 22nd position with 8 citations, with an average of 2.67 citations per article.

As of February 6, 2021, the 415 articles have 2,416 citations, with an average of 5.82 citations per article. Each article has an average of 0.83 citations per year. The year 2014 has the highest average with 3.5 citations per year. The 10 most cited

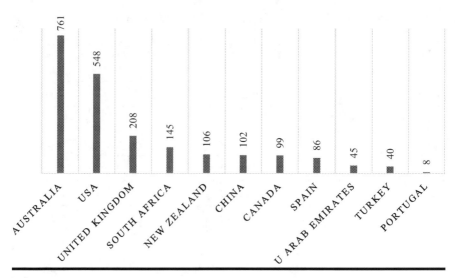

Figure 8.6 Total citations by country.

Number of citations / countries | own elaboration | Software: Excel

authors and articles in the entire database are presented in Table 8.5. Of the most cited articles, we identified 3 articles published by the Journal of business ethics that fall into the domains related to behavior, morality, and ethics. There are 2 articles related to education and research on educational issues, the rest of which are directly related to economic issues. The most quoted article is "The international integrated reporting framework: key issues and future research opportunities" (Cheng et al., 2014), with 120 citations and an average of 15 citations per year.

The authors used 1,166 keywords to index the 415 articles and WoS indexed it with 648 keywords-plus. Keywords-plus are more effective than the author's keywords for bibliometric analysis, when the goal is to investigate the structures of knowledge in scientific fields, but are less comprehensive in representing the content of an article (Zhang et al., 2016). The highlight is the keyword "accounting education" with 192 occurrences. Then "accounting", "education", and "learning" with 40, 24, and 14 occurrences. In Table 8.4, we can compare the words with the most occurrences in the four search fields. From the analysis of keywords-plus, we found that the most used words are "education", "perceptions", "students", and "skills". In order to be visually perceptible the size of the keywords, two "Wordcloud" were constructed with the authors' keywords and keywords-plus (Figures 8.7 and 8.8). Table 8.6 presents the 15 authors with the greatest impact on the researched topic.

The bibliographic lists of the 415 articles contain 15,741 references. Table 8.7 presents the 20 bibliographic references with the most citations, from which the articles "What skills and attributes does an accounting graduate need stand out? Evidence from student perceptions and employer expectations" (Kavanagh &

Table 8.4 Top10: Keywords, Keywords-Plus, Titles, and Summaries

Keywords	Occurrences	Keywords-Plus	Occurrences	Securities	Occurrences	Summaries	Occurrences
accounting education	192	education	61	Accounting	337	Accounting	1627
Accounting	40	perceptions	47	education	172	students	825
Education	24	students	40	students	71	education	584
Learning	14	skills	31	learning	56	study	475
Critical	12	performance	30	study	35	learning	422
Ethics	12	impact	29	perceptions	34	paper	320
higher education	12	Management	19	skills	32	skills	272
assessment	11	higher-education	18	teaching	28	findings	218
academic performance	9	Knowledge	17	performance	26	teaching	205
Accounting students	8	attributes	15	Student	25	Professional	183

Own elaboration | Software: Excel

Table 8.5 Authors and Articles Most Cited in WoS

AU	THEE	TC	OS	PY
Cheng m;green w;conradie p;konishi n;r omi a	The international integrated reporting framework: key issues and future research opportunities	120	Journal of international financial management & accounting	2014
Kaplan rs	Accounting scholarship that advances professional knowledge and practice	114	Accounting review	2011
Chiou cc	The effect of concept mapping on students' learning achievements and interests	75	Innovations in education and teaching international	2008
Liyanarachchi g;newdick c	The impact of moral reasoning and retaliation on whistle-blowing: new zealand evidence	48	Journal of business ethics	2009
Fischer m; rosenzweig k	Attitudes of students and accounting practitioners concerning the ethical acceptability of earnings management	47	Journal of business ethics	1995
Gendron	Accounting academy and the threat of the paying-off mentality	43	Critical perspectives on accounting	2015
Hiltebeitel km;jones sk	An assessment of ethics instruction in accounting education	43	Journal of business ethics	1992
Chabrak n; craig r	Student imaginings, cognitive dissonance and critical thinking	36	Critical perspectives on accounting	2013
Hopper T	Making accounting degrees fit for a university	36	Critical perspectives on accounting	2013
Evans e;tindale j;cable d; mead sh	Collaborative teaching in a linguistically and culturally diverse higher education setting: a case study of a post-graduate accounting program	36	Higher education research & development	2009

TI – Title | AU – Author | SO – Source | PY – Year | TC – Total citation | own elaboration | Software: Excel

Table 8.6 Impact of Authors: Top-15

Author	h_index	g_index	m_index	TC	NP	PY_start
Sangster to	4	7	0.133	71	7	1992
Dellaportas s	4	5	0.444	31	6	2013
Watty K	4	5	0.25	33	5	2006
Alanzi Ka	2	2	0.4	6	4	2017
Bayerlein L	2	4	0.286	24	4	2015
Cooper bj	3	3	0.429	14	4	2015
Kunz	3	4	0.429	19	4	2015
Stoner G	4	4	0.5	30	4	2014
Viviers Ha	2	4	0.333	24	4	2016
Alfraih mm	2	2	0.4	6	3	2017
Boyce G	3	3	0.333	37	3	2013
Brink ag	2	2	0.333	7	3	2016
Hassall T	3	3	0.333	28	3	2013
Howieson B	3	3	0.231	36	3	2009
Kirstein M	3	3	0.429	18	3	2015

TC – Total quotes | NP – Number of publications | PY_start – Year 1st publication | own elaboration | Software: Excel

Drennan, 2008), "Do Accounting Graduates' Skills Meet the Expectations of Employers? A Matter of Convergence or Divergence" (Jackling & De Lange, 2009) and "The Expectation-Performance Gap in Accounting Education: An Exploratory Study" (Bui & Porter, 2010). Through Reference Publication Year Spectroscopy analysis, we identified 3 years with relevant articles for this field of research. In 2000 we identified the publication of the work "Accounting education: Charting the course through a perilous future" (Albrecht & Sack, 2000). Later, in 2004, the article "Critical accounting education: teaching and learning outside the circle" (Boyce, 2004) and, in 2010, the work "The Expectation-Performance Gap in Accounting Education: An Exploratory Study" (Bui & Porter, 2010).

To answer the three research questions of this bibliometric analysis, we proceeded to analyze the three structures of knowledge: conceptual, intellectual, and social.

162 ■ *Technologies for Sustainable Global Higher Education*

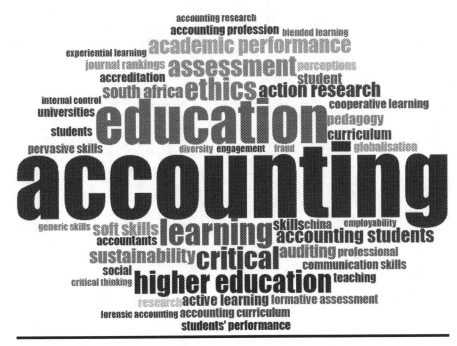

Figure 8.7   Wordcloud: Keywords.

Author's keywords | own elaboration | Software: Biblioshiny

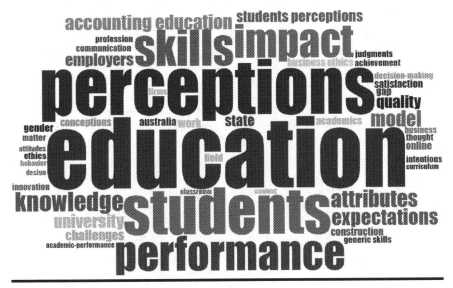

Figure 8.8   Wordcloud: "Keywords-plus".

"Keywords-plus" | own elaboration | Software: Biblioshiny

Table 8.7 Most Cited Bibliographic References

Reference	Year	Source	Quotes
Mh Kavanagh	2008	financ account	45
Jackling B	2009	account educ	40
Bui B	2010	account educ	28
Howieson B.	2003	Brit rev account	27
De lange p	2006	financ account	24
Albrecht w.	2000	accounting ed series	21
Apostolou b.	2013	j accounting ed	20
Boyce g.	2004	crit perspect accoun	20
Wells p	2009	account educ	18
Albrecht w.s.	2000	accounting ed charti	17
Boyce g.	2001	accounting ed int j	17
Gammie B.	2002	accounting edu int j	17
Barac K	2009	accountancy meditari	16
Apostolou b.	2010	j accounting ed	15
Ballantine J	2009	account educ	15
De villiers r.	2010	accountancy meditari	15
Doran b.m.	1991	iss account educ	15
Lawson Ra	2014	iss account educ	15
Mohamed E.K.A.	2003	financ manag	15
Pathways Commission	2012	chart nat strat next	15

Own elaboration | Software: Excel

8.4.1 Conceptual Structure of Knowledge

The conceptual structure of knowledge represents the relations between concepts and words in each set of articles, in order to map what science is studying and explore the different themes developed in research (Aria et al., 2020; Tijssen & Van Raan, 1989). Each field or scientific topic is characterized by author's keywords or "keywords-plus" (Garfield & Sher, 1993). To map the conceptual structure, we used two approaches: factor analysis and the network of keyword co-occurrences.

To reduce the dimensionality of the data, we performed a factor analysis of keywords-plus using the Multiple Match Analysis (MCA) technique. According to Abdi and Valentin (2007), this technique is an extension of correspondence analysis (CA), which analyzes the relationships of several categorical dependent variables. Analyzes a set of observations described by a set of nominal variables. In Figure 8.9, we present the factor analysis map. There are five clusters of keywords-plus, identified by different colors, and each represents the set of words closest to each other, on certain themes. It is visible the existence of a cluster on behavioral issues and related to ethics and morals, corroborating the results presented in the citations. There is a cluster related to the attributes and perspective of the employer, one about the difference in expectations and perceptions between the student, education, and the market, and finally, one that is related to education and knowledge.

In the visualization of the network of co-occurrence of keywords, we identify the words that appear in the articles indexed together and that are, consequently, related to each other. This conceptual structure of knowledge allows us to know the most addressed topics, and identify the most important research domains and the most recent research paths.

The visualization of the keyword co-occurrence network (Figure 8.10) showed that the keywords "accounting education" is the strongest word. With preponderance and strong links to it, we identified the words "accounting", "education", "learning", "skills", and "critical", with a close relationship between them coexisting in many of the articles.

In the visualization of the network map of co-occurrence by "keywords-plus" (Figure 8.11), we identified six clusters. The most related words in each of the clusters are "education", "perceptions", "students", "impact", "attributes", and "feedback". The mapping shows "education" with 37 links, and corroborates some of the central relationships of the keyword co-occurrence network. In both visualizations, we found strong links between "education" and "knowledge" or "perceptions", "skills", and "expectations".

8.4.2 Intellectual Structure of Knowledge

The intellectual structure of knowledge is used to detect changes in paradigms and schools of thought, through the influence of different authors in the scientific community. In bibliometry, the most common analysis is the so-called co-citation network (Small, 1973, 1997, 1999) to verify if there are relationships between bibliographic references. There is co-citation of two articles when both are quoted in a third. As we have seen, the bibliographic lists of the 415 articles contain 15,741 references.

In Figure 8.12, we visualize dwelled the network of co-citation scans by articles, where we identified 44 bibliographic references. The most prominent authors and bibliographic references with stronger links are: "Do accounting graduates'

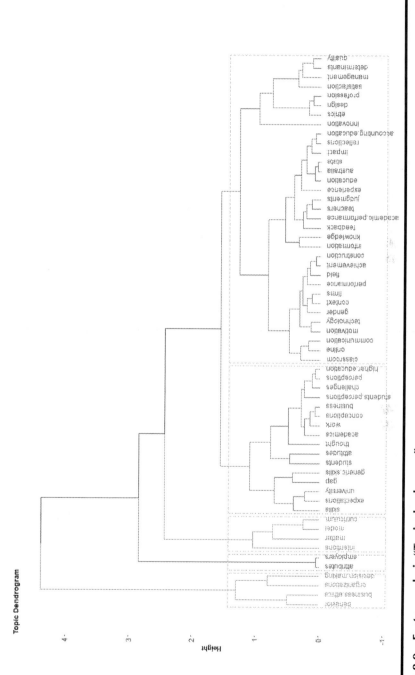

Figure 8.9 Factor analysis "Topic dendogram".
Own elaboration | Software: Biblioshiny

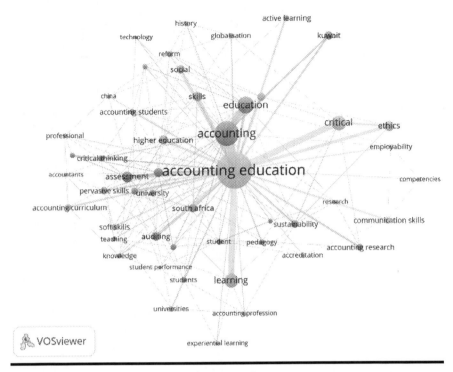

Figure 8.10 Keyword co-occurrence network.
Own elaboration | Software: VOSviewer

skills meet the expectations of employers? A matter of convergence or divergence" (Jackling & De Lange, 2009), "What skills and attributes does an accounting graduate need? Evidence from student perceptions and employer expectations" (Kavanagh & Drennan, 2008), "Accounting practice in the new millennium: is accounting education ready to meet the challenge?" (Howieson, 2003), "Accounting graduates' perceptions of skills emphasis in undergraduate courses: an investigation from two Victorian universities" (De Lange, Jackling & Gut, 2006), "The expectation-performance gap in accounting education: An exploratory study" (Bui & Porter, 2010). Noteworthy are the literature reviews "Accounting education literature review (2006–2009)" (Apostolou, Hassell, Rebele & Watson, 2010) and "Accounting education literature review (2010–2012)" (Apostolou, Dorminey, Hassell & Watson, 2013).

In the visualization of the co-citation network by authors (Figure 8.13) of the 15,741 bibliographic references, the strong link between Beverley Jackling (Victoria University), Marie Kavanagh (University of Southern Queensland), Binh Bui (Macquarie University), Paul de Lange (RMIT university), Paul Wells (Auckland University of Technology), and Trevor Hassall (Sheffield Hallam University) is visible.

Accounting Education ■ 167

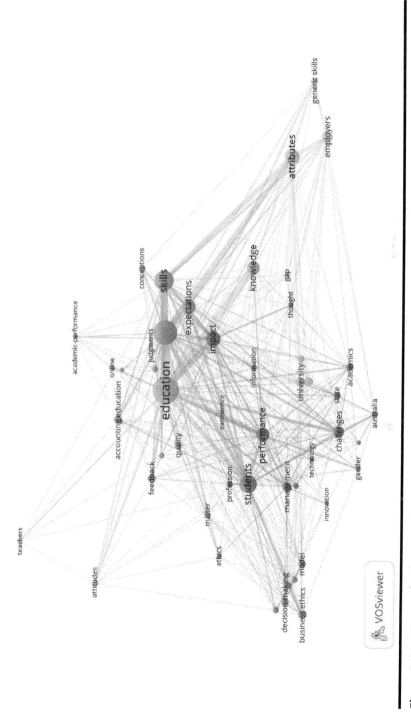

Figure 8.11 Keywords-plus co-occurrence network.
Own elaboration | Software: VOSviewer

168 ■ *Technologies for Sustainable Global Higher Education*

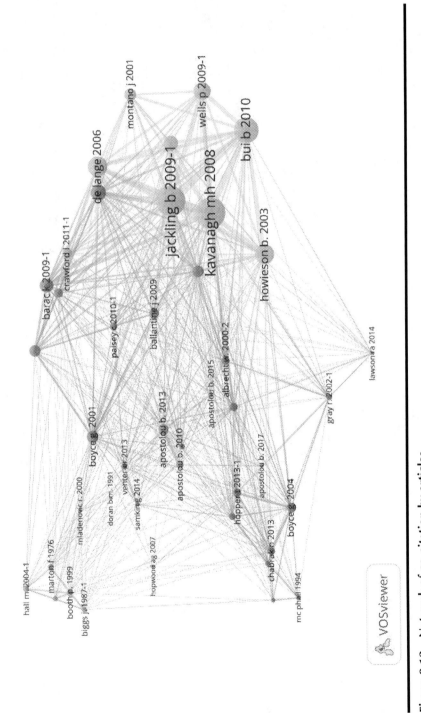

Figure 8.12 Network of co-citation by articles.
Own elaboration | Software: VOSviewer

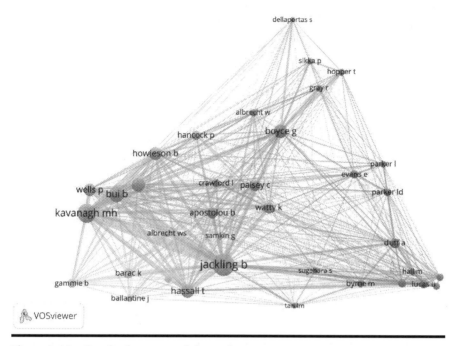

Figure 8.13 Co-citation network by authors.

8.4.3 Social Structure of Knowledge

Through the visualization of collaboration networks, the analysis of the social structure of knowledge shows how authors, institutions, and countries relate and verify the most influential authors, groups of authors, or relevant scientific research institutions (Glänzel, 2002). The most common social structure is the network of collaboration between authors (co-authorship), where the relationships between the different authors are usually constructed from the articles published together (Katz & Martin, 1997).

Figure 8.14 shows a network of collaboration between authors. This list of authors was determined based on the number of articles published in co-authorship. The map includes 10 circles representing the authors, grouped into different clusters by color. The closest circles indicate authors with closer collaboration. The author who most collaborates with other authors is Kim Watty of Deakin University. With "Developing a global model of accounting education and examining IES compliance in Australia, Japan, and Sri Lanka" (Watty et al., 2013), the author links Satoshi Sugahara from "Kwansei Gakuin University" and with "Social moderation, assessment and assuring standards for accounting graduates" (Watty et al., 2014) collaborates with a group of authors from different Australian universities, such as Mark Freeman of the University of Sydney, Bryan Howieson

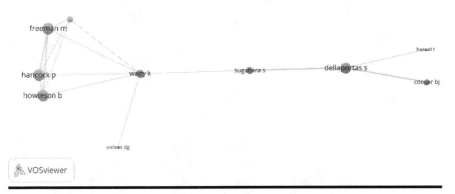

Figure 8.14 Network of collaboration between authors.

Own elaboration | Software: VOSviewer

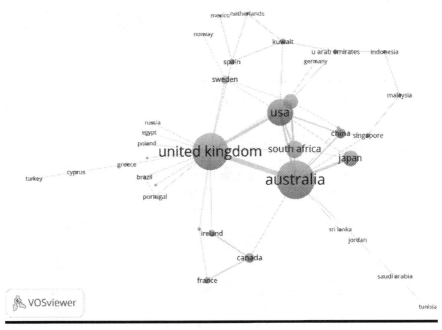

Figure 8.15 Network of international collaboration between countries.

Own elaboration | Software: VOSviewer

of the University of Adelaide, and Phil Hancock of the University of Western Australia.

In the network map of international collaboration between countries (Figure 8.15), Australia plays a significant role and shows strong collaboration with the USA and the UK, thus forming a strong triangle of collaboration. The most substantial collaborations, represented by thicker lines, are among the following pairs: Australia–UK, Australia–Japan, US–UK, South Africa–New Zealand, US–Australia, and US–South Africa. We identified 11 segmented clusters with different colors. The UK is the most collaborative, with 16 links to other countries. South Africa (Africa) and the United Kingdom (Europe) show themselves as the intercontinental bridges connecting the USA to Australia and Japan (Figure 8.17).

From the analysis of the network of international collaboration between institutions (Figure 8.16), we identified 18 institutions, and the "RMIT University" in Melbourne (Australia) with 10 relations and the "Deakin University" in Geelong (Australia) with 7 are the institutions that collaborate the most and the link with institutions from other continents. In addition to the diverse collaboration between Australian institutions, it is worth noting the collaboration of "Deakin University" with "Sheffield Hallam University" in Sheffield (United Kingdom) and "RMIT University" with the University of Glasgow in Glasgow (United Kingdom) and with the "Victoria University of Wellington" in Wellington (New Zealand).

8.5 Discussion and Conclusions

We obtained 779 publications in the initial research, covering all the years available in the central WoS collection. After applying the eligibility criteria and removing duplicates, we reviewed 415 articles. The results show an apparent increase in the number of publications [O1], authors, and collaborations, with an average annual growth rate of 6.94 %. Of 732 authors, the average number of authors per article is 1.76 and 0.567 articles per author. Published in 127 sources, we identified 612 authors collaborating on 277 articles, representing a collaboration index of 2.21 (Elango & Rajendran, 2012). Compared to other research subthemes, our study has a lower IC than "Social Media" with 3.4 (Martí-Parreño & Gómez-Calvet, 2020), Airbnb with 2.26 (Andreu, Bigne, Amaro & Palomo, 2020), but higher than "Revenue Management in Airline" with 1.85 (Raza, Ashrafi & Akgunduz, 2020), and "Information Technologies" with 0.71 (Khaparde & Pawar, 2013). This IC is probably the result of greater interdisciplinarity of education, better and easier communication between researchers from different institutions and countries, and increased pressure from institutions to publish.

The timeliness of the theme is demonstrated by the sharp growth of publications between 2015 and 2020, with an average of 52 articles per year. The highest productivity is even in 2020 with a total of 64 articles (15.42%), out of a total of 303 published in this period. Indeed, it is congruent with the overall growth of 3% of publications observed annually in all scientific disciplines. However, our study shows a growth rate over the past 5 years that reflects much faster growth than other disciplines. If, on the one hand, the number of researchers and the increase in the number of newspapers may be the reasons for this growth (Ware & Mabe, 2015),

172 ■ Technologies for Sustainable Global Higher Education

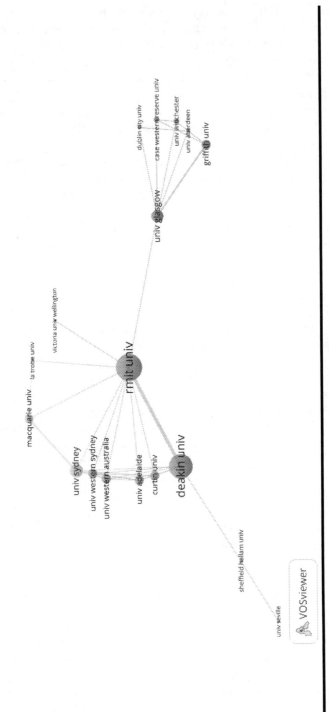

Figure 8.16 Network of international collaboration between institutions.
Own elaboration | *Software: VOSviewer*

Accounting Education ■ 173

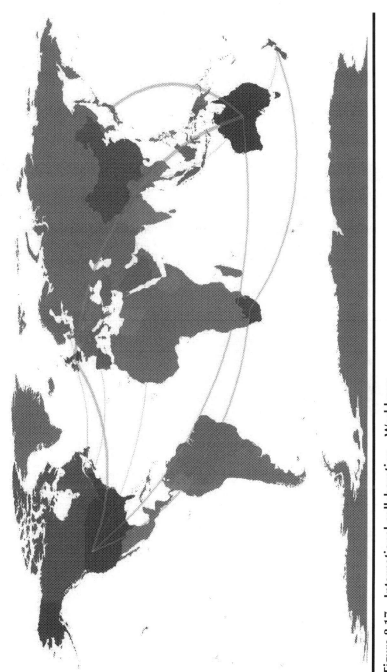

Figure 8.17 International collaboration – Worldmap.
Own elaboration | Software: Biblioshiny

on the other hand, there is a growing and current interest in education in general, namely about the future of education and a reorganization onto learning to learn (Trilling & Fadel, 2009).

This focus of interest is directly related to the capacity of polytechnic and university education, to be able to follow the whole process of change, to renew its courses according to the requirements of the new digital age to adapt the programs of the curricular units to the needs of the new labor markets, under penalty, of becoming obsolete itself, and this will be a disaster for any society. Factor analysis (Figure 8.9) shows some of these recent domains, essential for future research, related to perceptions, expectations, skills, and technology.

As for the [O6] objective, the 415 articles were published by 127 sources. Of the three sources with the most significant impact ("h-index", "g-index", "total citations"), the "Accounting review" is the source that published the first article in 1957and until 2014 assumed an active leadership role. From 2014 to 2020, "Accounting education" played a driving role with an upward and sharp curve in the number of publications, and the propensity of this source to publish on the subject was evident. Lawson et al. (2014), with the support of the IMA and the MAS of the AAA, publish the competency-based educational framework in the "Issues in accounting education" under the title "Focusing Accounting Curricula on Students' Long-Run Careers: Recommendations for an Integrated Competency-Based Framework for Accounting Education" which marks the moment from which the interest, in this field of research, increased.

Of the results obtained in the citations [08], the articles have 2416 citations on February 6, 2021, with an average of 5.82 citations per article. Each article has an average of 0.83 citations per year. This proportion is an insignificant average compared to other areas of science, such as "Educational research", with 44 average citations per article (Patience, Patience, Blais & Bertrand, 2017). However, it is superior to publications in arts, literature, and architecture, which have the lowest average citations per article (Patience et al., 2017).

The most quoted article throughout the database is "The international integrated reporting framework: key issues and future research opportunities" (Cheng, Green, Conradie, Konishi & Romi, 2014), with 120 citations and an average of 15 citations per year. The author with the highest number of citations is Alan Sangster, with 71citations and a longevity of scientific production of 28 years, among the articles "computer-based learning in UK accounting education - to support or to supplant" (Sangster, 1992) and "insights accounting into education in a COVID-19 world" (Sangster et al., 2020). This author's most quoted article is "you cannot judge a book by its cover: the problems with journal rankings" (Sangster, 2015).

The theme of the impact of COVID-19 on accounting education, namely on students and teachers (Sangster et al., 2020) showed that this crisis can also be seen as an opportunity to realign learning strategies. The application of experiential learning outside the classroom, with real experiences (Dellaportas & Hassall, 2013), active learning in the classroom (Sugahara & Dellaportas, 2018), the introduction of virtual internships (Bayerlein, 2015) or the implementation of games to develop personal skills and soft skills (Viviers et al., 2016), are innovations that can meet the perceptions of students, with an impact on their satisfaction (Bobe & Cooper, 2020).

In the most influential articles among the 415 of our research, there is a large line of research associated with the study of technical skills and soft skills (Abayadeera et al., 2016; Asonitou & Hassall, 2019; Papageorgiou & Callaghan, 2020; Samkin & Keevy, 2019) that future accounting professionals are expected to acquire. However, the characteristics of the students are not all the same. Learning styles, ability to grip communication, tolerance of ambiguity, languages, and linguistics are some of the characteristics that can create barriers to the development of these competencies and pedagogical change (Arquero et al., 2017).

Internationally, Duff et al. (2020) studied the role of professional associations and orders and the impact on research on accounting education and concluded that institutions and employers are the most interested parties in the development and updating of curriculum units. In our study, we identified international relations between countries, institutions, and authors. In the network map of international collaboration between countries [O2] (Figure 8.15), Australia plays a significant role and shows strong collaboration with the USA and the UK, thus forming a strong triangle of collaboration. For Australia, the institutions [O4] that have the most impact are RMIT University, Deakin University, Macquarie University, and Griffith University. Related to this country are the working groups of Leopold Bayerlein (Bayerlein, 2015, 2020; Bayerlein & Timpson, 2017; Vitale et al., 2020), Steven Dellaportas (Dellaportas, 2015; Dellaportas & Hassall, 2013; Sugahara & Dellaportas, 2018; Sugahara et al., 2016; Vesty et al., 2018; Wong et al., 2015; Wong et al., 2018) and Gordon Boyce (Boyce, 2004; Boyce & Greer, 2013; Boyce et al., 2012; Boyce et al., 2019; Boyce et al., 2001; Zhang et al., 2014). Associated with the United Kingdom are "Glasgow University" and "Huddersfield University" and the works of Alan Sangster (Mari et al., 2020; Marriott et al., 2014; Sangster, 1992, 2015; Sangster et al., 2015; Sangster et al., 2020). The impact in the USA is related to the task force created with the support of the IMA and the AAA, led by Raef A. Lawson, whose work became known as the Pathways Commission 2012. South Africa (Africa) and the United Kingdom (Europe) show themselves as the intercontinental bridges connecting the USA to Australia and Japan (Figure 8.17).

Regarding the [O3] objective, the Economist (2016) reported an average number of 4.4 authors per article in 2015. This average is higher than our results, with 1.76 authors per article and 2.16 co-authors. With regard to the distribution of the number of authors and their scientific productivity, we found that our articles comply with Lotka's Law (Lokta, 1926), with a very asymmetric distribution where many authors publish few articles, and few authors publish many articles. Of the 732 authors, 609 are occasional and wrote only one article. Of the 20 most relevant authors, only 3 have a longevity of 10 or more years of scientific production.

Regarding research themes, through the analysis of the conceptual structure of knowledge, according to the map of keywords-plus themes [O7] the most important and transversal cluster to the scientific field is the "education" associated with keywords-plus: "skills", "perceptions", "knowledge", "expectations", and "employers". We identified the "students" cluster from the perspective of "impact" and "intentions", and the cluster "students perceptions" from the perspective of "satisfaction" of the student, namely with "technology", "learning styles", and "behaviors". The cluster of "performance" is related to "gender", and "classroom".

8.6 Implications of the Research

8.6.1 Theoretical Implications

In order to incorporate and balance the various objectives of education for the 21st century, Fadel, Bialik & Trilling, 2016 (Four-Dimensional Education: The Competencies Learners Need to Succeed, CCR) have developed a structure that supports the holistic view of the student, and define four dimensions necessary for an integral education: the dimension of knowledge, the dimension of skills, the dimension of attitudes and meta-learning. For effective learning, the four dimensions must be interconnected and interact with each other. The student needs to gain a deeper understanding of the relevant knowledge. The areas of knowledge that are currently part of academic curricula should be redesigned to include modern disciplines such as "Entrepeunership", as well as a selected set of traditional disciplines, with options for interdisciplinary exploration of topics such as: "Digital literacy", "Environmental literacy", "Global literacy", "Information literacy", "Design thinking", and "Systems thinking". The student needs skills to be ready to use and apply their knowledge in real-world issues and problems with creativity, critical thinking, communication, and collaboration. The different components of critical thinking originate from Bloom's Taxonomy of Educational Goals (1956) in its revisions. The dimension of attitudes is related to the way the student behaves, motivates himself, and commits to the objectives. The student must develop six attitudes ("Mindfulness", curiosity, Courage, Resilience, Ethics, and Leadership), to apply it during its existence. Finally, students need to learn to learn. Reflect on the ability to learn and manage learning challenges. Meta-learning amplifies the other three dimensions.

Accounting as a discipline of knowledge has the responsibility to include learning skills, attitudes, and meta-learning strategies. Financial accounting can be well suited to teaching creativity and collaboration, resilience, and metacognition. Students may be instructed to practice leadership and collaboration skills while working as a team to develop and analyze financial statements, applying a wide variety of technical, scientific, and technological skills, with the ultimate goal of making decisions for real-world problems. In the future, these skills should be included and intertwined within the relevant parts of learning activities as they will be best apprehended when placed in the field of concrete knowledge.

8.6.2 Practical Implications

A teaching that prepares future professionals for the business needs of the present is obsolete. It urgently needs a visionary strategy, aggregator of professional practice, which defines a global transformation of teaching in accounting, innovating in the training offer, readapting or recreating current curricula, in order to exponentially increase its adaptability to new realities such as "Smart Contracts", "Big Data", "Metaverse", "Blockchain" or sustainability, environment, and innovation. It is time to redesign strategies for the profession, rethink plans and methods of learning and teaching, and follow the new research agenda for accounting education.

8.6.3 Limitations

Our analysis has some limitations. Although WoS is one of the most reputable and complete databases, there are sources that are not indexed and, therefore, these publications have been lost. Some authors may have more than one name, use different initials, or have different names in different publications. This limitation can create an inaccuracy in the productivity of institutions or authors and generate some divergences in bibliographic analysis. Our option was to analyze the data without any manual processing. We can only compare the geographical distributions of publications without correcting the population of countries. If this correction were possible, the results could be different.

References

Abayadeera, N., Watty, K., & Zhou, H. (2016). Generic skills in accounting education in a developing country: Exploratory evidence from Sri Lanka. *Asian Review of Accounting*, 24(2).

Abdi, H. & Valentin, D. (2007). Multiple correspondence analysis. *Encyclopedia of Measurement and Statistics*, 2(4), 651–657.

Albrecht, W. S., & Sack, R. J. (2000). *Accounting education: Charting the course through a perilous future* (Vol. 16). American Accounting Association Sarasota, FL.

Allen, R. D. (2019). "The Winter Oak": Inspiring passion for teaching. *Issues in Accounting Education*, 34(2), 11–21.

Andreu, L., Bigne, E., Amaro, S. & Palomo, J. (2020). Airbnb research: an analysis in tourism and hospitality journals. *International Journal of Culture, Tourism and Hospitality Research*, 14(1), 2–20.

Apostolou, B., Dorminey, J. W., & Hassell, J. M. (2020). Accounting education literature review (2019). *Journal of Accounting Education*, 51, 100670.

Apostolou, B., Dorminey, J. W., Hassell, J. M., & Rebele, J. E. (2015). Accounting education literature review (2013–2014). *Journal of Accounting Education*, 33(2), 69–127.

Apostolou, B., Dorminey, J. W., Hassell, J. M. & Watson, S. F. (2013). Accounting education literature review (2010–2012). *Journal of Accounting Education*, 31(2), 107–161.

Apostolou, B., Hassell, J. M., Rebele, J. E., & Watson, S. F. (2010). Accounting education literature review (2006–2009). *Journal of Accounting Education, 28*(3–4), 145–197.

Apostolou, B., Watson, S. F., Hassell, J. M., & Webber, S. A. (2001). Accounting education literature review (1997–1999). *Journal of Accounting Education, 19*(1), 1–61.

Ardianto, A., & Anridho, N. (2018). Bibliometric analysis of digital accounting research. *The International Journal of Digital Accounting Research, 18*(1), 141–159.

Aria, M. & Cuccurullo, C. (2017). bibliometrix: An R-tool for comprehensive science mapping analysis. *Journal of Informetrics, 11*(4), 959–975.

Aria, M., Misuraca, M. & Spano, M. (2020). Mapping the evolution of social research and data science on 30 years of Social Indicators Research. *Social Indicators Research, 149*, 1–29.

Arquero, J. L., Fernández-Polvillo, C., Hassall, T., & Joyce, J. (2017). Relationships between communication apprehension, ambiguity tolerance and learning styles in accounting students. *Revista de Contabilidad, 20*(1), 13–24.

Asonitou, S., & Hassall, T. (2019). Which skills and competences to develop in accountants in a country in crisis? *The International Journal of Management Education, 17*(3), 100308.

Awuson-David, K., Al-Hadhrami, T., Funminiyi, O., & Lotfi, A. (2020). Using hyperledger fabric blockchain to maintain the integrity of digital evidence in a containerised cloud ecosystem. In *Emerging Trends in Intelligent Computing and Informatics: Data Science, Intelligent Information Systems and Smart Computing 4* (pp. 839–848). Springer International Publishing.

Azzari, V., Mainardes, E. W., & da Costa, F. M. (2020). Accounting services quality: a systematic literature review and bibliometric analysis. *Asian Journal of Accounting Research, 6*(1), 80–94.

Bailey, C. D. (2017). Psychopathy and accounting students' attitudes towards unethical professional practices. *Journal of Accounting Education, 41*, 15–32.

Bailey, C. D. (2019). The joint effects of narcissism and psychopathy on accounting students' attitudes towards unethical professional practices. *Journal of Accounting Education, 49*, 100635.

Balios, D. (2021). The impact of Big Data on accounting and auditing. *International Journal of Corporate Finance and Accounting (IJCFA), 8*(1), 1–14.

Ballantine, J., & McCourt Larres, P. (2009). Accounting undergraduates' perceptions of cooperative learning as a model for enhancing their interpersonal and communication skills to interface successfully with professional accountancy education and training. *Accounting Education: An International Journal, 18*(4–5), 387–402.

Bayerlein, L. (2015). Curriculum innovation in undergraduate accounting degree programmes through "virtual internships". *Education and Training, 57*(6), 673–684. https://doi.org/10.1108/et-09-2014-0110

Bayerlein, L. (2020). The impact of prior work-experience on student learning outcomes in simulated internships. *Journal of University Teaching and Learning Practice, 17*(4), 18, Article 4. <Go to ISI>://WOS:000562829400004

Bayerlein, L., & Timpson, M. (2017). Do accredited undergraduate accounting programmes in Australia meet the needs and expectations of the accounting profession? *Education and Training, 59*(3), 305–322. https://doi.org/10.1108/et-04-2016-0074

Bialik, M., Martin, J., Mayo, M., & Trilling, B. (2016). *Evolving assessments for a 21st century education*. Assessment Research Consortium.

Birkey, R., & Hausserman, C. (2019). Inducing creativity in accountants' task performance: the effects of background, environment, and feedback. In *Advances in accounting education: Teaching and curriculum innovations* (Vol. 22, pp. 109–133). Emerald Publishing Limited.

Blankley, A., Kerr, D., & Wiggins, C. (2018). An Examination and analysis of technologies employed by accounting educators. *The Accounting Educators' Journal, XXVIII,* 75–98.

Blanthorne, C. (2017). Designing a theme-based ethics course in accounting. In *Advances in accounting education: Teaching and curriculum innovations* (Vol. XXVIII, 135–140). Emerald Publishing Limited.

Blay, A. D., & Fennema, M. (2017). Are accountants made or born? An analysis of self-selection into the accounting major and performance in accounting courses and on the CPA exam. *Issues in Accounting Education, 32*(3), 33–50.

Bobe, B. J., & Cooper, B. J. (2020). Accounting students' perceptions of effective teaching and approaches to learning: Impact on overall student satisfaction. *Accounting & Finance, 60*(3), 2099–2143.

Bonsón, E., & Bednárová, M. (2019). *Blockchain and its implications for accounting and auditing.* Meditari Accountancy Research.

Boyce, G. (2004). Critical accounting education: Teaching and learning outside the circle. *Critical Perspectives on Accounting, 15*(4–5), 565–586.

Boyce, G., & Greer, S. (2013). More than imagination: Making social and critical accounting real. *Critical Perspectives on Accounting, 24*(2), 105–112. https://doi.org/10.1016/j.cpa.2012.06.002

Boyce, G., Greer, S., Blair, B., & Davids, C. (2012). Expanding the horizons of accounting education: Incorporating social and critical perspectives. *Accounting Education, 21*(1), 47–74.

Boyce, G., Narayanan, V., Greer, S., & Blair, B. (2019). Taking the pulse of accounting education reform: Liberal education, sociological perspectives, and exploring ways forward. *Accounting Education, 28*(3), 274–303. https://doi.org/10.1080/09639284.2019.1586552

Boyce, G., Williams, S., Kelly, A., & Yee, H. (2001). Fostering deep and elaborative learning and generic (soft) skill development: The strategic use of case studies in accounting education. *Accounting Education, 10*(1), 37–60.

Boyle, D. M., Carpenter, B. W., Hermanson, D. R., & Mero, N. P. (2015). Examining the perceptions of professionally oriented accounting faculty. *Journal of Accounting Education, 33*(1), 1–15.

Bradford, S. C. (1934). Sources of information on specific subjects. *Engineering, 137,* 85–86.

Brookes, B. C. (1969). Bradford's law and the bibliography of science. *Nature, 224*(5223), 953–956.

Brukhansky, R., & Spilnyk, I. (2021). Digital accounting: concepts, roots and current discourse. *The Institute of Accounting, Control and Analysis in the Globalization Circumstances, 1*(3–4), 7–20.

Bui, B. & Porter, B. (2010). The expectation-performance gap in accounting education: An exploratory study. *Accounting Education: An International Journal, 19*(1–2), 23–50.

Bujaki, M., Lento, C. & Sayed, N. (2019). Utilizing professional accounting concepts to understand and respond to academic dishonesty in accounting programs. *Journal of Accounting Education, 47,* 28–47.

Butler, M. G., Church, K. S., & Spencer, A. W. (2019). Do, reflect, think, apply: Experiential education in accounting. *Journal of Accounting Education, 48,* 12–21.

Cheng, M., Green, W., Conradie, P., Konishi, N., & Romi, A. (2014). The international integrated reporting framework: Key issues and future research opportunities. *Journal of International Financial Management & Accounting*, 25(1), 90–119. https://doi.org/10.1111/jifm.12015

Christensen, J., Harrison, J. L., Hollindale, J., & Wood, K. (2019). Implementing team-based learning (TBL) in accounting courses. *Accounting Education*, 28(2), 195–219.

Cloete, M. (2018). The impact of an integrated assessment on the critical thinking skills of first-year university students. *Accounting Education*, 27(5), 479–494.

Coady, P., Byrne, S., & Casey, J. (2018). Positioning of emotional intelligence skills within the overall skillset of practice-based accountants: Employer and graduate requirements. *Accounting Education*, 27(1), 94–120.

Coetzee, S. A., Schmulian, A., & Coetzee, R. (2018). Web conferencing-based tutorials: Student perceptions thereof and the effect on academic performance in accounting education. *Accounting Education*, 27(5), 531–546.

De Lange, P., Jackling, B., & Gut, A. M. (2006). Accounting graduates' perceptions of skills emphasis in undergraduate courses: An investigation from two Victorian universities. *Accounting & Finance*, 46(3), 365–386.

De Villiers, R. (2010). *The incorporation of soft skills into accounting curricula: preparing accounting graduates for their unpredictable futures*. Meditari Accountancy Research.

Dellaportas, S. (2015). Reclaiming 'Sense' from 'Cents' in accounting education. *Accounting Education*, 24(6), 445–460. https://doi.org/10.1080/09639284.2015.1114456

Dellaportas, S., & Hassall, T. (2013). Experiential learning in accounting education: A prison visit. *British Accounting Review*, 45(1), 24–36. https://doi.org/10.1016/j.bar.2012.12.005

Demirkan, S., Demirkan, I., & McKee, A. (2020). Blockchain technology in the future of business cyber security and accounting. *Journal of Management Analytics*, 7(2), 189–208.

Deniz, F. (2021). Strategies for digital transformation in business: Digital accounting strategy. In *Disruptive technology and digital transformation for business and government* (pp. 153–171). IGI Global. DOI: 10.4018/978-1-7998-8583-2.ch008

Deshmukh, A. (2006). *Digital accounting: The effects of the internet and ERP on accounting*. IGI Global.

Diane, J., Joy, G., & Boss, S. (2020). Accountants, Cybersecurity isn't just for 'Techies': Incorporating Cybersecurity into the Accounting Curriculum.

Dias, L. (2020). ERA DIGITAL–desafios e avanços dos processos em escritórios de contabilidade. https://repositorio.pucgoias.edu.br/jspui/handle/123456789/1343

Djatej, A., Chen, Y., Eriksen, S., & Zhou, D. (2015). Understanding students' major choice in accounting: An application of the theory of reasoned action. *Global Perspectives on Accounting Education*, 12, 53.

Douglas, S., & Gammie, E. (2019). An investigation into the development of non-technical skills by undergraduate accounting programmes. *Accounting Education*, 28(3), 304–332.

Duff, A., Hancock, P., & Marriott, N. (2020). The role and impact of professional accountancy associations on accounting education research: An international study. *The British Accounting Review*, 52(5), 100829.

Elango, B. & Rajendran, P. (2012). Authorship trends and collaboration pattern in the marine sciences literature: a scientometric study. *International Journal of Information Dissemination and Technology*, 2(3), 166–169.

Fadel, C., Bialik, M. & Trilling, B. (2016). Educación en cuatro dimensiones: las competencias que los estudiantes necesitan para su realización.

Fisher, E., McLeod, A. J., Savage, A., & Simkin, M. G. (2016). Ghostwriters in the cloud. *Journal of Accounting Education*, 34, 59–71.

Forum, W. E. (2020). The Future of Jobs Report 2020. *Retrieved from Geneva.*
Freeman, M., & Burkette, G. (2019). Storytelling in the accounting classroom. *The Accounting Educators' Journal, 29*(1), 29–39.
Frolova, O. A., Milgunova, I. V., Sidorova, N. P., Kulkova, N. S., & Kitaeva, E. N. (2020). Development of accounting in digital economy ERA. In *Integrated Science in Digital Age 2020* (pp. 53–59). Cham: Springer International Publishing.
Gammie, B., Gammie, E., & Cargill, E. (2002). Personal skills development in the accounting curriculum. *Accounting Education, 11*(1), 63–78.
Garfield, E. & Sher, I. H. (1993). Key words plus [TM]-algorithmic derivative indexing. *Journal-American Society For Information Science, 44*, 298–298.
Glänzel, W. (2002). Coauthorship patterns and trends in the sciences (1980-1998): A bibliometric study with implications for database indexing and search strategies.
Grossman, A. M., & Johnson, L. R. (2016). Employer perceptions of online accounting degrees. *Issues in Accounting Education, 31*(1), 91–109.
Hammour, H. (2018). Influence of the attitudes of Emirati students on their choice of accounting as a profession. *Accounting Education, 27*(4), 433–451.
Hassall, T., Joyce, J., Montaño, J. L. A., & Anes, J. A. D. (2005). Priorities for the development of vocational skills in management accountants: A European perspective. In *Accounting Forum* (Vol. 29, No. 4, pp. 379–394). No longer published by Elsevier.
Holmes, A. F., Zhang, S., & Harris, B. (2019). An analysis of teaching strategies designed to improve written communication skills. *Accounting Education, 28*(1), 25–48.
Holt, T., Burke-Smalley, L. A., & Jones, C. (2017). An empirical investigation of student career interests in auditing using the big five model of personality. In *Advances in accounting education: Teaching and curriculum innovations* (Vol. 20, pp. 1–31). Emerald Publishing Limited.
Howcroft, D. (2017). Graduates' vocational skills for the management accountancy profession: Exploring the accounting education expectation-performance gap. *Accounting Education, 26*(5–6), 459–481.
Howieson, B. (2003). Accounting practice in the new millennium: Is accounting education ready to meet the challenge? *The British Accounting Review, 35*(2), 69–103.
Hutchins, R., & Roberts, D. (2019). Factors that determine the decision to major in accounting: A survey of accounting graduates. *The Accounting Educators' Journal, 28*, 159–167.
Ionescu, L., & Andronie, M. (2019). The future of Jobs in the digital world. *International Conference ICESBA*, Bucharest.
Jackling, B., & De Lange, P. (2009). Do accounting graduates' skills meet the expectations of employers? A matter of convergence or divergence. *Accounting Education: An International Journal, 18*(4–5), 369–385.
Jill, M., Wang, D., & Mattia, A. (2019). Are instructor generated YouTube videos effective in accounting classes? A study of student performance, engagement, motivation, and perception. *Journal of Accounting Education, 47*, 63–74.
Katz, J. S. & Martin, B. R. (1997). What is research collaboration? *Research Policy, 26*(1), 1–18.
Kavanagh, M. H., & Drennan, L. (2008). What skills and attributes does an accounting graduate need? Evidence from student perceptions and employer expectations. *Accounting & Finance, 48*(2), 279–300.
Kelton, K., Fleischmann, K. R., & Wallace, W. A. (2008). Trust in digital information. *Journal of the American Society for Information Science and Technology, 59*(3), 363–374.

Khaparde, V. & Pawar, S. (2013). Authorship pattern and degree of collaboration in Information Technology. *Journal of Computer Science & Information Technology*, *1*(1), 46–54.

Khuntia, J., Saldanha, T. J., Mithas, S., & Sambamurthy, V. (2018). Information technology and sustainability: Evidence from an emerging economy. *Production and Operations Management*, *27*(4), 756–773.

Kohlmeyer, J. M., Seese, L. P., & Sincich, T. (2015). Online accounting degrees: Hiring perceptions of accounting professionals. In *Advances in accounting education teaching and curriculum innovations*. Emerald Group Publishing Limited.

Koseoglu, M. A. (2016). Growth and structure of authorship and co-authorship network in the strategic management realm: Evidence from the Strategic Management Journal. *BRQ Business Research Quarterly*, *19*(3), 153–170.

Koseoglu, M. A. (2019). Evolution of the social structure of hospitality management literature: 1960-2016. *International Journal of Contemporary Hospitality Management*, *32*(2), 489–510.

Kotb, A., Abdel-Kader, M., Allam, A., Halabi, H. & Franklin, E. (2019). Information technology in the British and Irish undergraduate accounting degrees. *Accounting Education*, *28*(5), 445–464.

Lawson, R. A., Blocher, E. J., Brewer, P. C., Cokins, G., Sorensen, J. E., Stout, D. E., Sundem, G. L., Wolcott, S. K., & Wouters, M. J. (2014). Focusing accounting curricula on students' long-run careers: Recommendations for an integrated competency-based framework for accounting education. *Issues in Accounting Education*, *29*(2), 295–317.

Leitner-Hanetseder, S., Lehner, O. M., Eisl, C., & Forstenlechner, C. (2021). A profession in transition: actors, tasks and roles in AI-based accounting. *Journal of Applied Accounting Research*, *22*(3), 539–556.

Lento, C., Sayed, N. & Bujaki, M. (2018). Sex role socialization and perceptions of student academic dishonesty by male and female accounting faculty. *Accounting Education*, *27*(1), 1–26.

Liu, Y., Xu, H., & Krahel, J. P. (2019). Improving writing self-efficacy of accounting students. *The Accounting Educators' Journal*, *29*(1), 41–59.

Lokta, A. (1926). The frequency distribution of scientific distribution. *Journal of the Washington Academcy of Sciences*, *16*, 317–323.

Loo, I. D., & Bots, J. (2018). The life of an accounting information systems research course. *Accounting Education*, *27*(4), 358–382.

Maffei, M., Casciello, R., & Meucci, F. (2021). Blockchain technology: Uninvestigated issues emerging from an integrated view within accounting and auditing practices. *Journal of Organizational Change Management*, *34*(2), 462–476.

Mari, L. M., Picciaia, F., & Sangster, A. (2020). Manzoni's sixteenth-century 'Quaderno Doppio': The evolution of accounting education towards modern times. *Accounting History*, *25*(4), 580–601, Article 1032373220942330. https://doi.org/10.1177/1032373220942330

Marriott, N., Stoner, G., Fogarty, T., & Sangster, A. (2014). Publishing characteristics, geographic dispersion and research traditions of recent international accounting education research. *British Accounting Review*, *46*(3), 264–280. https://doi.org/10.1016/j.bar.2013.11.003

Martí-Parreño, J., & Gómez-Calvet, R. (2020, March). Social Media and Sustainable Tourism: A Literature Review. In *ICTR 2020 3rd International Conference on Tourism Research* (p. 148). Academic Conferences and publishing limited.

Mauldin, S., Braun, R. L., Viosca, C., & Boldt, M. N. (2019). CPAs' evaluations of accounting graduates: An empirical investigation of face-to-face and online degrees. *The Accounting Educators' Journal, 28*, 99–115.

McCarthy, M., Kusaila, M., & Grasso, L. (2019). Intermediate accounting and auditing: Does course delivery mode impact student performance? *Journal of Accounting Education, 46*, 26–42.

McKinney Jr, E., Yoos II, C. J., & Snead, K. (2017). The need for 'skeptical' accountants in the era of Big Data. *Journal of Accounting Education, 38*, 63–80.

Mesquita, H. A. (2021). Accounting assistance for decision-making: A theoretical study. *Revista de Estudos Interdisciplinares do Vale do Araguaia-REIVA, 4*(01), 21–21.

Mosweu, O., & Ngoepe, M. (2021). Trustworthiness of digital records in government accounting system to support the audit process in Botswana. *Records Management Journal, 31*(1), 89–108.

Opdecam, E., & Everaert, P. (2019). Choice-based learning: lecture-based or team learning? *Accounting Education, 28*(3), 239–273.

Palácios, H., Almeida, H. D., & Sousa, M. J. (2021a). A bibliometric analysis of service climate as a sustainable competitive advantage in hospitality. *Sustainability, 13*(21), 12214.

Palácios, H., de Almeida, M. H., & Sousa, M. J. (2021b). A bibliometric analysis of trust in the field of hospitality and tourism. *International Journal of Hospitality Management, 95*, 102944. https://doi.org/10.1016/j.ijhm.2021.102944

Palácios, H., Fernandes, J. S. a., Gonçalves, C., Gonçalves, G., & Sousa, C. (2017). The influence of ethical dilemmas in the accounting. *Tourism & Management Studies, 13*(3), 49–57.

Papageorgiou, E., & Callaghan, C. W. (2020). Accountancy learning skills and student performance in accounting education: Evidence from the South African context. *Accounting Education, 29*(2), 205–228.

Patience, G. S., Patience, C. A., Blais, B. & Bertrand, F. (2017). Citation analysis of scientific categories. *Heliyon, 3*(5), e00300.

Raza, S. A., Ashrafi, R. & Akgunduz, A. (2020). A bibliometric analysis of revenue management in airline industry. *Journal of Revenue and Pricing Management, 19*, 1–30.

Reid, A., & Petocz, P. (2004). Learning domains and the process of creativity. *The Australian Educational Researcher, 31*(2), 45–62.

Richardson, V. J., & Shan, Y. (2019). Data analytics in the accounting curriculum. *Advances in accounting education: Teaching and curriculum innovations* (Vol. 23, pp. 67–79). Emerald Publishing Limited.

Samkin, G., & Keevy, M. (2019). Using *a stakeholder developed case study to develop soft skills.* Meditari Accountancy Research.

Samuel, S. (2018). A conceptual framework for teaching management accounting. *Journal of Accounting Education, 44*, 25–34.

Sangster, A. (1992). Computer-based learning in UK accounting education - to support or to supplant. *British Journal of Educational Technology, 23*(2), 136–138. https://doi.org/10.1111/j.1467-8535.1992.tb00319.x

Sangster, G., Garcia-R, J. C., & Trewick, S. A. (2015). A new genus for the Lesser Moorhen Gallinula angulata Sundevall, 1850 (Aves, Rallidae). *European Journal of Taxonomy*, (153).

Sangster, A., Stoner, G., & Flood, B. (2020). Insights into accounting education in a COVID-19 world. *Accounting Education, 29*(5), 431–562.

Sayed, N., & Lento, C. (2016). Accounting professors' perceptions of academic dishonesty: Motivations, controls and the impact of technology. *The Accounting Educators' Journal, 26*(special edition), 65–87.

Shaub, M. K. (2017). A wisdom-based accounting ethics course. In *Advances in accounting education: Teaching and curriculum innovations* (Vol. 20, pp. 181–216). Emerald Publishing Limited.

Shauki, E. R., & Benzie, H. (2017). Meeting threshold learning standards through self-management in group oral presentations: Observations on accounting postgraduate students. *Accounting Education, 26*(4), 358–376.

Silva, R., Rodrigues, R., & Leal, C. (2019). Play it again: How game-based learning improves flow in Accounting and Marketing education. *Accounting Education, 28*(5), 484–507.

Sledgianowski, D., Gomaa, M., & Tan, C. (2017). Toward integration of Big Data, technology and information systems competencies into the accounting curriculum. *Journal of Accounting Education, 38*, 81–93.

Small, H. (1973). Co-citation in the scientific literature: A new measure of the relationship between two documents. *Journal of the American Society for information Science, 24*(4), 265–269.

Small, H. (1997). Update on science mapping: Creating large document spaces. *Scientometrics, 38*(2), 275–293.

Small, H. (1999). Visualizing science by citation mapping. *Journal of the American Society for information Science, 50*(9), 799–813.

Smith, K. J., Emerson, D. J., Haight, T. D., Mauldin, S., & Wood, B. G. (2019). An examination of the psychometric properties of the Connor-Davidson Resilience Scale-10 (CD-RISC10) among accounting and business students. *Journal of Accounting Education, 47*, 48–62.

Stanley, T., & Xu, J. (2019). Work-Integrated Learning in accountancy at Australian universities–forms, future role and challenges. *Accounting Education, 28*(1), 1–24.

Steenkamp, N., & Roberts, R. (2017). Unethical practices in response to poor student quality: An Australian perspective. *The Accounting Educators' Journal, 26*, 89–119.

Sugahara, S., & Dellaportas, S. (2018). Bringing active learning into the accounting classroom. *Meditari Accountancy Research, 26*(4), 576–597. https://doi.org/10.1108/medar-01-2017-0109

Sugahara, S., Sugao, H., Dellaportas, S., & Masaoka, T. (2016). The effect of body-movement teaching, learning motivation and performance. *Meditari Accountancy Research, 24*(3), 414–437. https://doi.org/10.1108/medar-02-2015-0006

Sweileh, W. M., Al-Jabi, S. W., AbuTaha, A. S., Sa'ed, H. Z., Anayah, F. M. & Sawalha, A. F. (2017). Bibliometric analysis of worldwide scientific literature in mobile-health: 2006–2016. *BMC Medical Informatics and Decision Making, 17*(1), 72.

Tan, H. C. (2019). Using a structured collaborative learning approach in a case-based management accounting course. *Journal of Accounting Education, 49*, 100638.

Tan, L. M., & Laswad, F. (2018). Professional skills required of accountants: What do job advertisements tell us? *Accounting Education, 27*(4), 403–432.

Taplin, R., Kerr, R., & Brown, A. (2017). Monetary valuations of university course delivery: The case for face-to-face learning activities in accounting education. *Accounting Education, 26*(2), 144–165.

Taylor, M., Marrone, M., Tayar, M., & Mueller, B. (2018). Digital storytelling and visual metaphor in lectures: A study of student engagement. *Accounting Education, 27*(6), 552–569.

Tijssen, R. & Van Raan, A. (1989). Mapping co-word structures: A comparison of multidimensional scaling and LEXIMAPPE. *Scientometrics, 15*(3–4), 283–295.

Trilling, B., & Fadel, C. (2009). *21st Century skills, enhanced edition: Learning for life in our times*. John Wiley & Sons.

Troshani, I., Locke, J., & Rowbottom, N. (2018). Transformation of accounting through digital standardisation: Tracing the construction of the IFRS taxonomy. *Accounting, Auditing & Accountability Journal, 32*(1), 133–162.

Tugui, A. (2015). Meta-digital accounting in the context of cloud computing. In *Encyclopedia of Information Science and Technology* (Third Edition, pp. 20–32). IGI Global.

Van Eck, N. J. & Waltman, L. (2010). Software survey: VOSviewer, a computer program for bibliometric mapping. *Scientometrics, 84*(2), 523–538.

Vesty, G., Sridharan, V. G., Northcott, D., & Dellaportas, S. (2018). Burnout among university accounting educators in Australia and New Zealand: Determinants and implications. *Accounting and Finance, 58*(1), 255–277. https://doi.org/10.1111/acfi.12203

Vitale, C., Bowyer, D., & Bayerlein, L. (2020). Developing and presenting a framework for meeting industry, student and educator expectations in university degrees. *E-Journal of Business Education & Scholarship of Teaching, 14*(1), 57–65. <Go to ISI>://WOS:000587615300005

Viviers, H. A., Fouché, J. P., & Reitsma, G. M. (2016). Developing soft skills (also known as pervasive skills). *Meditari Accountancy Research, 24*(3), 368–389.

Waltman, L., Van Eck, N. J. & Noyons, E. C. (2010). A unified approach to mapping and clustering of bibliometric networks. *Journal of Informetrics, 4*(4), 629–635.

Ware, M. & Mabe, M. (2015). The STM report: An overview of scientific and scholarly journal publishing.

Warren Jr, J. D., Moffitt, K. C., & Byrnes, P. (2015). How big data will change accounting. *Accounting horizons, 29*(2), 397–407.

Watty, K., Freeman, M., Howieson, B., Hancock, P., O'Connell, B., De Lange, P., & Abraham, A. (2014). Social moderation, assessment and assuring standards for accounting graduates. *Assessment & Evaluation in Higher Education, 39*(4), 461–478.

Watty, K., McKay, J., & Ngo, L. (2016). Innovators or inhibitors? Accounting faculty resistance to new educational technologies in higher education. *Journal of Accounting Education, 36*, 1–15.

Watty, K., Sugahara, S., Abayadeera, N., & Perera, L. (2013). Developing a global model of accounting education and examining IES compliance in Australia, Japan, and Sri Lanka. *Accounting Education, 22*(5), 502–506.

Wells, P., Gerbic, P., Kranenburg, I., & Bygrave, J. (2009). Professional skills and capabilities of accounting graduates: The New Zealand expectation gap? *Accounting Education: an International journal, 18*(4–5), 403–420.

Wells, P. K. (2019). How does contact with accountants influence perceptions of accounting? *Accounting Education, 28*(2), 127–148.

Whitman, C., & Sobczak, M. (2018). AI: Overrated or the Future of Accounting. Undergraduate Student Research Awards. 45. https://digitalcommons.trinity.edu/infolit_usra/45

Wong, G., Cooper, B. J., & Dellaportas, S. (2015). Chinese students' perceptions of the teaching in an Australian accounting programme - An exploratory study. *Accounting Education*, *24*(4), 318–340. https://doi.org/10.1080/09639284.2015.1050678

Wong, G., Dellaportas, S., & Cooper, B. J. (2018). Chinese learner in a linguistically challenged environment - an exploratory study. *Asian Review of Accounting*, *26*(2), 264–276. https://doi.org/10.1108/ara-07-2017-0123

Wulandari, S. S., & Ali, S. (2019). Incorporating XBRL topics into the accounting curriculum: Empirical evidence from Indonesia. *Accounting Education*, *28*(6), 597–620.

Wygal, D. E., Stout, D. E., & Cunningham, B. M. (2017). Shining additional light on effective teaching best practices in accounting: Self-reflective insights from Cook Prize winners. *Issues in Accounting Education*, *32*(3), 17–31.

Zhang, G. H., Boyce, G., & Ahmed, K. (2014). Institutional changes in university accounting education in post-revolutionary China: From political orientation to internationalization. *Critical Perspectives on Accounting*, *25*(8), 819–843. https://doi.org/10.1016/j.cpa.2013.10.007

Zhang, J., Yu, Q., Zheng, F., Long, C., Lu, Z. & Duan, Z. (2016). Comparing keywords plus of WOS and author keywords: A case study of patient adherence research. *Journal of the Association for Information Science and Technology*, *67*(4), 967–972.

Chapter 9

International Mobility Challenges in Higher Education in the Digital Era

Maria do Carmo Botelho and Nuno Nunes
Instituto Universitário de Lisboa (ISCTE-IUL), CIES-Iscte, Lisboa, Portugal

Catarina Ferreira da Silva
Instituto Universitário de Lisboa (ISCTE-IUL), ISTAR-Iscte, Lisboa, Portugal

Isabel Machado Alexandre
Instituto Universitário de Lisboa (ISCTE-IUL), IT-Iscte, Lisboa, Portugal

Maria das Dores Guerreiro
Instituto Universitário de Lisboa (ISCTE-IUL), CIES-Iscte, Lisboa, Portugal

Maria José Sousa
Instituto Universitário de Lisboa (ISCTE-IUL), BRU-Iscte, Lisboa, Portugal

Contents

9.1 Introduction 188
      9.1.1 Research Agenda for Digital International Mobility in Higher Education 188
      9.1.2 The Emergent Importance of Digital International Mobility in Higher Education 189
9.2 The Internationalization of Universities and Student Mobility 194
9.3 The Case of Iscte in Europe 196
      9.3.1 Giving Voice to Students 196
      9.3.2 International Mobility and Digital Teaching 203
9.4 Conclusion 206
Acknowledgments 207
Notes 207
References 207
References of the Systematic Literature Review 208

9.1 Introduction

9.1.1 Research Agenda for Digital International Mobility in Higher Education

To understand concepts associated with digital international mobility in higher education and develop an overview of research trends in this field, a systematic literature review was performed based on the PRISMA protocol (Page et al., 2021). The main keywords "students AND international AND mobility AND higher AND education AND digital" were used for the article search. The latter was conducted on the scientific search engine B-On (Online Knowledge Library, n.d.), which aggregates and provides access to all major scientific databases. The analysis was performed for the entire database until the beginning of September 2022, then reduced to the last four years (see Table 9.1).

After applying the exclusion criteria defined in Table 9.1, the final number of papers used in the analysis was 27 ($n = 27$). The analysis was guided by the following research question: "What are the main concepts associated with digital international mobility in higher education?" To answer the research question, the papers' research attributes and keywords network were analyzed (see Table 9.2).

For further analysis, the scientific software VOSviewer was used to visualize the keywords networks present in the articles ($n = 27$). A network of all of the main research keywords in the analyzed articles is shown in Figure 9.1.

The network contains four clusters. The red cluster focuses on international mobility of the student's research, the blue cluster focuses on innovation and the digitalization of internationalization of the university's research, the yellow cluster focuses on COVID-19 and pandemic research, and the green cluster focuses on students' virtual mobility.

Table 9.1 Summary of Articles Found According to the Exclusion Criteria

Search keywords	Students + international + mobility + higher education + digital
Number of publications retrieved	268,687
Number of publications retrieved in the last four years (2018–2022)	69,959
Description of exclusion criteria (EC1)	EC1: The study is a non-scientific or non-peer-reviewed paper or report (gray literature). EC2: The study is written in a language other than English. EC3: The study is not electronically available. EC4: The study is a duplication of another publication. EC5: The study is a short paper (less than four pages).
Total number of publications excluded according to ECs	82
Total number of publications with integral text available	49
Number of papers that matched the research scope after reading	27

9.1.2 The Emergent Importance of Digital International Mobility in Higher Education

The systematic literature review enabled an examination of the ways in which higher education institutions (HEIs) have started to change their global mobility policies to incorporate digital strategies. Among HEIs, there is already an understanding of the necessity for more fundamental quality and longer-term reforms in higher education. Such institutions are shifting to online teaching formats to ensure short-term continuity and develop administrative and didactic competence and confidence in digital teaching. Alongside practical concerns about the drawbacks of digital education and losses in student enrolment, there is also an increasing understanding of inclusion opportunities and the value of international cooperation.

In international mobility programmes, digital learning is used when academic staff and students take online courses offered by a partner university rather than traveling overseas or to another country as part of their mobility programme.

Table 9.2 Research Attributes

Research Attributes	Author(s)	Year
Virtual mobility Digital storytelling Blended learning Student experiences	Otto, Daniel	2018
Foreign language teaching Financial and credit field Euro integration Globalization	Semenchenko, T O	2018
International exchange of ideas Student-interactive video conferences Intercultural understanding Student teachers	Sundh, Stellan	2018
Role of virtual exchange Transnational mobility	Barbier, R and Benjamin, E	2019
Virtual exchange Teacher education European policy	Baroni, Alice et al.	2019
Academic mobility Financial stability Erasmus student exchange Programme	Kabanbayeva, Gulbakyt et al.	2019
Virtual internationalization Higher education Innovative university Digital – international – transformative	Bruhn, Elisa	2020
Multilingual project International mobility	Griggio, L and Pittarello, S	2020
Asian studies in the West Autoethnographic reflection on mobility Knowledge production Academic discourses	Kelley, Liam C	2020
Measurement and assessment Virtual internationalization Higher agrarian education	Kobzhev, Alexander et al.	2020
Learner skills Open virtual mobility	Rajagopal, Kamakshi et al.	2020

(Continued)

Table 9.2 (Continued)

Research Attributes	Author(s)	Year
Transcultural practices International students Digital settings	Solmaz, Osman	2020
Postgraduate students Course selection Decision-making process Digitalization	Towers, A and Towers, N	2020
Teaching and engaging International students	Tran, Ly Thi	2020
Internationalization of higher education Armenia	Aperyan, Yevgine	2021
Digital technologies Artificial intelligence Education	Barakina, Elena et al.	2021
Impact of mobility Internationalization of higher education	Dias, Gonçalo Paiva et al.	2021
International student mobility Research mentions Social media	Park, H and Park, H W	2021
International student mobilities Higher education	Sidhu, Ravinder et al.	2021
COVID-19 Pandemic Development of higher education	Sultanova, Leila et al.	2021
Internationalization United Kingdom Higher education	Al-Mahdawi, Emad	2022
Erasmus Programme Higher education Europe	Carola, M B and Demiray, Z E G	2022
Educational management Pandemic reality State universities	Lukhutashvili, Nana et al.	2022

(Continued)

Table 9.2 (Continued)

Research Attributes	Author(s)	Year
Internationalization Russian universities COVID-19 Pandemic	Minaeva, E and Taradina, L	2022
Recruitment and mobility International students Chinese universities	Oladipo, O A and Sugandi, B	2022
Teaching and learning COVID-19 Pandemic Higher education Global health networks	Puradiredja, Dewi Ismajani et al.	2022
Digital learning International mobility programme University students and staff Europe	Leek, Joana and Rojek, Marcin	2022

Thus, it is crucial to analyze how digital environments promote digital learning while in mobility programmes, determine the purpose of digital learning, and outline opportunities and difficulties faced by students who participate in global mobility. For people who travel internationally, self-directed learning and a focus on course material are both components of the learning process in digital environments. The goal is to promote flexibility and motivation to learn among learners.

Students and staff become more autonomous in their learning and more open to confronting problems encountered in various educational environments when they participate in international digital learning. In the latter, online courses are distinguished by their pedagogical approaches to innovation and evaluation. In the context of mobility, digital learning refers to the extension of course material through oral expression, such as speaking and interacting with peers and teachers, and imparting meaning to one's actions in a digital environment.

The idea of internationalization at home (IaH), which is based on digital technology's ability to create learning possibilities, is also crucial. The integration of IaH assignments with the pedagogy course at the home university, convenient online access for students, and consideration of the various academic calendars at international partner universities are all crucial considerations. The following sections of this chapter explore the specificities of the internationalization of universities and student mobility by analyzing the unique case of Iscte.

Digital Era: Higher Education International Mobility Challenges ■ 193

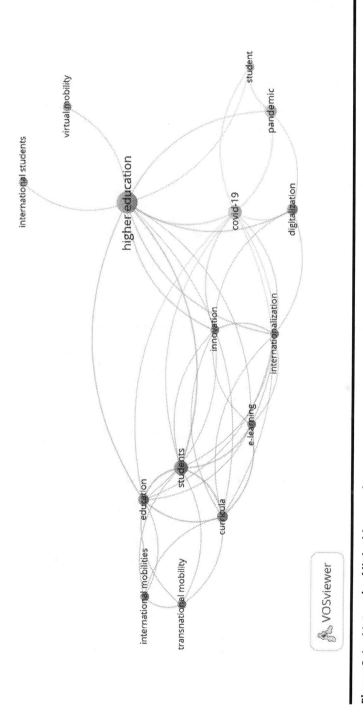

Figure 9.1 Network of linked keywords.

9.2 The Internationalization of Universities and Student Mobility

Over time, progress in human societies and the dissemination of knowledge have been based on population mobility and the exchange of knowledge between cultures. Thus, globalization processes have contributed to the universalization of knowledge. Along with Greek philosophy, the decimal system of Western mathematics – which was developed in India and later brought to Europe by the Arabs – and the printing technologies developed by China and various Buddhist cultures, a wide range of contributions from non-European societies have been incorporated into the creation of a universal culture (Sen, 2006).

Despite the asymmetry existing in the different regions of the globe, with high levels of concentration of science and technology in a small constellation of countries, fundamental research – the main source of knowledge generation – occurs at universities, in an open public system, providing access to academics from all over the world (Castells, 2010). The scientific research system assumes a global nature, based on the internationalization of researchers and teachers who specialize in different domains of knowledge, promote permanent communication, and share processes through scientific meetings, mobility missions, networks and thematic associations, publications, and other forms of contact and idea exchange (Castells, 2010). Therefore, the internationalization of universities becomes an intrinsic aspect of their existence and provides teachers, researchers, and students with opportunities for permanent updating and insertion into global academic communities. It is important to follow and participate in a scientific agenda of research, innovation, production, and knowledge dissemination as actively as possible; this agenda is anchored in an international framework that prepares current generations to address the challenges of the global era, which require multidimensional skills (European Universities Association [EUA], 2020; OECD, 2018).

Bearing in mind the United Nations Sustainable Development Goals, the American Council of Education (ACE, n.d.) advocates for a comprehensive internationalization process that, in the current globalization framework, would be based on a set of assumptions and focus on three main angles: (a) diversity, equity, and inclusion; (b) institutional transformation; and (c) decision-making based on data and research, which would integrate policies, programmes, initiatives, and people to transform universities into more globally oriented institutions. Thus, internationalization should cut across each university's strategy and policies (EUA, 2020).

The realization of such an academic internationalization agenda may unfold over a broad set of dimensions: (a) participation in research teams of international scope; (b) development of research based on topics on the global agenda; (c) integration of regional and local problems in research that addresses global challenges; (d) updating of teaching contents with new research results; (e) establishment of university partnerships for teaching and research; (f) creation of joint programmes; (g) integration of international networks and associations that represent different areas of action at universities and promote interdisciplinarity; (h) updating of pedagogical practices and teaching–learning methodologies while taking into consideration digital technologies; and (i) contact with lecturers, students, researchers, and other staff with different realities, cultures, and ways of doing and thinking through sustainable programmes of mobility and exchange *incoming* and *out*going that combine face-to-face and virtual experiences.

In the context of European universities, these various dimensions of internationalization have been greatly supported by European Commission programmes. Among these, a standout is the Erasmus Programme, especially in the domain of education. With its multiple developments and lines of action, the Erasmus Programme must be acknowledged as perhaps the most successful European programme and a leading contributor to the internationalization of HEIs and the mobility of their students and teaching and administrative staff. Over the past 35 years, generating a new phenomenon of "lifestyle mobility" (Wickham, 2016), the Erasmus Programme undoubtedly represents a "success story" that has promoted several million mobilities, greater employability, and a stronger European identity (Cojocaru, 2019).

As a university institution that has promoted the Erasmus Programme since its first years of existence, Iscte-Instituto Universitário de Lisboa has anchored itself on this important pillar to foster internationalization. Through the establishment of near half a thousand inter-university partnerships over several decades, with the support of the Erasmus Programme, Iscte has provided internationalization experiences in education to some tens of thousands of students, faculty members, administrative staff, and researchers. First involving universities from European Union countries, and more recently addressing also universities from out of the European Union scope, the different kinds of Erasmus actions are enabling Iscte students' internationalization through semesters abroad, internships, dual degrees, Erasmus Mundus Joint Masters as well through the development of strategic partnerships and capacity-building programmes, namely those involving other Portuguese-speaking countries from the Global South (European Commission, 2022).

The ambition of the current Erasmus 2021–2027 Programme raises the bar of internationalization even higher. In particular, with the European Universities Initiative, it aims for the transformation of HEIs at all levels[1] and expects that at least 50% of all European students should participate in an international experience along their studies pathway. These goals bring new challenges for HEIs and their modalities of doing mobility programmes. To understand students' position on this topic, a questionnaire was administered in the context of the European Pioneer[2] consortium, of which Iscte is a member. Selected results from the questionnaire are analyzed in this chapter.

9.3 The Case of Iscte in Europe

9.3.1 Giving Voice to Students

International mobility activities conducted by university students from different educational cycles have different motivations, interests, and barriers. To study students' practices and perceptions, Iscte developed research involving a survey in collaboration with other European universities. The survey was administered online in February 2022 through Google Forms, and the survey link was disseminated to all Iscte students (11,406 individuals, of whom around 20% are from other nationalities than Portuguese).

The 412 respondents in the sample (see Table 9.3) were mainly national students, and approximately 10% were international students (including students in Erasmus programmes). Most respondents were female (62%) and under 25 years of age (52%). Regarding the study programme, the highest frequency observed in the sample was second-cycle students (43%) and first-cycle students (39%). Around 46% of respondents were full-time students, but 24.5% of respondents maintained full-time employment; the vast majority were students in advanced education programmes (i.e., master's and doctorate programmes).

Regarding mobility practices, 26% of respondents (106) said they had already undertaken a mobility action during their higher education studies. As shown in Figure 9.2, students in all higher education programmes had international experience, with a higher number of master's and doctoral students reporting mobility experience (34% and 36%, respectively).

Within the group of respondents with mobility experience, studying abroad for one semester was the most frequent mobility action for bachelor's and master's students (see Figure 9.3), while studying abroad for a year was the most frequent option for doctoral students and the second most frequent for master's students. Moreover, traveling for short-term studies (i.e., less than a semester) was more frequent among undergraduate students (25%) than students in other educational programmes.

Studying abroad for one semester was also the most frequent option among most full-time students (54%) and students with another employment status (34%). Short-term studies and internships or professional mobility were more frequent among students with another employment status (26% and 16%, correspondingly) than full-time students.

Most respondents (74%) reported that they had not undertaken any mobility actions during their higher education studies. Financial, family, or health constraints were the most frequently mentioned reasons for not undertaking a mobility action, as mentioned by 31% of full-time students and 37% of part-time students (see Figure 9.4). The COVID-19 pandemic of the last few years was cited by 18% of respondents as a barrier to mobility. It should be noted that 15% of respondents indicated an intention to pursue a mobility action in the future; this response was most frequent among undergraduate and full-time students.

Table 9.3 Characteristics of the Sample of Iscte Students

Student Characteristics		n	%
Nationality	**National**	372	**90.3**
	International	40	9.7
Total		412	100.0
Gender	**Female**	257	**62.4**
	Male	144	35.0
	Other/unspecified	11	2.7
Total		412	100.0
Age (in years)	**< 25**	215	**52.2**
	25–34	91	22.1
	35–44	52	12.6
	≥ 45	54	13.1
Total		412	100.0
Programme	**Bachelor**	162	**39.3**
	Master's	179	**43.4**
	Doctorate	59	14.3
	Other	12	2.9
Total		412	100.0
Employment status	**Employed full-time**	101	**24.5**
	Employed part-time	36	8.7
	Self-employed	30	7.3
	Unemployed	54	13.1
	Full-time student	191	**46.4**
Total		412	100.0

Note: Portuguese results from the Pioneer Alliance (2022) university students survey, 2022.

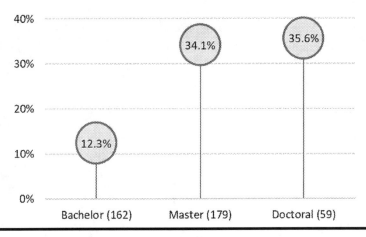

Figure 9.2 Student mobility by programme type.

Note: Portuguese results from the Pioneer Alliance university students survey, 2022.

The results also demonstrated that 13% of respondents did not feel the need to pursue mobility experiences during their higher education studies. This sentiment was more common among male respondents than female respondents. Moreover, 7% of respondents did not feel that they were able to pursue mobility experiences due to linguistic or academic limitations. Also of note was the manifestation of lack of information mentioned by 11% of respondents.

Regarding the benefits of mobility, the main advantages cited by respondents were the development of their ability to adapt to new environments and improvements in language skills (see Figure 9.5). When comparing national and international students, the results show that national students considered the three main benefits of mobility to be improvements in language skills, the development of their ability to adapt to new environments, and growth in their employability through curriculum enhancement. For international students, the most frequently reported benefits were the development of their ability to adapt to new environments, improvements in language skills, and new experiences. Thus, international students' perceptions of the benefits of mobility appeared to reflect the experience of new realities, while national students' perceptions of the benefits of mobility appeared to reflect the possibility of improving their employability.

The survey also asked about respondents' preferences for possible means of pursuing future higher education programmes, including double or joint degrees (see Figure 9.6). Overall, 43% of participants reported a preference for combined experiences (e.g., face-to-face and online degree attainment). Traditional education (e.g., onsite or on campus) was the second most frequent option selected by respondents. Finally, only 13% preferred to attend classes exclusively online.

As shown in Table 9.4., a deeper analysis of respondents' preferences and characteristics demonstrated that female participants preferred the combined learning

Digital Era: Higher Education International Mobility Challenges ■ 199

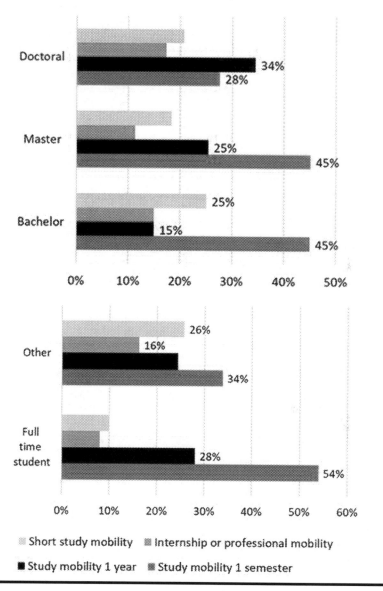

Figure 9.3 Type of mobility actions by programme and employment status.

Note: Portuguese results from the Pioneer Alliance university students survey, 2022.

modality (46.3%), while male participants were divided between onsite or on-campus (37.5%) and combined learning (36.1%). In addition, undergraduate students expressed a preference for onsite or on-campus learning, but master's and doctoral students most frequently selected combined learning (40.2% and 64.4%,

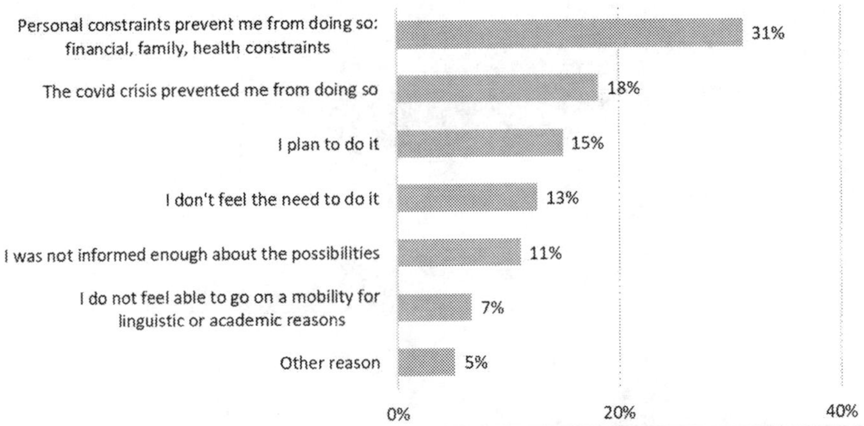

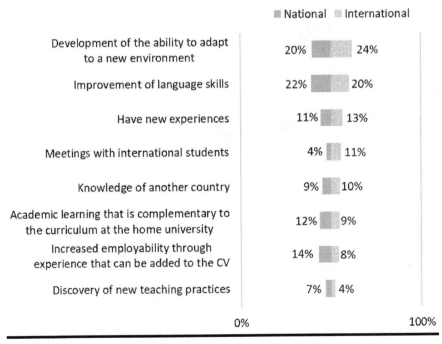

Figure 9.4 Reasons cited by respondents for not pursuing mobility actions.

Note: Portuguese results from the Pioneer Alliance university students survey, 2022.

Figure 9.5 Benefits of mobility.

Note: Portuguese results from the Pioneer Alliance university students survey, 2022.

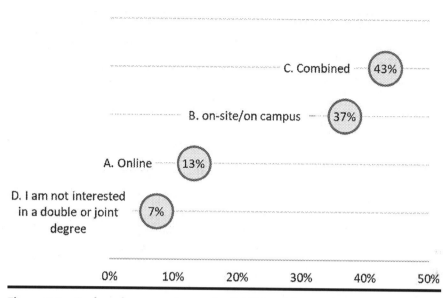

Figure 9.6 Preferred means of pursuing additional future degrees (Double and Joint Degrees).

Note: Portuguese results from the Pioneer Alliance university students survey, 2022.

respectively). Notably, 18.6% of PhD students indicated a preference for online learning. Finally, full-time students preferred onsite or on-campus learning (46.6%) and combined learning (40.8%), but 44.1% of students with another employment status preferred combined learning and 19% preferred online learning.

The skills that respondents most frequently wanted to develop to increase their employability were language and communication skills (26%), digital skills (18%), and technical skills in the respondent's area of interest (14%; see Figure 9.7).

It can be underlined that most students did not undertake any mobility actions during their higher education studies, probably due to financial, family, and academic reasons (in addition to the pandemic), but some of them intended to do so in the future.

Several respondents recognized benefits associated with new experiences, adaptation to new environments (see Figure 9.5), and the development of language and communication skills (see Figure 9.7). It is also noteworthy that the skills that respondents wished to develop to increase their employability were also recognized as benefits of mobility and online learning, as they are associated with the development of digital skills.

Student mobility can be promoted based on some of the results from this study. Some students reported that they did not feel the need to pursue these experiences or felt unable to do so due to linguistic or academic limitations. Therefore, future

Table 9.4 Preferred Means of Pursuing Additional Future Degrees (Double and Joint Degrees) by Gender, Programme, and Employment Status

Way to Study Additional Degree			A. Online	B. On-site/ On campus	C. Combined	D. Not Interested in a Double or Joint Degree	Total of Responses
Gender							
Male		n	23	54	52	15	144
		%	16.0	**37.5**	**36.1**	10.4	100.0
Female		n	30	93	119	15	257
		%	11.7	36.2	**46.3**	5.8	100.0
Programme							
Bachelor		n	16	73	63	10	162
		%	9.9	**45.1**	38.9	6.2	100.0
Master		n	23	68	72	16	179
		%	12.8	38.0	**40.2**	8.9	100.0
Doctoral		n	11	6	38	4	59
		%	18.6	10.2	**64.4**	6.8	100.0
Employment status							
Full-time student		n	12	89	78	12	191
		%	6.3	**46.6**	40.8	6.3	100.0
Other		n	42	62	99	18	221
		%	19.0	28.1	**44.8**	8.1	100.0

Note: Portuguese results from the Pioneer Alliance university students survey, 2022.

communication strategies could include empowerment and encouragement measures, such as dissemination of the aforementioned benefits and experiences of students who have experienced international mobility.

The offer of new training proposals, such as the double degree or other modalities of joint programmes, may be proposed in the future by HEIs through different

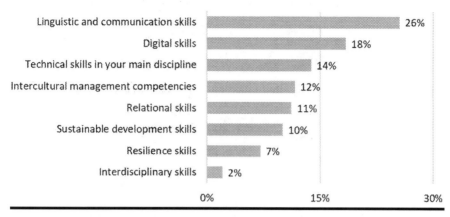

Figure 9.7 Skills that respondents want to develop to increase their employability.
Note: Portuguese results from the Pioneer Alliance university students survey, 2022.

modes, such as combined education (e.g., B-learning that combines national and European or international programmes exclusively onsite or online). It was found that online education was preferred by a public associated with higher academic degrees, and professionals. This is possibly related to the fact that Portuguese students engaged in higher academic studies that have a professional activity, find it more difficult to combine with on-site abroad mobility. Furthermore, international mobility programmes should be heterogeneous in the sense that universities should tailor educational offerings to the needs of specific segments of students.

9.3.2 International Mobility and Digital Teaching

For universities, a major challenge is to equip students with global skills that enable them to participate in a globalized economy while striving to be sustainable and inclusive and keeping pace with constant change. International student mobility poses two different challenges: promoting and providing the requirements for students to go abroad and providing home students with adequate "abroad" conditions. These challenges arise from the two-pillar model of internationalization (see Figure 9.8).

This urgent need for knowledge without borders was even more evident during the COVID-19 pandemic, as most students could access new knowledge and follow their studies through online media despite being at home. In this case, the pillar of IaH had a different conceptualization/realization since students were obliged to be at their facilities but could experience a different learning context (i.e., being forced to follow online teaching). The pandemic confirmed the urgent need to adapt to e-learning strategies and pedagogies.

Figure 9.8 Two pillars of internationalization: At home and abroad/cross-border.
Note: From Knight (2012).

However, now that the world has returned to its usual pace (albeit a different one), it is time to investigate students' needs and requirements. International mobility and curricular programmes should be led by the concept of global competence, which the Organisation for Economic Co-operation and Development (OECD, 2018) defined as follows:

> the capacity to examine local, global and intercultural issues, to understand and appreciate the perspectives and worldviews of others, to engage in open, appropriate and effective interactions with people from different cultures, and to act for collective well-being and sustainable development.
>
> (p. 7)

Based on the results of the survey conducted for this study, only 26% of participants reported having studied abroad during their higher education studies. Thus, most respondents had yet to go abroad for their studies. However, 15% planned to pursue international mobility (see Figure 9.4).

This intention is predominantly motivated by opportunities to be immersed in a different learning context, learn new languages and communications skills, and be embedded in a different culture. However, researchers have identified several obstacles to a full learning experience abroad. According to Lomer and Anthony-Okeke (2019), there is evidence that, in the British context, some international students lack the necessary linguistic and academic skills, which prevents them from effectively and actively participating in academic life; in addition, some intercultural tensions occur, especially in collaborative work. The authors also indicated that pedagogies must change to foster genuine international learning contexts and experiences.

The results from the survey also provide evidence of these issues, as most respondents reported that one of the most important reasons for studying abroad is to improve their language skills and be immersed and active in a different environment. Van Maele et al. (2016) obtained similar results in a study conducted on the IEREST (Intercultural Education Resources for Erasmus Students and their Teachers) project, in which international students stated that major factors that contribute to a successful study abroad experience are the opportunity to acquire a new language, personal development, and experiences in a different social context. Similarly, Kjellgren and Richter (2022) found that major obstacles to traveling abroad to conduct studies include poor timing, financial considerations, and a mismatch between the study or course plan and other private or personal obligations that may take priority. The results from the study showed that most students justified not being able to go abroad with personal constraints, including financial, family, and health constraints. Moreover, attention should be paid to the subgroup of students who do not view mobility experiences as relevant or stated that they did not have access to information about the opportunities and advantages of mobility. Therefore, institutions should more effectively disseminate information about mobility programmes, scholarships, and the long-term benefits of mobility actions within their communities.

Online micro-credential programmes (Oliver, 2019) can boost undergraduate students' interest in short-term mobilities while avoiding the obstacles related to finances, family, and health highlighted by respondents in the survey conducted for the current study (see Figure 9.4). Short-term online micro-credentials can also address the needs of professionals and advanced students who cannot leave their job location for long-term stays but are interested in developing their skills. Micro-credentials have several benefits, including personalization of the learning pathway, increased competency, uplevel skillsets, flexibility, cost efficiency, and collaboration. These make them appealing to both learners and the institutions that provide them. The development of micro-credentials enables institutions to diversify their educational offerings and target various publics, such as lifelong learning. Learners can personalize their continuous education credits and maximize competency-based learning by selecting micro-credential courses that most closely correspond to their career development needs.

According to Kjellgren and Richter (2021), HEIs should engage in joint efforts to establish a global competence and mobility strategy plan that

- provides global competence training for all that is tailored to individual needs, such as addressing the concerns of professionals and advanced studies for online offers, namely by including micro-credential strategies;
- fosters diversity among faculty, staff, and students;
- improves institutional clarity about goals and concepts related to global competence;
- assesses outputs and outcomes to ensure the attainment of desired goals;
- and evaluates results and adjusts further mobility strategies.

Emirza et al. (2021, p. 1) advocated for international mobility programmes to be designed in a challenging but not too challenging manner, which would provide an opportunity for students to succeed without becoming bored or overly frustrated when they fail. They also found evidence that "(…) both general self-efficacy and by extension job search self-efficacy could be enhanced through properly designed international student mobility programs." This aligns with the results of this study and respondents' belief that engaging in international mobility would foster the development of some capacities (mainly digital, linguistic, and communication skills) and increase employment opportunities.

The Pioneer Alliance partnership with other European universities through the European Union-funded project InCITIES (University Institute of Lisbon, 2022) will help Iscte and its partners to develop, implement, and foster mutual mobility strategies that benefit both participating institutions and learners.

9.4 Conclusion

The current research focuses on the internationalization of universities, specifically student mobility in a border sense. The chapter began with an overview of research published on digital international mobility in higher education, within the last four years, to identify main trends and network relations on research attributes studied by a high number of researchers. There have been numerous studies on this topic, and the main research attributes were found to be digital learning, digitalization, the Erasmus Programme, innovative universities, international mobility, international student mobility, international students, internationalization, open virtual mobility, the role of virtual exchange, student-interactive video conferences, teaching and learning, transcultural practices, transnational mobility, university students and staff, virtual exchange, virtual internationalization, and virtual mobility.

The chapter also presented the results of a survey administered to Iscte students on their reasons for studying abroad, which included the improvement of language skills and the opportunity to immerse themselves and be active in a different environment for personal development and experience a different social context. The results also demonstrated that there is scarce information about the opportunities and advantages of international mobility programmes.

Acknowledgments

Work supported by the Fundação para a Ciência e Tecnologia, within the Projects UIDB/3126/2020, UIDB/04466/2020, and UIDP/04466/2020 and by the European Union under the Grant Agreement n° 101071330.

Notes

1 On what concerns the way they are organized, the processes of teaching and doing research, how to get funds, the links with their ecosystems and their service to society
2 https://pioneer-alliance.eu/

References

American Council of Education. (n.d.). *Comprehensive internationalization*. Retrieved on August 25, 2022, from https://www.acenet.edu/Research-Insights/Pages/Internationalization/Comprehensive-Internationalization.aspx

Castells, M. (2010). *The rise of network society*. Willey-Blackwell.

Cojocaru, C. (2019). Erasmus mobilities and European identity: An exploratory incursion. *Journal of Educational Sciences*, *40*(2), 66–78. https://doi.org/10.35923/jes.2019.2.06

Emirza, S., Öztürk, E. B., & Şengönül, A. S. (2021). The quality of international mobility experiences, general self-efficacy, and job search self-efficacy: A time-lagged investigation. *Current Psychology*, *40*(4), 1580–1591. https://doi.org/10.1007/s12144-021-01394-3

European Commission. (2022, January 26). *Erasmus+ Programme Guide 2022 (Version 2)*. https://erasmus-plus.ec.europa.eu/sites/default/files/2022-01/2022-erasmusplus-programme-guide-v2_en_0.pdf

European Universities Association. (2020, March). *Learning & teaching paper #9: Internationalisation in learning and teaching*. https://eua.eu/downloads/publications/eua%20report%20internationalisation_web.pdf

Kjellgren, B., & Richter, T. (2021). Education for a sustainable future: Strategies for holistic global competence development at engineering institutions. *Sustainability*, *13*(20), Article 11184. https://doi.org/10.3390/su132011184

Kjellgren, B. O., & Richter, T. (2022). Redesigning international student mobility for global competence development. In *IEEE Global Engineering Education Conference* (pp. 1104–1112). IEEE. https://doi.org/10.1109/EDUCON52537.2022.9766799

Knight, J. (2012). Concepts, rationales, and interpretive frameworks in the internationalization of higher education. In D. K. Deardorff, H. de Witt, J. D. Heyl, & T. Adams (Eds.), *The SAGE handbook of international higher education* (pp. 27–42). Sage. https://doi.org/10.4135/9781452218397.n2

Lomer, S., & Anthony-Okeke, L. (2019). Ethically engaging international students: Student-generated material in an active blended learning model. *Teaching in Higher Education, 24*(5), 613–632. https://doi.org/10.1080/13562517.2019.1617264

OECD. (2018). *Preparing our Youth for an Inclusive and Sustainable World*. https://eric.ed.gov/?id=ED581688

Oliver, B. (2019, August). *Making micro-credentials work for learners, employers, and providers*. Deakin University. https://dteach.deakin.edu.au/wp-content/uploads/sites/103/2019/08/Making-micro-credentials-work-Oliver-Deakin-2019-full-report.pdf

Online Knowledge Library. (n.d.). *What is B-On?* https://www.b-on.pt/en/what-is-b-on/

Page, M., McKenzie, J., Bossuyt, P., Boutron, I., Hoffmann, T., Mulrow, C., & Al, E. (2021). The PRISMA 2020 statement: An updated guideline for reporting systematic reviews. *Research Methods & Reporting, 372*(1), Article 71. https://doi.org/10.1136/bmj.n71

Pioneer Alliance. (2022). Pioneer Alliance - A new generation of learners, knowledge producers, and entrepreneurs for sustainable cities. https://pioneer-alliance.eu/

Sen, A. (2006). *Identity and violence. The illusion of destiny*. W.W. Norton & Company.

University Institute of Lisbon. (2022, July 27). *Iscte leads European InCITIES consortium*. https://www.iscte-iul.pt/news/2044/iscte-leads-european-incities-consortium

Van Maele, J., Vassilicos, B., & Borghetti, C. (2016). Mobile students' appraisals of keys to a successful stay abroad experience Hints from the IEREST project. *Language and Intercultural Communication, 16*(3), 384–401. https://doi.org/10.1080/14708477.2016.1168050

Wickham, J. (2016). *Unequal Europe. Social divisions and social cohesion in an old continent*. Routledge.

References of the Systematic Literature Review

Al-Mahdawi, E. (2022). An overview on internationalisation within the United Kingdom higher education. *Social Sciences, Humanities and Education Journal, 3*(1). https://doi.org/10.25273/she.v3i1.11925

Aperyan, Y. (2021). The internationalization of higher education in armenia nowadays the analysis of the existing problems. *Banber Erevani Hamalsarani. Sots'iologia, 12*(1 (33)). https://doi.org/10.46991/BYSU:F/2021.12.1.079

Barakina, E. Y., Popova, A. V., Gorokhova, S. S., & Voskovskaya, A. S. (2021). Digital technologies and artificial intelligence technologies in education. *European Journal of Contemporary Education, 10*(2), 285–296. https://doi.org/10.13187/ejced.2021.2.285

Barbier, R., & Benjamin, E. (2019). From "CoCo" to "FloCoCo": The Evolving Role of Virtual Exchange (Practice Report). In *Research-publishing.net*. https://eric.ed.gov/contentdelivery/servlet/ERICServlet?accno=ED596479

Baroni, A., Dooly, M., García, P. G., Guth, S., Hauck, M., Helm, F., Lewis, T., Mueller-Hartmann, A., O'Dowd, R., Rienties, B., & Rogaten, J. (2019). Evaluating the Impact of Virtual Exchange on Initial Teacher Education: A European Policy Experiment. In *Research-publishing.net*. https://eric.ed.gov/contentdelivery/servlet/ERICServlet?accno=ED593741

Bruhn, E. (2020). *Virtual Internationalization in Higher Education. Innovative University: Digital – International – Transformative*. https://eric.ed.gov/contentdelivery/servlet/ERICServlet?accno=ED610050

Carola, M. B., & Demiray, Z. E. G. (2022). *The impact of the Erasmus Programme on higher education in Europe*. http://hdl.handle.net/10400.14/38281

Dias, G. P., Barbosa, B., Santos, C. A., Pinheiro, M. M., Simões, D., & Filipe, S. (2021). Between promises and pitfalls: the impact of mobility on the internationalization of higher education. *Journal of Further & Higher Education, 45*(1), 79–94. https://doi.org/10.1080/0309877X.2020.1735321

Griggio, L., & Pittarello, S. (2020). How a Multilingual Project Can Foster and Enhance International Mobility. In *Research-publishing.net*. https://eric.ed.gov/contentdelivery/servlet/ERICServlet?accno=ED610275

Kabanbayeva, G., Gureva, M., Bielik, P., & Ostasz, G. (2019). Academic mobility and financial stability: A case of Erasmus student exchange program. *Journal of International Studies (2071-8330), 12*(1), 324–337. https://doi.org/10.14254/2071-8330.2019/12-1/22

Kelley, L. C. (2020). The decline of Asian studies in the west and the rise of knowledge production in Asia: An autoethnographic reflection on mobility, knowledge production, and academic discourses. *Research in Comparative and International Education, 15*(3), 273–290. https://search.ebscohost.com/login.aspx?direct=true&db=eric&AN=EJ1265425&site=eds-live

Kobzhev, A., Bilotserkovets, M., Fomenko, T., Gubina, O., Berestok, O., & Shcherbyna, Y. (2020). Measurement and assessment of virtual internationalization outcomes in higher agrarian education. *Postmodern Openings / Deschideri Postmoderne, 11*, 78–92. https://doi.org/10.18662/po/11.1sup1/124

Leek, J., & Rojek, M. (2022). Functions of digital learning within the international mobility programme - perspectives of university students and staff from Europe. In *Education and information technologies* (Vol. 27, Issue 5, pp. 6105–6123). https://doi.org/10.1007/s10639-021-10855-y

Lukhutashvili, N., Valishvili, T., & Genelidze, L. (2022). Challenges of educational management in pandemic reality (On the example of Akaki Tsereteli State University). ეკონომიკური პროფილი, *17*(1(23)), 98–108. https://doi.org/10.52244/ep.2022.23.12

Minaeva, E., & Taradina, L. (2022). Internationalization in Russian universities during the pandemic of COVID-19: Lessons for succeeding in the new reality. *Higher Education Quarterly, 76*(2), 293–310. https://doi.org/10.1111/hequ.12387

Oladipo, O. A., & Sugandi, B. (2022). Recruitment and mobility of international students: Spotlight on a Chinese university. *Globalisation, Societies & Education, 20*(5), 655–668. https://doi.org/10.1080/14767724.2021.1988522

Otto, D. (2018). Using virtual mobility and digital storytelling in blended learning: Analysing students' experiences. *Turkish Online Journal of Distance Education, 19*(4), 90–103. https://eric.ed.gov/contentdelivery/servlet/ERICServlet?accno=EJ1192803

Park, H., & Park, H. W. (2021). Global-level relationships of international student mobility and research mentions on social media. *El Profesional de La Información, 30*(2), 1–11. https://doi.org/10.3145/epi.2021.mar.14

Puradiredja, D. I., Kintu-Sempa, L., Eyber, C., Weigel, R., Broucker, B., Lindkvist, M., Casamitjana, N., Reynolds, R., Klinkel, H.-F., Matteelli, A., & Froeschl, G. (2022). Adapting teaching and learning in times of COVID-19: A comparative assessment among higher education institutions in a global health network in 2020. *BMC Medical Education, 22*(1), 1–12. https://doi.org/10.1186/s12909-022-03568-4

Rajagopal, K., Firssova, O., Beeck, I. Op de, Stappen, E. Van der, Stoyanov, S., Henderikx, P., & Buchem, I. (2020). Learner skills in open virtual mobility. *Research in Learning Technology*, *28*(0), 1–18.

Semenchenko, T. O. (2018). Peculiarities of foreign language teaching to future specialists of financial and credit field In circumstances of eurointegration and globalisation. *Financial & Credit Activity: Problems of Theory & Practice*, *3*(26), 510–515. https://doi.org/10.18371/fcaptp.v3i26.143870

Sidhu, R., Cheng, Y. E., Collins, F., Ho, K. C., & Yeoh, B. (2021). International student mobilities in a contagion: (Im)mobilising higher education? *Geographical Research*, *59*(3), 313–323. https://doi.org/10.1111/1745-5871.12471

Solmaz, O. (2020). Transcultural practices of international students as identity performances in digital settings. *Journal of Interdisciplinary Studies in Education*, *9*(2), 276–300. https://eric.ed.gov/contentdelivery/servlet/ERICServlet?accno=EJ1294632

Sultanova, L., Milto, L., & Zheludenko, M. (2021). The impact of the Covid-19 pandemic on the development of higher education. *Acta Paedagogica Vilnensia*, *46*, 132–147. https://doi.org/10.15388/ActPaed.46.2021.9

Sundh, S. (2018). International exchange of ideas in student-interactive video conferences – sustainable communication for developing intercultural understanding with student teachers. *Discourse and Communication for Sustainable Education*, *9*(2), 123–133. https://search.ebscohost.com/login.aspx?direct=true&db=eric&AN=EJ1202620&site=eds-live

Towers, A., & Towers, N. (2020). Re-evaluating the postgraduate students' course selection decision-making process in the digital era. *Studies in Higher Education*, *45*(6), 1133–1148. https://search.ebscohost.com/login.aspx?direct=true&db=eric&AN=EJ1257832&site=eds-live

Tran, L. T. (2020). Teaching and engaging international students. *Journal of International Students*, *10*(3). https://doi.org/10.32674/jis.v10i3.2005

Chapter 10

Artificial Intelligence: Applicability of This Technology to Higher Education – A Scoping Review

Andreia de Bem Machado,
Gertrudes Aparecida Dandolini,
and João Artur de Souza
Federal University of Santa Catarina, Florianópolis, Brazil

Miltiades Demetrios Lytras
Effat University, Jeddah, Saudi Arabia

Maria José Sousa
ISCTE – University Institute of Lisbon, Lisbon, Portugal

Contents

10.1 Introduction 212
10.2 Artificial Intelligence 213
10.3 Methodology 215

DOI: 10.1201/9781003424543-11

10.4 Result 218
    10.4.1 Bibliometric Analysis of the Selected Publications 218
    10.4.2 Main Scientific Sources 224
10.5 Artificial Intelligence: The Applicability of This Technology to
Higher Education 229
    10.5.1 Artificial Intelligence in Higher Education 229
    10.5.2 Applicability of AI to Higher Education 230
    10.5.3 Synthesis 232
10.6 Final Conclusion 233
References 233

10.1 Introduction

The world is undergoing transformations that can be noticed in all dimensions of society. With regard to education, the influence that the COVID-19 pandemic has had on the lives of education professionals, especially teachers, is noted. In this context, many problems previously discussed have taken on a much greater development (Alyahyan & Düştegör, 2020). Several questions about the competencies in teacher training for the teaching–learning process were again gaining prominence in training centers. Among them can be highlighted the applications of artificial intelligence (AI) in education, which are on the rise and have received much attention in these two pandemic years. Artificial intelligence and technologies used for learning are highlighted as important developments in educational technology (Zawacki-Richter et al., 2019).

Digital technologies have been widely used in education to facilitate the learning process (Chun Lam et al., 2020). Students can take advantage of opportunities to learn using digital technologies tied to more sustainable actions (Sousa et al., 2022). In the context of higher education, educational technologies and strategies adopted in digital education are a key tool to facilitate fairness and inclusive access to education, eliminate barriers to learning, broaden the vision of teachers, and to qualify the student learning process (de Bem Machado et al., 2022).

In this regard, artificial intelligence has been standing out both in the academic scenario and in the context of organizations that envision new approaches and funding opportunities arising from it. Concepts such as machine learning (ML), deep learning (DL), and others are terms commonly used nowadays (José Sousa et al., 2021).

The concept of artificial intelligence originated from the Dartmouth Society in 1956 (Dodigovic, 2007) and has been applied to an increasing number of aspects of our lives, among them in the educational context. The purpose of AI is to build intelligent machines, or at least machines that behave as if they were intelligent. As an essential branch of computer science, artificial intelligence technology is dedicated to the research and development of technical sciences used to simulate, extend, and expand human intelligence. In recent years, thanks to the tremendous advances in machine learning and the exponential growth of data, artificial intelligence has ushered in an explosive period. Due to its advantages in analysis, prediction, judgment, and decision-making, artificial intelligence can fundamentally empower sectors such as security, finance, retail, transportation, and education (Massaro, Dumay & Guthrie, 2016).

In the educational field, AI applications are becoming more popular and have received attention in recent years (Zawacki-Richter et al., 2019). In the 2018 Horizon study (Educause, 2018), AI and adaptive learning technologies are highlighted as major advances in educational technology, with an implementation time of two to three years. According to the survey conducted, the use of AI in education is assumed to increase by 43% between 2018 and 2022. However, the Horizon Report 2019 Higher Education Edition (Educause, 2019) anticipates that AI applications related to teaching and learning will develop even faster through a bibliometric review of how artificial intelligence can be applied to education as a technology for higher education. This chapter contributes to reflecting on the following research questions:

What is AI in higher education?
How is AI being applied as a technology to higher education?

This research discusses the concepts of artificial intelligence and its applicability as a technology in higher education. To this end, a systematic search was conducted in the Web of Science and Scopus databases. The research is divided into six parts. The first is this introduction, the second deals with the concept of artificial intelligence, the third deals with the methodology adopted in this research, the fourth discusses the research results, the fifth discusses the applicability of artificial intelligence in higher education, and finally, the last part presents the final considerations and future work.

10.2 Artificial Intelligence

Although various definitions of artificial intelligence have emerged in recent decades, John McCarthy was the first to define it in a two-month workshop at Dartmouth College in the US. AI is a field of study that focuses on artificially replicating the cognitive abilities of human intelligence to create software or machines capable of performing tasks typically performed by humans. The term "artificial intelligence" is used, according to Russell and Norvig (2013, p. 24), when a machine imitates the cognitive functions that humans associate with other human minds, such as learning and problem-solving. In the workshop proposal, McCarthy first used the term artificial intelligence in 1956 (Russell & Norvig, 2013). Their defined concept spells out that AI is the science and engineering of making intelligent machines, especially intelligent computer programs. AI Is related to the similar task of using computers to understand human intelligence, but it is not necessarily limited to methods that are biologically observable.

Artificial intelligence must proceed on the conjecture that every aspect of learning or any other feature of intelligence can, in principle, be described so accurately that a machine can be made to simulate it. An attempt will be made to figure out how to make machines use language, form abstractions and concepts, solve types of problems now reserved for humans, and improve themselves (Zawacki-Richter et al., 2019).

Baker and Smith (2019) explain that AI has the following concept: computers that perform cognitive tasks, generally similar to the human mind, particularly learning and problem-solving. They explain that AI does not describe a single technology. It is an umbrella term to describe a variety of technologies and methods, such as machine learning, natural language processing (NLP), data mining, neural networks, and genetic algorithms.

One can also characterize AI as a collection of models, techniques, and technologies (knowledge search, reasoning, and representation; perception, planning, and decision mechanisms; NLP; uncertainty handling; and machine learning) that, alone or in groups, solve problems involving logical reasoning (Sichman, 2021). The main paradigms used in AI are symbolic, connectionist, evolutionary, and probabilistic.

In the symbolic paradigm (Sichman, 2021), one must first identify the domain-expert knowledge (problem model), and then represent it using a formal representation language and implement an inference mechanism to use this knowledge. Examples are expert systems, fuzzy expert systems, and hybrid systems.

In the connectionist paradigm (Sichman, 2021), language is a network of simple elements, inspired by the functioning of the brain, where artificial neurons, connected in a network, are able to learn and generalize from examples. The reasoning consists in directly learning the input-output function. Mathematically, for example, this can be a technique for approximating functions by non-linear regression. Here are the artificial neural networks, which can be supervised or unsupervised.

The evolutionary paradigm (Sichman, 2021) uses a probabilistic method of finding solutions to problems (optimization), where solutions are represented as individuals, to which techniques "inspired" by the theory of evolution, such as heredity, mutation, natural selection, and recombination (or crossing over) are applied, to select for the following generations the most adapted individuals. Genetic algorithms are examples of this paradigm.

The probabilistic paradigm uses models to represent the statistical concept of conditional independence, based on causal relationships in the domain (Sichman, 2021).

Artificial intelligence and machine learning are often mentioned at the same time. Machine learning is an AI method for the classification and creation of supervised and unsupervised profiles, for example, to predict the likelihood of a student dropping a course or being admitted to a program or to identify topics in projects. Popenici and Kerr (2017) explain machine learning as a subfield of artificial intelligence that includes software that can recognize patterns, make predictions, and apply newly discovered patterns to situations that were not included or covered by its initial design.

As such, the definition of AI is broad and comprises several areas, such as knowledge, reasoning, problem-solving, perception, learning, planning, and the ability to manipulate and move objects (Vieira Barros & Guerreiro, 2019). In this scenario, it is considered its presence in different contexts, including the educational one, which has increasingly incorporated technological tools into pedagogical practice.

10.3 Methodology

This research was conducted using the systematic scoping review methodology, suitable when a better understanding of a concept or phenomenon is desired, contemplating several data sources and types of publications, theoretical and empirical (Munn et al., 2018).

Tricco et al. (2018) adapted the PRISMA methodology for scoping reviews, calling it PRISMA-ScR. Having a protocol for conducting scoping reviews ensures greater methodological rigor to research and increases its relevance, transparency, and replicability.

It was sought to use descriptors that could encompass the main terms related to the research and their respective synonyms adopted by the literature. Two databases were chosen – Scopus (Elsevier) and Web of Science (Clarivate Analytics) – because they are multidisciplinary and have peer-review methods. The justifications for choosing these bases for the electronic searches were because they are multidisciplinary and have the peer-review method, and are the largest indexing services today (Mongeon & Paul-Hus, 2016), concentrating most of the publications on the topic of artificial intelligence and higher education (Ouyang et al., 2022).

According to the flowchart of PRISMA-ScR, it was sought to fulfill the steps of identification, selection, eligibility, and inclusion of articles, shown in Table 10.1.

The methodological steps of the PRISMA-ScR protocol include determining and justifying the eligibility criteria, describing the information sources, presenting

Table 10.1 PRISMA Scoping Review Table

	Searched terms: "Artificial Intelligence" and "higher education" and "technology" and "application"
	Research carried out in the Scopus and WoS databases between March and April 2022
IDENTIFICATION		Total found in the databases	Scopus	WoS	Total
			169	308	477
SELECTION	Inclusion criteria	Publication type: peer-reviewed review and research articles,	42	149	191
		Linked to the terms AI, education, and higher education	13	10	23
	Exclusion criteria	Language: articles in English, Spanish, or Portuguese	0	0	0
		Publication type: books and articles from event proceedings	127	159	286
ELIGIBILITY		Analysis of titles and abstracts and cross-checking between databases to remove duplicates	13	10	23
INCLUSION		Total included	13	5	18

Source: Prepared by the authors (2022).

the database search strategy, the data presentation process, and summarizing the results. All steps are presented below.

Step 1: Identification

In the identification step, the terms used in the searches were "artificial intelligence" and "higher education" and "technology" and "application". The searches were carried out between 03/15/2022 and 04/04/2022. A total of 477 articles were identified, distributed as 308 articles in the Web of Science and 169 in Scopus. Then, to ensure scientific rigor, only articles from peer-reviewed academic journals were included, resulting in 286 articles.

Step 2: Selection

In order to obtain the largest number of publications, only two inclusion criteria were adopted: 1) the publications must be made available as "open access", in line with the growing global movement of policies of open access to research (Xavier, 2019); 2) the researches must be classified as peer-reviewed articles. Due to the nature of this article, in systematic reviews, it is recommended to analyze only this type of document.

In the selection step, articles were first selected by reading the titles, abstracts, and keywords, leaving 42 publications from Scopus and 149 from Web of Science for the next step, and five articles appeared in duplicity in the two databases, leaving 186 articles.

Step 3: Eligibility

In this step, as eligibility criteria, the titles and abstracts were analyzed, and the databases were cross-checked to remove duplicates. After the triage, 13 articles selected from the Scopus database and 10 from the Web of Science that met the eligibility criteria went to full-text analysis. As 5 articles are duplicates in both databases, a total of 18 articles resulted in full-text reading.

Step 4: Inclusion

Finally, 18 articles were included in the qualitative and quantitative synthesis. In the PRISMA recommendation, there is no rule regarding the minimum or maximum number of articles to be included. According to Moher et al. (2009), the review team should search the available literature. This search results in the number of reports found. Once these reports were examined and the eligibility criteria were applied, a smaller number of articles remained.

The following research inclusion criteria were defined: a) peer-reviewed articles, in order to guarantee the quality of the selected publications; b) the descriptors should appear in the title, abstract, or keywords, in both bases; c) without chronological delimitation; d) with a connection to the researched theme (artificial intelligence in higher education).

The exclusion criteria were: a) books and conference papers; b) articles without adherence to the research objectives; and c) unavailability of full access to the article, either through the base itself, contact with the authors, or through parallel platforms such as Google Scholar, Research Gate, and Emerald Insight.

Thus, a bibliometric analysis was performed first, followed by a careful reading of the selected publications, in order to answer the research questions.

10.4 Result

10.4.1 Bibliometric Analysis of the Selected Publications

To analyze the bibliometric data of the 23 articles, the Bibliometrix software was used, because it has, through the R Bibliometrix package, called Biblioshiny, the most extensive and adequate set of techniques among the researched tools for bibliometric analysis (Moral-Muñoz et al., 2020). The summary of this information is presented in Table 10.2.

Table 10.2   Summary of the Information Found in the Databases

Main Information About the Data	Scopus	Web of Science
Timespan	1992–2022	2019–2021
Sources (Journals, Books, etc)	11	9
Documents	13	10
Average years from publication	3.69	1.5
Average citations per document	9.385	8
Average citations per year per doc	29.86	2.492
References	1	497
DOCUMENT CONTENTS		
Keywords Plus (ID)	62	43
Author's Keywords (DE)	55	54
AUTHORS		
Authors	49	34
Author appearances	49	34
Authors of single-authored documents	1	1
Authors of multi-authored documents	48	33
AUTHORS COLLABORATION		
Single-authored documents	1	1
Documents per Author	0.265	0.294
Authors per document	3.77	3.4
Co-Authors per documents	3.77	3.4
Collaboration Index	4	3.67

Source: Prepared by the authors (2022).

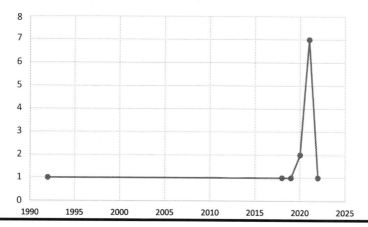

Figure 10.1 Distribution of publications over the years – Scopus.

Source: Prepared by the authors (2022).

The analysis started by referencing the global growth rate in the number of scientific publications, which increased by 34% in 2021. Figure 10.1 indicates the growing interest in the topic verified in the Scopus database and, in Figure 10.2, in the Web of Science.

This analysis began by identifying the 20 most relevant authors on the theme of this research in Scopus and Web of Science, which are detailed in Figure 10.3 and Figure 10.4, respectively.

It can be seen that there is no author that stands out as a reference in both databases.

The country that published the most on artificial intelligence and higher education in both Scopus and Web of Science was China, with eight publications in Scopus and seven in Web of Science. Figures 10.5 and 10.6 present the intensity

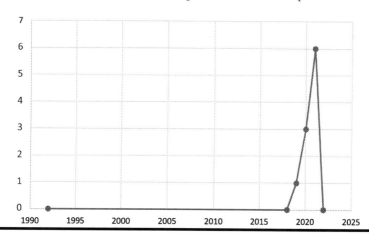

Figure 10.2 Distribution of publications over the years – Web of Science.

Source: Prepared by the authors (2022).

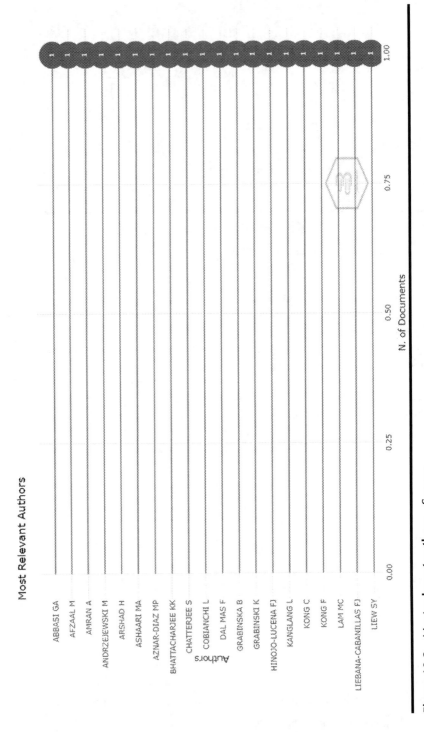

Figure 10.3 Most relevant authors – Scopus.
Source: Prepared by the authors (2022).

Artificial Intelligence ■ 221

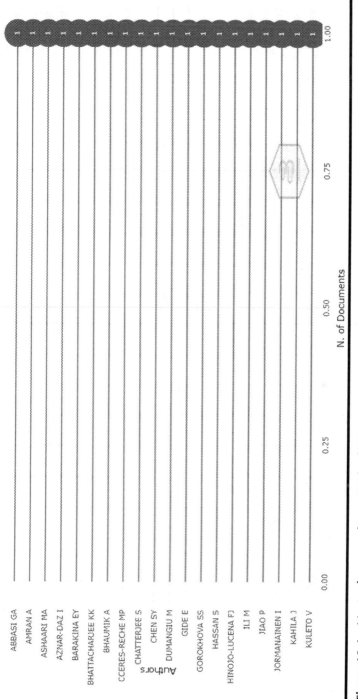

Figure 10.4 Most relevant authors – Web of Science.
Source: Prepared by the authors (2022).

222 ■ *Technologies for Sustainable Global Higher Education*

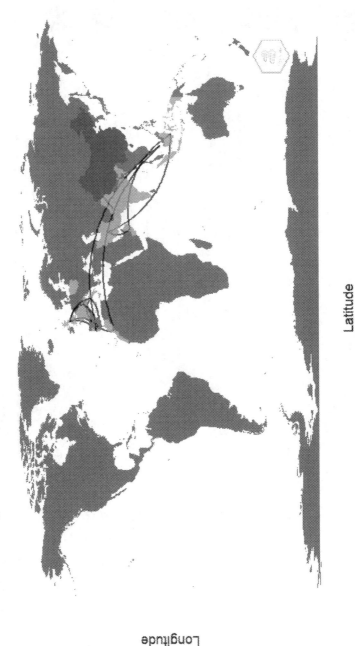

Figure 10.5 Country collaboration map – Scopus.
Source: Prepared by the authors (2022).

Artificial Intelligence ■ 223

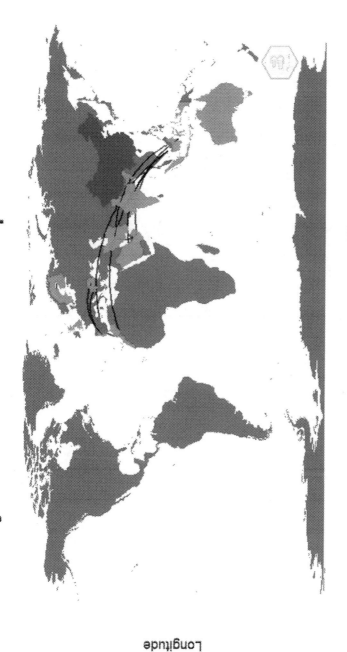

Figure 10.6 Country collaboration map – Web of Science.
Source: *Prepared by the authors (2022).*

of publications by country and the relationship established between them, through citations between papers published in Scopus and Web of Science, respectively.

It was found that the largest concentration of publications is located in Europe, Asia, Oceania, and Africa.

10.4.2 Main Scientific Sources

The documents analyzed were published in nine different journals, with two studies published in two journals in the Scopus database: *Education And Information Technologies* and *Sustainability*. In the Web of Science database, two were published in only one journal, *Tem Journal – Technology Education Management Informatics*, as presented in Table 10.3, with the nine most relevant scientific sources on the themes of artificial intelligence and higher education.

Table 10.3 Main Scientific Sources in Scopus and Web of Science

\multicolumn{4}{c|}{Databases}			
\multicolumn{2}{c	}{Scopus}		\multicolumn{2}{c}{Web of Science}	
Sources	Articles	Sources	Articles
Education and Information Technologies	2	TEM Journal – Technology Education Management Informatics	2
Sustainability (Switzerland)	2	E-Mentor	1
Computers And Education	1	Education and Information Technologies	1
Education Sciences	1	Education Sciences	1
European Journal of Contemporary Education	1	Fresenius Environmental Bulletin	1
Frontiers In Psychology	1	Heliyon	1
Heliyon	1	International Journal of Educational Sciences	1
IEEE Access	1	International Journal of Emerging Technologies in Learning	1
International Journal of Interactive Mobile Technologies	1	Technological Forecasting and Social Change	1

Source: Prepared by the authors (2022).

Artificial Intelligence ■ 225

[Tag cloud image with prominent terms: decision making, data analytics, machine learning, classroom teaching, neural networks, developing world, how people learn, artificial intelligence technologies, advanced analytics, big data, performance, data set, academic performance, building blockes, power, knowledge, ir4 0, exploration, curricula, data mining, malaysia, serbia, contextualization, academic research, deep learning, organization, artificial intelligence techniques, policy making, artificial neural network, data management, operating modes, big data analytic capability, computation theory, computing curricula, decision theory, behavioral research, neural-networks]

Figure 10.7 Tag cloud – Scopus.
Source: Prepared by the authors (2022).

The tag clouds below were constructed from the bibliometric analysis, based on the groups of papers retrieved from the two databases, and 55 keywords were indicated by the authors from Scopus and 54 from Web of Science.

Highlighted in the Scopus database were: *higher education*, which appears four times, and *artificial intelligence*, which appears three times, according to Figure 10.7.

In the second database, *artificial intelligence* and *higher education* appear with four occurrences, according to Figure 10.8. The emphasis on the term *higher education* indicates that it is an area of application of artificial intelligence technology.

The five most cited documents globally in Scopus and Web of Science are listed in Table 10.4.

The paper that gained prominence with 49 citations in Scopus and 35 in Web of Science was *Artificial Intelligence in Higher Education: A Bibliometric Study on its Impact in the Scientific Literature*, by authors Francisco-Javier Hinojo-Lucena, Inmaculada Aznar-Díaz, María-Pilar Cáceres-Reche, and José-María Romero-Rodríguez, published in 2019. The article analyzes the studies on artificial intelligence in higher education indexed in Web of Science and Scopus during the period 2007–2017.

To answer the research questions (What is AI in higher education? How is AI being applied as a technology to higher education?), the 18 articles described in Table 10.5 were read and analyzed.

The analysis of the 18 articles is presented in the next section.

Figure 10.8 Tag cloud – Web of Science.

Source: Prepared by the authors (2022).

Table 10.4 Most Cited Documents in Scopus and Web of Science

Author/Scientific Source	DOI	No. of Citations in Scopus	No. of Citations in WoS
Hinojo-Lucena FJ, 2019, Education Sciences	10.3390/educsci9010051	49	35
Chatterjee S, 2020, Education and Information Technologies	10.1007/s10639-020-10159-7	37	28
Tanveer M, 2020, Sustainability	10.3390/su12229435	7	–
Kong F, 2020, International Journal Emergence Technologies in Learning	10.3991/ijet.v15i13.15351	–	7
Nazari N, 2021, Heliyon	10.1016/j.heliyon.2021.e07014	6	2
Sousa MJ, 2021, TEM Journal – Technology Education Management Informatics	10.18421/TEM102-02	–	3
Kuleto V, 2021, Sustainability	10.3390/su131810424	5	–

Source: Prepared by the authors (2022).

Table 10.5 Selected Articles for Reading and Analysis

Year	Authors	Article
1992	Noel Williams	The artificial intelligence applications to learning programme
2018	Nitirajsingh Sandu and Ergun Gide	Analysis of the main factors affecting the adoption of cloud based interactive mobile learning in the Australian higher education sector
2019	Francisco-Javier Hinojo-Lucena, Inmaculada Aznar-Díaz, María-Pilar Cáceres-Reche, and José-María Romero-Rodríguez	Artificial intelligence in higher education: A bibliometric study on its impact in the scientific literature
2020	Muhammad Tanveer, Shafiqul Hassan, and Amiya Bhaumik	Academic policy regarding sustainability and artificial intelligence (Ai)
2020	Sheshadri Chatterjee and Kalyan Kumar Bhattacharjee	Adoption of artificial intelligence in higher education: a quantitative analysis using structural equation modelling
2020	Meng Chun Lam, Hwei Kei Tee, Siti Soleha Muhammad Nizam, Nurhazarifah Che Hashim, Nur Asylah Suwadi, Siok Yee Tan, Nazatul Aini Abd Majid, Haslina Arshad, and Sook Yee Liew	Interactive augmented reality with natural action for chemistry experiment learning
2020	Liu Kanglang, and Muhammad Afzaal	Artificial intelligence (AI) and translation teaching: A critical perspective on the transformation of education
2020	Fanwen Kong	Application of artificial intelligence in modern art teaching
2021	Mohamed Azlan Ashaari, Karpal Singh Dara Singh, Ghazanfar Ali Abbasi, Azlan Amran, and Francisco J. Liebana-Cabanillas	Big data analytics capability for improved performance of higher education institutions in the Era of IR 4.0: A multi-analytical SEM & ANN perspective.

(Continued)

Table 10.5 (Continued)

Year	Authors	Article
2021	Valentin Kuleto, Milena Ilić, Mihail Dumangiu, Marko Ranković, Oliva M. D. Martins, Dan Păun, and Larisa Mihoreanu	Exploring opportunities and challenges of artificial intelligence and machine learning in higher education institutions
2021	Elena Y. Barakina, Anna V. Popova, Svetlana S. Gorokhova, and Angela S. Voskovskaya	Digital technologies and artificial intelligence technologies in education
2021	Nabi Nazari, Muhammad Salman Shabbir, and Roy Setiawan	Application of artificial intelligence powered digital writing assistant in higher education: Randomized controlled trial
2021	Yu-Shan Lin, Shih-Yeh Chen, Chia-Wei Tsai, and Ying-Hsun Lai	Exploring computational thinking skills training through augmented reality and AIoT learning
2021	Ruishu Wang, Jiannan Li, Wanbing Shi, and Xin Li	Application of artificial intelligence techniques in operating mode of professors' academic governance in American research universities
2021	Matti Tedre, Tapani Toivonen, Juho Kahila, Henriikka Vartiainen, Teemu Valtonen, Ilkka Jormanainen, and Arnold Pears	Teaching machine learning in K-12 classroom: Pedagogical and technological trajectories for artificial intelligence education
2021	Barbara Grabińska, Mariusz Andrzejewski, and Konrad Grabiński	The students' and graduates' perception of the potential usefulness of artificial intelligence (AI) in the academic curricula of finance and accounting courses
2021	Maria José Sousa, Francesca Dal Mas, António Pesqueira, Carlos Lemos, Juan Manuel Verde, and Lorenzo Cobianchi	The potential of AI in health higher education to increase the students' learning outcomes
2022	Fan Ouyang, Luyi Zheng, and Pengcheng Jiao	Artificial intelligence in online higher education: A systematic review of empirical research from 2011 to 2020

Source: Prepared by the authors (2022).

10.5 Artificial Intelligence: The Applicability of This Technology to Higher Education

Of the 18 articles that comprised the corpus of analysis, seven were systematic literature reviews, two were literature reviews added to the analysis of documents and/or projects, and nine were empirical studies with application of a questionnaire. After the researchers read and analyzed the articles, they identified some themes that stood out in the two questions that were the focus of this study and that will be addressed in the following subsections.

10.5.1 Artificial Intelligence in Higher Education

In the educational context, AI has been defined as the ability of machines, i.e., computers to achieve goals through learning based on prior experiences associated with humans (Chatterjee & Bhattacharjee, 2020). AI is the ability of a system to learn from input data to achieve a defined goal (Kaplan & Haenlein, 2019). Its recognition goes beyond computer science, involving disciplines such as information science, psychology, linguistics, mathematics, and others. AI is an interdisciplinary field, which integrates methods and results from other sciences, with the goal of developing integrative, adaptive environments that complement and optimize traditional forms of education (Popenici & Kerr, 2017). AI can be established as computing systems capable of developing processes such as learning, adaptation, self-correction, and the employment of data to process complex tasks (Baker & Smith, 2019).

Baker and Smith (2019) present AI in higher education from three different perspectives: a) student-oriented, b) teacher-oriented, and c) system-oriented. Student-oriented AI enables a personalized learning system; teacher-oriented AI can automate activities such as assessments and administrative procedures; and system-oriented AI also assists teachers and managers in monitoring student learning and decision-making.

In higher education, AI enables institutions to make available interfaces capable of dialoguing with students (through AI there are already chatbots as tutors). Thus, students will be able to clear their doubts by asking questions directly to the machine, without having to take teachers' time (Grabiński, 2021).

Artificial intelligence allows teachers to have a holistic view of their students while being able to visualize them in a specific way. AI can provide personalized resources, learning paths, and learning services for students. Through various communication tools, it can also conduct effective teacher–student and computer–human interactions, provide rich information sources and a good navigation structure, as well as intelligently guide students to learn, and provide suggestions on their further study content. AI can free up students' imagination space. AI can process, classify, and organize knowledge, systematically divide knowledge according to students' habits and help them build their own knowledge base; it can improve students' learning efficiency (Kong, 2020).

10.5.2 Applicability of AI to Higher Education

Industry 4.0 technologies (José Sousa et al., 2021), such as cloud computing, automation, blockchain, additive manufacturing, immersive technologies, robotics, and the Internet of Things (IoT), integrate AI to promote intelligent systems and devices, leading to the creation of new models that can be adopted by higher education institutions.

Artificial intelligence in higher education is studied by several authors in order to contribute to the application of AI in terms of learning opportunities for students and management systems. NLP is connected to ML techniques to find patterns in large datasets (human-written sources), which recognize natural language. Its use includes analyzing customers' feelings about some products or services by searching social media posts. AI technologies can be used to ensure equitable and inclusive access to education. AI provides opportunities for people with disabilities, refugees, and people living in isolated communities (Jose Sousa et al., 2021).

Artificial intelligence can be used in higher education for personalized education through the automation of administrative teaching tasks, software programs that foster the detection of topics that need reinforcement in the classroom, the guidance and support of students outside the classroom, and the use of data intelligently to teach and support students (Hinojo-Lucena et al., 2019). In addition to personalized education, AI can be applied through Augmented Reality, Adaptive Learning Platforms, Intelligent Tutoring Systems, Chatbots, Adaptive Learning, Computer-Assisted Instruction, Direct Feedback, Massive Open Online Courses (MOOCs), and Robotics, which will be described next.

Augmented Reality (AR) is an educational innovation that has the ability to attract student attention to an interesting and fun learning environment through the implementation of AI technology (Chun Lam, 2020).

Adaptive Platforms are resources that enable students to travel through individualized knowledge trails, taking their already acquired knowledge as a starting point, in order to stimulate their cognitive development and autonomy. In the context of higher education, universities must establish a clear division of power and good communication platforms based on artificial intelligence (Wang et al., 2021).

Intelligent Tutoring Systems are a part of the AI narrative that makes it possible, through the development of tutoring programs, to personalize education by promoting interactive learning (Tanveer et al., 2020). They are part of the new technological possibilities to extend educational learning (Jose Sousa et al., 2021). Intelligent tutors act as a guide for student learning, detecting the student's progress in learning based on content knowledge and the student's personal characteristics, while distributed intelligent teaching systems favor student collaboration through software programs that support and encourage interactions (Hinojo-Lucena et al., 2019).

A Chatbot is a software used to simulate interactions with humans by means of text or voice. It can understand natural language and learns according to usage. In the academic context of higher education, interactive chatbots are very appropriate since with AI the responses to students are refined over time. Higher education institutions have created chatbots designed to engage students, accumulate candidate data, and create virtual teaching assistants using that data (Kuleto et al., 2021). Some examples of known virtual assistants (Grabiński, 2021): Watson Assistant (IBM), Siri (Apple), Alexa (Amazon), and Google Assistant (Google).

In Adaptive Learning, students use AI technology to personalize their educational paths in the context of higher education. Many universities believe that AI has the potential to facilitate adaptive learning and increase student success. Although this technology is widely used, most people are not using it because it has not entered their daily lives. Interactive technologies create mediation and thus indicate a learning path when the student interacts with the system. Once the tools are in place, they can measure and respond to student progress moment by moment using actual student activities, learning analytics data, and machine learning (Kuleto et al., 2021). Machine Learning, which drives adaptive learning, addresses the question of how to build information systems to automatically improve through experience (Sandu & Gide, 2018). Machine learning is a technology that emerged from AI and allows computers to learn (Cho et al., 2020; Grabiński, 2021). Learning with the help of AI technologies (Elena et al., 2021), which on the one hand is a toolkit for the broader use of these technologies by students in various spheres of public life is, on the other hand, the result of the study of various academic disciplines that consider AI and interact with it. Thus, representatives of generation Alpha (the first generation to be born in the 21st century) will learn almost exclusively from AI technology. This generation has, like other generations, distinctive characteristics that must be taken into account when developing and implementing training tools. Changes in educational interaction are happening for Generation Z and the next, generation Alpha, in schools, namely the transition from structured, auditory learning to the attraction of visual, multimodal, and hands-on teaching methods for these new generations (Education, 2021; Eskidarov–Student, 2021). Thus, teachers can use components of AI to develop teaching materials that enable adaptive learning (Williams, 1992).

Computer-Assisted Instruction (Kong, 2020) applies computer technologies such as multimedia, hypertext, artificial intelligence, network communication, and knowledge base to overcome the shortcomings of traditional teaching in teaching scenarios. It can shorten the learning time and improve the quality and efficiency of teaching to achieve the teaching objectives. According to research by Kong (2020), there are many cases of AI applications in education in the United States – for example, there are self-adaptive learning systems for teachers and college students; there are teaching materials that can interact with students and change course content according to students' responses on random tests; there are intelligent textbooks customized according to students' personalized requirements; and there are cases that lead to more suitable designs in the interface according to the analysis of images to improve the user experience.

Artificial intelligence as a technology in higher education can be applied with Direct Feedback, which is associated with greater commitment, involvement, and better performance of teachers and students because it can provide feedback based on mistakes made in some activity. Thus, students can perform the tasks and exercises by receiving an evaluation of the wrong questions through feedback (Kuleto et al., 2021). One of the most important contributions of AI to education and meaningful learning is to give immediate feedback to students about their learning progress. Hence, it can promote more student engagement and improve performance, motivation, and self-regulation through direct feedback that makes students more engaged, knowledge builders, active, and autonomous (Raza et al., 2021).

MOOCs can be used in conjunction with AI, for example, in individualized solutions for people with disabilities (José Sousa et al., 2021). Also, with the use of AI, online micro-class videos, flipped classrooms, and PAD (Presentation-Assimilation-Discussion) classes allow students to use dispersed time to learn and effectively control the speed of learning; at the same time, it breaks the location limit, effectively solves the shortcomings of the traditional offline teaching mode, and vastly increases the utilization rate of teachers (Kong, 2020).

Robotics can be used as a technology in higher education as automation software solutions applied to repetitive tasks (Seasongood, 2016; Grabiński, 2021; Tedre et al., 2021).

10.5.3 Synthesis

Artificial intelligence was defined by Russell and Norvig (2013) as the ability of machines, i.e., computers to achieve goals through learning based on prior experiences associated with humans. In the context of higher education, AI is an interdisciplinary field that brings together methods and results from other sciences, with the aim of developing integrative, adaptive, and interactive environments that complement the methodologies of the teaching–learning process.

Among others, technologies that can be related to AI in higher education are ML, DL, and NLP (José Sousa et al., 2021). Machine Learning refers to machines that learn from data and achieve results autonomously. Deep Learning involves machines that use complex algorithms to imitate the neural network of the human brain and learn an area of knowledge with virtually no supervision. NLP is connected to ML techniques to find patterns in large data sets (sources written by humans), which recognize natural language (José Sousa et al., 2021).

In this context, some applications of AI to higher education take place through Augmented Reality, Adaptive Platforms, Intelligent Tutoring Systems, Chatbots, Adaptive Learning, Computer-Assisted Instruction, Direct Feedback, MOOCs, Robotics, and Personalized Education, which bring the possibility of flexibility, personalization, and support of collaborative learning.

10.6 Final Conclusion

The main purpose of this systematic review was to map in light of the bibliometric review how artificial intelligence can be applied to education as a technology for higher education. This study aimed to answer two research questions: (1) What is artificial intelligence in higher education? (2) How can artificial intelligence be applied as a technology to higher education? To answer the first research question, the 18 articles identified with the theme "artificial intelligence as a technology in higher education" were reviewed. China is the country with the largest production, with eight articles in Scopus and seven in Web of Science. However, several other countries from different continents (Europe, Asia, Africa, and Oceania) have shown interest in the theme, since there is intensity in the network of relationships established among the countries, through citations between papers published in Scopus and Web of Science, placing them among the most productive countries. Thus, it can be concluded that this phenomenon is of global interest.

The paper that gained the most prominence, with 49 citations in the Scopus database and 35 in the Web of Science, was *Artificial Intelligence in Higher Education: A Bibliometric Study on its Impact in the Scientific Literature*, by Francisco-Javier Hinojo-Lucena, Inmaculada Aznar-Díaz, María-Pilar Cáceres-Reche, and José-María Romero-Rodríguez, published in 2019. The article analyzes the studies on artificial intelligence in higher education indexed in the Web of Science and Scopus during the period 2007–2017.

To answer the research question about the application of artificial intelligence as a technology in higher education, several artifacts were identified, such as Augmented Reality, Adaptive Platforms, Intelligent Tutoring Systems, Engagement Chatbots, Adaptive Learning, Personalized Education, Computer-Assisted Instruction, Direct Feedback, Moocs, And Robotics.

For future research, it is intended to map how blockchain and artificial intelligence can serve as tools for technological innovation in the context of higher education.

References

Alyahyan, E. & Düştegör, D. (2020). Predicting academic success in higher education: Literature review and best practices. *International Journal of Educational Technology in Higher Education*, 17(1). doi:10.1186/s41239-020-0177-7

Ashaari, M. A., Singh, K. S. D., Abbasi, G. A., Amran, A., & Liebana-Cabanillas, F. J. (2021). Big data analytics capability for improved performance of higher education institutions in the Era of IR 4.0: A multi-analytical SEM & ANN perspective. *Technological Forecasting and Social Change*, 173(121119), 121119. doi:10.1016/j.techfore.2021.121119

Baker, T. & Smith, L. (2019). Educ-AI-tion rebooted? Exploring the future of artificial intelligence in schools and colleges. Retrieved from Nesta Foundation website: https://media.nesta.org.uk/documents/Future_of_AI_and_education_v5_WEB.pdf

de Bem Machado, A., Sousa, M. J., & Dandolini, G. A. (2022). Digital learning technologies in higher education: A bibliometric study. In Abrar Ullah, Sajid Anwar, Álvaro Rocha, & Steve Gill (Eds.), *Lecture Notes in Networks and Systems* (pp. 697–705). Singapore: Springer Nature Singapore.

Chatterjee, S. & Bhattacharjee, K. K. (2020). Adoption of artificial intelligence in higher education: A quantitative analysis using structural equation modelling. *Education and Information Technologies*, 25(5), 3443–3463. doi:10.1007/s10639-020-10159-7

Cho, D., Yoo, C., Im, J., & Cha, D. H. (2020). Comparative assessment of various machine learning-based bias correction methods for numerical weather prediction model forecasts of extreme air temperatures in urban areas. *Earth and Space Science*, 7(4), e2019EA000740.

Chun Lam, M., Kei Tee, H., Muhammad Nizam, S. S., Che Hashim, N., Asylah Suwadi, N., Yee Tan, S., & Yee Liew, S. (2020). Interactive augmented reality with natural action for chemistry experiment learning. doi:10.18421/TEM91-48.

Dodigovic, M. (2007). Artificial intelligence and second language learning: An efficient approach to error remediation. *Language Awareness*, 16(2), 99–113. doi:10.2167/la416.0.

EDUCAUSE. (2018). Horizon report: 2018 higher education edition. Retrieved from EDUCAUSE Learning Initiative and The New Media Consortium website: https://library.educause.edu/-/media/files/library/2018/8/2018horizonreport.pdf.

EDUCAUSE. (2019). Horizon report: 2019 higher education edition. Retrieved from EDUCAUSE Learning Initiative and The New Media Consortium website: https://library.educause.edu/-/media/files/library/2019/4/2019horizonreport.pdf

Eskidarov–Student (2021), D. Organization of work in a distributed center of a courier company3. НАУЧНИ ТРУДОВЕ.

Grabiński, B. G. M. A. (2021). e-mentor: The students' and graduates' perception of the potential usefulness of Artificial Intelligence (AI) in the academic curricula of Finance and Accounting Courses. Recuperado 23 de abril de 2022, de Edu.pl website: https://www.e-mentor.edu.pl/artykul/index/numer/92/id/1544

Hinojo-Lucena, F.-J., Aznar-Díaz, I., Cáceres-Reche, M.-P., & Romero-Rodríguez, J.-M. (2019). Artificial intelligence in higher education: A bibliometric study on its impact in the scientific literature. *Education Sciences*, 9(1), 51. doi:10.3390/educsci9010051

José Sousa, M., Dal Mas, F., Pesqueira, A., Lemos, C., Manuel Verde, J., & Cobianchi, L. (2021). The potential of AI in health higher education to increase the students' learning outcomes. *TEM Journal*, 488–497. doi:10.18421/tem102-02

Kaplan, A., & Haenlein, M. (2019). Siri, Siri, in my hand: Who's the fairest in the land? On the interpretations, illustrations, and implications of artificial intelligence. *Business Horizons*, 62(1), 15–25. doi:10.1016/j.bushor.2018.08.004

Kong, F. (2020). Application of artificial intelligence in modern art teaching. *International Journal of Emerging Technologies in Learning (iJET)*, 15(13), 238. doi:10.3991/ijet.v15i13.15351

Kuleto, V., Ilić, M., Dumangiu, M., Ranković, M., Martins, O. M. D., Păun, D., & Mihoreanu, L. (2021). Exploring opportunities and challenges of artificial intelligence and machine learning in higher education institutions. *Sustainability*, 13(18), 10424. doi:10.3390/su131810424

Lin, Y.-S., Chen, S.-Y., Tsai, C.-W., & Lai, Y.-H. (2021). Exploring computational thinking skills training through Augmented Reality and AIoT learning. *Frontiers in Psychology,* 12, 640115. doi:10.3389/fpsyg.2021.640115

Massaro, M., Dumay, J., & Guthrie, J. (2016). On the shoulders of giants: Undertaking a structured literature review in accounting. *Accounting, Auditing & Accountability Journal,* 29(6), 767–801. doi: 10.1108/AAAJ-01-2015-1939

Moher, D., Liberati, A., Tetzlaff, J., Altman, D. G., & PRISMA Group, T. (2009). Preferred reporting items for systematic reviews and meta-analyses: the PRISMA statement. *Annals of Internal Medicine,* 151(4), 264–269.

Mongeon, P. & Paul-Hus, A. (2016). The journal coverage of Web of Science and Scopus: A comparative analysis. *Scientometrics,* 106(1), 213–228. doi:10.1007/s11192-015-1765-5.

Moral-Muñoz, J. A., Herrera-Viedma, E., Santisteban-Espejo, A., & Cobo, M. J. (2020). Software tools for conducting bibliometric analysis in science: An up-to-date review. *El profesional de la información,* 29(1), e290103.

Munn, Z., Peters, M. D. J., Stern, C., Tufanaru, C., McArthur, A., & Aromataris, E. (2018). Systematic review or scoping review? *BMC Medical Research Methodology,* 18(143), 1–7.

Ouyang, F., Zheng, L., & Jiao, P. (2022). Artificial intelligence in online higher education: A systematic review of empirical research from 2011 to 2020. *Education and Information Technologies.* doi:10.1007/s10639-022-10925-9

Popenici, S. & Kerr, S. (2017). Exploring the impact of artificial intelligence on teaching and learning in higher education. *Research and Practice in Technology Enhanced Learning.* doi:10.1186/s41039-017-0062-8

Raza, S. A., Qazi, Z., Qazi, W., & Ahmed, M. (2021). E-learning in higher education during COVID-19: Evidence from blackboard learning system. *Journal of Applied Research in Higher Education.* doi:10.1108/jarhe-02-2021-0054

Russell, S. & Norvig, P. (2013). *Artificial intelligence - a modern approach.* New Jersey: Pearson Education.

Sandu, N., & Gide, E. (2018). Analysis of the main factors affecting the adoption of Cloud based interactive mobile learning in the Australian Higher Education sector. *International Journal of Interactive Mobile Technologies (iJIM),* 12(4), 43. doi:10.3991/ijim.v12i4.9200

Seasongood, S. (2016). Not just for the assembly line: A case for robotics in accounting and finance. *Financial Executive,* 32, 31–39.

Sichman, J. S. (2021). Inteligência Artificial e sociedade: avanços e riscos. *Estudos Avançados,* 35(101), 37–50. doi:10.1590/s0103-4014.2021.35101.004

Sousa, M. J., Marôco, A. L., Gonçalves, S. P., & Machado, A. D. B. Digital Learning Is an Educational Format towards Sustainable Education. *Sustainability* 2022, 14, 1140. doi:10.3390/su14031140

Tanveer, M., Hassan, S., & Bhaumik, A. (2020). Academic policy regarding sustainability and artificial intelligence (AI). *Sustainability,* 12(22), 9435. doi:10.3390/su12229435

Tedre, M., Toivonen, T., Kahila, J., Vartiainen, H., Valtonen, T., Jormanainen, I., & Pears, A. (2021). Teaching machine learning in K–12 classroom: Pedagogical and technological trajectories for artificial intelligence education. *IEEE Access: Practical Innovations, Open Solutions,* 9, 110558–110572. doi:10.1109/access.2021.3097962

Tricco et al. (2018). PRISMA extension for scoping reviews (PRISMA-ScR): Checklist and explanation. *Annals of Internal Medicine,* 169(7), 467–473.

Vieira Barros, D. & Guerreiro, A. (2019). Novos desafios da educação a distância: programação e uso de Chatbots. *Revista Espaço Pedagógico*, 26(2), 410–431. doi:10.5335/rep.v26i2.8743

Wahyuni, A., Utami, A. R., & Education, E. (2021). The use of youtube video in encouraging speaking skill. *Pustakailmu. Id*, 7(3), 1–9.

Wang, R., Li, J., Shi, W., & Li, X. (2021). Application of artificial intelligence techniques in operating mode of professors' academic governance in American research universities. *Wireless Communications and Mobile Computing*, 2021, 1–7. doi:10.1155/2021/3415125

Williams, N. (1992). The artificial intelligence applications to learning programme. *Computers & Education*, 18, 101–107. Recuperado de https://eric.ed.gov/?id=EJ441698

Xavier, R. F. (2019). Evolução das plataformas de acesso aberto brasileiras: Propriedades e perspectivas. *Ciência Da Informação*, 48(3). Recuperado de http://revista.ibict.br/ciinf/article/view/4949

Zawacki-Richter, O., Marín, V. I., Bond, M., & Gouverneur, F. (2019). Systematic review of research on artificial intelligence applications in higher education – where are the educators? *International Journal of Educational Technology in Higher Education*, 16(1). doi:10.1186/s41239-019-0171-0

Chapter 11

Case Study of Two Higher Education Institutions in the Use of a National MOOC Platform Toward Sustainable Development

Pedro Barbosa Cabral
NAU Project, FCCN, Lisboa, Portugal

Célio Gonçalo Marques and Inês Araújo
LIED, Polytechnic Institute of Tomar, Tomar, Portugal

José Miguel Padilha, Francisco Vieira, and Luís Carvalho
Nursing School of Porto, Porto, Portugal

Contents

11.1 Introduction 238
11.2 Role of MOOC in the Portuguese Higher Education Context 238
       11.2.1 NAU Platform 240
11.3 Methodology 241
11.4 The Case at the Polytechnic Institute of Tomar (IPT) 242
       11.4.1 MOOC in Sustainable Tourism 242

DOI: 10.1201/9781003424543-12   **237**

11.4.2 MOOC in Introduction to Programming 248
11.5 MOOCs in Health: A Case Study Based on the Nursing School of
Porto Experience 251
11.5.1 The Ecare-COPD Training Program 253
11.5.2 The Ecare-COVID19 Professional Update Program 254
11.5.3 Further Developments 255
11.6 Conclusions 255
References 256

11.1 Introduction

MOOCs have emerged with the intention of reaching those interested in specific scientific content without the need to attend a degree course. Higher education institutions have implemented this methodology reaching thousands of students who otherwise would not have had access to this knowledge.

In Portugal, only three institutions have created the conditions for MOOCs, but they are often mere experiments with no continuity due to sustainability issues. The development of the NAU platform created the right conditions for the MOOCs to take on a new dimension at a national level.

Several institutions have implemented MOOCs using the NAU Platform, reaching thousands of trainees and a completion rate above 45%. It is now important to know the experience of different institutions to understand the development of MOOCs. This will allow us to highlight both the positive and negative aspects of these experiences so that solutions can be found to increase the completion rate and/or attract even more trainees.

In this chapter, we will present the evolution of MOOCs at the international level, contextualizing the Portuguese reality that led to the emergence of the NAU Platform. Also will be described the case studies carried out by the Polytechnic Institute of Tomar and the Nursing School of Porto, two higher education institutions in Portugal, about their experience in creating and promoting two MOOCs in 2021. This will allow us to get to know concrete cases so that we can infer new lines of action at the level of MOOC creation, but also at the research level.

11.2 Role of MOOC in the Portuguese Higher Education Context

The last 10 years have been quite valuable in the development of MOOC's pedagogy. If the discussion around this topic started with the distinction between Connectivism MOOC (cMOOC), based on the ideas of George Siemens, and eXtension MOOC (xMOOC), centered in the replication of existing face-to-face courses into an online environment (Rhoads, 2015), what we have witnessed later was the explosion of other models, such as Social MOOC (sMOOC) or Innovative MOOC (iMOOC), and so many others. Nonetheless, the characteristics of all models are established by four main ideas: the capability of reaching a large number of people (M for Massive); the fact that they are open somehow and not specifically that they are connected to the Open Educational Practice's movement (O for Open); it is offered in an online environment (O for Online); and we are talking about a course with dates, time effort, syllabus, assessment and so many other elements that we often identify in courses (C for Course).

During the pandemic period we witnessed, according to Class Central (2019, 2021), an enormous growth in this area moving from 120 million learners to 220 million, more than 5900 new courses, the duplication of microcredentials to 1670, an increase of 20 MOOC based degrees, and Coursera and EdX changing their approach by having more non-universities institutions offering courses.

In Portugal, the idea of developing MOOC platforms is not that strange. There are various experiences in this area, not exclusive to Higher Education. Regarding academia, we can see, from the different approaches, two that are most common; on the one hand, institutions developing their own platform and promoting there their courses or, on the other hand, using major MOOC players to accommodate their courses, such as MiriadaX. From these experiences only three entities still have their platforms operating (Universidade Aberta, Instituto Politécnico de Leiria, and Instituto Superior Técnico) and most of the courses that ran in MOOC providers were mere experiences that have not continued. We can consider that the lack of strategy to maintain a MOOC production is caused by many factors and to have such a short number of entities that continue to develop MOOC is related to the sustainability of the business model implemented.

EADTU (2016) identifies that the main reasons for Higher Education Institutions to develop MOOCs are related to increasing student visibility, reaching new students, creating flexible learning opportunities, or innovating their pedagogical approaches. Looking into these four reasons, it is easier to reach the first two if you have your courses exposed to a MOOC provider and have a shared marketing strategy with them. Considering the other two reasons, which are focused on pedagogical aspects, you can implement it independently of having or not having a MOOC provider, because you might just need a specialized e-learning team or educational advisors helping to build your MOOC, a learning management system (LMS) or digital learning tools that allow you either to create flexible learning opportunities or to try out new pedagogical approaches. Nonetheless, each of the reasons taken in here needs investment in human resources, services, and infrastructure, having a big impact on the organization's cost–benefit, and therefore in the sustainability of an ecosystem that contributes to the different activities and outputs that you can find in a higher education institution.

Bearing in mind that the two main reasons to develop a MOOC are related to having new students, either online or on campus, the impact observed with the three Portuguese higher education institutions referred previously, might be lower than the expected one when compared to a general MOOC provider. In the case of Universidade Aberta, we can find a course that has reached, in two editions, 263 participants (Bastos, Cabral & Rocio, 2019). This course has a specific target audience related to librarian teachers at primary and secondary schools. Another course, from the Instituto Politécnico de Leiria, where the topic addressed was about the use of e-books in education, had 184 enrolments in one edition (Gonçalves, 2019). In this case, about 60% of the users were from the location area of the institution and eight lived abroad from Portugal. Regarding Instituto Superior Técnico, a school from Universidade de Lisboa, Dias (2021) refers that the total amount of users registered in the organization's MOOC platform was 20,240 at the end of July 2021, and that the platform exists since 2016, representing an average of about 4000 new registered users per year. Even though these figures might be perceived with high impact, all the effort and cost with staff, services, and infrastructure may possibly have a lower cost–benefit if the courses were implemented in a MOOC provider.

One of the biggest MOOC providers around the world is EdX, initially a nonprofit organization with a mission to (EdX, 2022) "increase access to high quality (…), enhance teaching and learning on campus and online, and advance teaching and learning through research", it was responsible for the initial development of the LMS Open EdX. Currently, with the acquisition of EdX by 2U, the Open EdX Project moved to another nonprofit organization led by MIT and Harvard University called the Center for Reimagining Learning (tCRIL). This software is being used by a large community of entities which are responsible for local, regional, and national MOOC platforms, such as the France platform FUN-MOOC. Exactly inspired by the French experience, Portugal implemented, in 2019, a MOOC platform based on Open EdX Software to provide a service for Higher Education and the Public Administration for the development of courses in the Portuguese language, and it was named NAU (https://www.nau.edu.pt/).

11.2.1 NAU Platform

The platform had two European structural funding (02/SAMA2020/2016 and POCI-05-5762-FSE-000266) that enabled the creation of an infrastructure for MOOC which can be easily scalable and built around it a group of services that provides good support and learning experience for the users, and, at the same time, a quality cycle that empowers the course development teams to produce MOOC with higher quality for free. Since 2019, the year that the platform was launched, NAU has been working with more than 40 national entities, that created over 150 courses for different target audiences in areas such as Cybersecurity, Health, Digital Skills, Education, Inclusion, and many others. Commonly, these courses easily reach 1000 users, and the most successful course has more than 80,000 users enrolled. With more than 190,000 users registered and 410,000 enrolments, the average completion rate of the courses is above 45%. Even though, these numbers are far behind from what we can find in Coursera, EdX, or FutureLearn, when compared to the national examples given before, the two main objectives related to achieving new students seem to be more efficient in a platform like NAU since it covers a wider audience brought by the ecosystem that exists around the platform.

Currently, NAU has eight higher education institutions with activity in the platform (https://bit.ly/nau-dashboard). In total, these institutions have developed 17 courses and 27 editions of these courses. With a total of 31,792 students enrolled in these courses, we have an average of 1870 students per course.

11.3 Methodology

For the present study, we proposed to two higher education institutions in Portugal to conduct a case study with their students. They are the Polytechnic Institute of Tomar (Instituto Politécnico de Tomar – IPT) and the Nursing School of Porto.

The IPT, located in Tomar, a city in the central interior zone of Portugal, has been training students in science, technology, arts, and humanities since the 1980s. In 2019, the Laboratory for Pedagogical Innovation and Distance Education (LIED) was created to accomplish objectives such as the dissemination of active learning methodologies (i.e. Project-Based learning, Flipped classroom) as well as the inclusion of distance learning methodologies. It is in this context and in partnership with the NAU platform that the first MOOCs produced by LIED were created and implemented.

The Nursing School of Porto (NSP), located in Porto, the second major city of Portugal, was created in 2007 through the fusion of three institutions dedicated to higher education in nursing. The oldest of which dates back to 1896, one of the first Portuguese institutions. The current lifelong learning needs of nurses drove the Nursing School of Porto to develop MOOCs in partnership with the NAU platform.

Both institutions were invited to present in this chapter their experience through a Case Study. Yin (2014) outlines that "a case study allows to focus on a 'case' and retain a holistic and real-world perspective" (p. 4). Case study methodology can be applied in four different ways: 1) to explain a particular case, 2) to describe an intervention, 3) to illustrate, or 4) to highlight unclear aspects. The aim of the current chapter is to use a multiple-case study to "describe an intervention and the real-world context in which it occurred" (Yin, 2014, p. 19).

Two MOOCs carried out by each of the institutions are presented and the results obtained are analyzed futher in this chapter. To characterizing the trainees who enrolled in the MOOCs, IPT applied documental analysis to the data available from the NAU platform. Also applied a survey, using a questionnaire online at the end of the MOOC with the aim of understanding the usefulness of attending this training. NSP presents the application of a first MOOC and an updated version of the same course, analyzing both results. The data in this case was obtained through a survey using 5-point Likert scale course evaluation questions. Both institutions carried out a description of the cases and a statistical analysis of the quantitative data.

11.4 The Case at the Polytechnic Institute of Tomar (IPT)

The creation of the LIED reinforced the IPT's focus on the development of contents for Massive Open Online Courses (MOOCs). In 2021, its first two MOOCs were launched through the NAU platform: Sustainable Tourism and Introduction to Programming. These courses are organized in two strategic areas of the Polytechnic Institute of Tomar (Tourism and Computer Science) and their topics were chosen according to their relevance.

If on the one hand, it was intended to meet the demand for these fields, on the other hand, it was also intended to meet the needs of IPT students. Currently, there is no specific module on sustainable tourism in the Tourism and Cultural Heritage Management degree nor in the CTeSP (foundation program) in Tourism Management, so the MOOC on this topic has allowed students of these courses to increase their knowledge and skills in the field. The programming modules, on the contrary, are in all courses related to computer science, but present high failure rates, namely the introductory ones (Butler & Morgan, 2007; Jenkins, 2002; Lahtinen, Mutka & Jarvinen, 2005). The MOOC created in this domain was a great help for IPT students with difficulties in learning how to program.

In order to successfully complete the courses, the participant needed to complete at least 50% of the required coursework. In line with the development of transversal skills, two modules were created based on the MOOCs mentioned above whose assessment consisted of an oral test. Besides, the certificate issued by the NAU platform, the participants could enroll in these modules, and, in case of a successful completion, they could also obtain a certificate issued by IPT. If the participants are already students of the Polytechnic Institute of Tomar, reference to those modules is made in the Diploma Supplement.

11.4.1 MOOC in Sustainable Tourism

The MOOC in Sustainable Tourism started on 13 July 2021 and ended on 28 December and addressed the concepts of sustainability, the importance of sustainable tourism, tangible and intangible heritage, innovation, and tourism trends, with a total of 29 hours and distributed over three modules.

Each module was presented by a specialist teacher (Maria Rita Nunes, Eunice Ramos Lopes, and João Tomaz Simões) who was responsible for curating and presenting the content. Videos were presented in each module and the participants were challenged to rethink the way tourism has been practiced and how the precepts of sustainability can help in a more responsible and committed use of environmental resources. The MOOC has an estimated duration of 29 working hours.

There were 1340 individuals enrolled in the course, but only 1274 were identified as active enrolments. Even so, and since the survey that serves as the basis for our analysis was not mandatory, we do not have demographic, educational, or gender data on all active enrollees.

Of the 1274 registered participants, only 65.3% reported their age. Of these, 20.6% are aged up to 25 years, 32% are aged between 26 and 40 years, and 47.4% are aged over 41 years. With regard to schooling/education, only 62.4% reported it. Of these, 35.7% have a high school diploma or below, 36.9% have an academic degree, and 27.4% have an advanced degree.

Only 70% of the individuals reported their gender. Of these, 61.2% identified themselves as female, 37% identified themselves as male, and 1.8% identified themselves as other.

Regarding the location of the students, although not all provide this information, from the data collected (close to 50% of active enrolments), 90.1% indicated being from Portugal; 7.7% from Brazil; 1% from Mozambique; 0.6% from Cape Verde; 0.2% from Guinea Bissau; 0.2% from São Tomé and Príncipe; and 0.2% from Australia. We can see that we have participants from two-thirds of the countries of the Community of Portuguese Language Countries (CPLP).

Of the respondents, the majority claimed to work in the public sector (36%); followed by respondents who claimed to be students (22%); then private sector workers (18%); there are also individuals who are unemployed (10%), self-employed (8%) and in another employment situation (6%).

456 certificates were issued through the NAU platform. The completion rate was 34%, which required approval in at least 50% of the proposed activities. The average rating was 92.3% with 71,000 complete activities registered in the course, through 45, 39, and 45 questions distributed respectively by the three modules, which made up a total of 102 questions to evaluate knowledge acquisition in the course.

At the end of the course, the participants were asked to complete a survey about the course and how it could be improved. This survey was created in Microsoft Forms and was available between 13 July 2021 and 9 March 2022.

Two hundred and ninety responses were obtained. The questions were anonymous and optional, so the total number of respondents was not equal in all questions.

On the question about expectations, 65% of the respondents said that expectations were met and 32% of the individuals even said that expectations were exceeded. Only 3% of the individuals mentioned that the course was below their expectations (Figure 11.1).

With regard to quizzes, 69.3% of the participants reported that they were adequate and easy and 30.7% indicated that they were adequate and easy but too long. No participant considered the quizzes to be bad and difficult (Figure 11.2).

Almost half of the participants (48.9%) considered that the course was very well organized; 44.4% stated that the course was well organized; and only 6.7% of the participants indicated that improvements are needed (Figure 11.3). No participant chose the disorganized option.

In terms of overall rating (stars from 1 to 5), the course scored 4.36 stars (n = 247).

Participants were also given the opportunity to respond about the likelihood of recommending the course on a scale of 0–10, where zero (0) is not at all likely and 10 is extremely likely. The most frequent response was 10 (extremely likely), with 41.7% of responses, followed by assessment 9 with 18.6% responses and assessment 8 with 17.2% of responses (Figure 11.4).

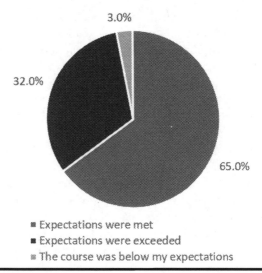

Figure 11.1 Opinion of participants in the MOOC in sustainable tourism about expectations about the course (n = 290).

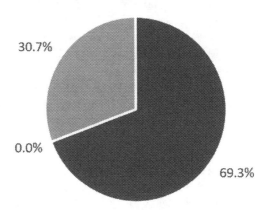

Figure 11.2 Opinion of participants in the MOOC in sustainable tourism about the course quizzes (n = 264).

The same survey requested three sentences that best characterized the MOOC in Sustainable Tourism. We received 484 sentences/expressions on which a content analysis was performed. Only 11 comments with negative criticism were registered, all the other comments report positive aspects, which we divide into the following categories: 19 comments that focus on the structure and organization of the course,

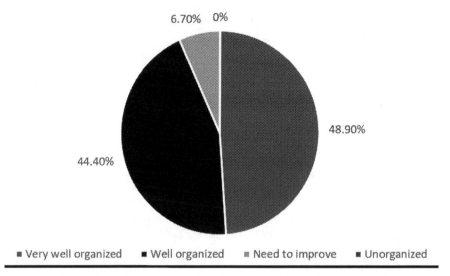

Figure 11.3 Opinion of the participants of the MOOC in sustainable tourism about the organization of the course (n = 270).

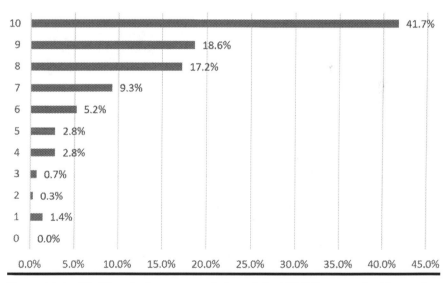

Figure 11.4 Likelihood of recommendation of the MOOC on sustainable tourism by participants (n = 290).

127 comments that enumerate the relevance or usefulness of the course; and 190 comments that make an evaluation of the course through phrases and/or adjectives. We had 54 comments about the objectivity and clarity of the course and 83 comments about the topic of sustainability (and not specifically about the course) (Table 11.1).

Table 11.1 Analysis of the Sentences Prepared by the Participants to Characterize the MOOC on Sustainable Tourism

Category	Examples of Expressions Used in this Category (with Expressions and Adjectives)	Number of Sentences/ Adjectives
Course structure	"It is an accurate and well-structured course"; "well structured"; "the sustainable tourism course is quite up to date and organised"; "well organised in the presentations"; "well-structured and easy to internalise"; "very well structured".	19
Relevance/ usefulness of the course	"relevant themes"; "with this course we got to know better what to do"; "very complete course in terms of explanations"; "very relevant information"; "the course offers us a range of knowledge and analysis on how sustainability is the best weapon to turn around the current context"; "the course succinctly managed to include a large amount of interesting and innovative concepts and contents", "it is a course of great interest for the current days we are going through"; "it is a relevant course for the general public"; "it allows tourists to become aware and improve the quality of tourism"; "it is a comprehensive, interesting training with a wide range of topics"; "the course was very useful"; "the course makes you think"; "it is a very interesting, relevant and pertinent course for today"; "very pertinent and useful".	127
Rating/ evaluative adjectives	"Good course"; "interesting"; "Innovative"; " up-to-date"; "enriching"; "enlightening"; "innovative and easy to understand"; "well presented and quite enlightening"; "impressive"; "interesting"; "arouses interest"; " it was a very interesting and complete course"; "effective"; "Excellent"; "Proactive"; "excellent course"; "quite educational"; "inspiring"; "interesting"; "I learned a lot"; "thorough"; "very good"; "I liked it".	190

(Continued)

Table 11.1 (Continued)

Category	Examples of Expressions Used in this Category (with Expressions and Adjectives)	Number of Sentences/ Adjectives
Objectivity/ clarity	"clarity of information"; "easy to understand"; "simple and objective"; "fast"; "simplicity in the way it is expressed and defined"; "simple approach"; "the texts are short and easy to understand"; "the course is practical"; "it is a very practical course"; "information transmitted clearly".	54
Other (mostly personal reflections on the theme of the course and not specifically about the course)	"Sustainable tourism is the mode of tourism in which the tourist himself is responsible for the environmental quality and heritage of the place he visits"; "there is still time to save Nature"; "sustainable tourism is a concept that adds concern for the environment, society and the economy to the tourism agenda"; "it should be faced with the importance of the commitment and involvement of all sectors of activity"; "travelling is good"; "sustainable tourism is the best tourism".	83
Negative criticism	"too expository"; "less videos"; "too much information in video"; "could be more complete"; "more interaction videos"; "a bit theoretical".	11

Also in the survey students were asked to make suggestions for future editions; 116 comments were made which will be used to improve the next edition of the MOOC. We reproduce some of these comments: "I recommend"; "none"; "nothing to add"; "nothing, keep going"; "yes, I recommend the course"; "well done"; "rural tourism and the future"; "do not make the attempt of unlimited answers, because then some of the trainees end up disinterested because they already know that they will always get the answers right"; "only as a suggestion, the transcription of the contents could make the videos accessible to audiences that do not have the necessary conditions to listen to them in their entirety"; "deepen sustainability, tourism / mobility in cities; tourism and senior citizens"; "fewer videos and some text support"; "correct the quality of the videos and the elements provided"; "in module 3, there should be more images to accompany the speech"; "more courses in the area of sustainability and environmental preservation"; "food waste"; "course more focused on AL tourism (local accommodation)"; "the programme is very well structured. Congratulations"; "A second course with more depth on the subject"; "less extensive questionnaires"; "it would be recommended that in a next edition there are more modules with more subjects about sustainable tourism"; "I think the course is great!"; "there should be more courses on natural and environmental issues".

11.4.2 MOOC in Introduction to Programming

The MOOC in Introduction to Programming started on 20 July 2021 and was divided into six modules: 1) methodologies and tools; 2) sequential processing; 3) conditional decision; 4) repetition; 5) modularization; 6) complex computational calculus. Each module was coordinated by a specialist teacher in the subject (Paulo Santos, António Manso). Twenty-three exercises were provided that were automatically evaluated by the Algorithmi application (Manso, Marques & Santos, 2018). The course has an estimated duration of 128 working hours, a figure that is justified by the course specificities.

There were 2761 individuals enrolled in the course, but only 2562 were identified as active enrolments. Of these, only 65.9% reported their age: 17% reported being up to 25 years old; 34.5% indicated being between 26 and 40 years old, and 48.5% mentioned being over 41 years old.

With regard to schooling/education, we obtained answers from 64.41% of the participants. Of these, 38.6% stated having a high school diploma or below; 32.9% indicated having an academic degree and 28.5% mentioned an advanced degree.

In terms of gender, we obtained responses from 70.18% of the participants. Of these, 56.2% identified themselves as female, 43.3% identified themselves as male and 0.5% chose the option "other".

Only 44% of the participants mentioned their country of origin. Of these, 95.9% indicated being from Portugal; 2.7% from Brazil; 0.4% from Mozambique; 0.3% from Angola; 0.2% from Cape Verde; 0.2% from Great Britain; 0.2% from Ireland; and 0.1% from Paraguay.

The majority of respondents stated that they work in the public sector (38%), followed by the private sector with 20% and students with 19%. There are also 11% of individuals who mentioned being unemployed, 8% who referred to being in another employment situation, and 4% who indicated being self-employed.

There were 238 certificates issued through the NAU platform, which represents a completion rate of 8.62%, a situation that may be related to the estimated duration of the course. The average grade was 76.5% and more than 63,000 activities were reported.

At the end of the course, the participants were asked to complete a survey about the course. This survey was created in Microsoft Forms and was available between 29 October 2021 and 9 May 2022.

The survey was answered by 155 participants. The authors of the MOOC considered it pertinent to assess only the likelihood of recommending the course, ask

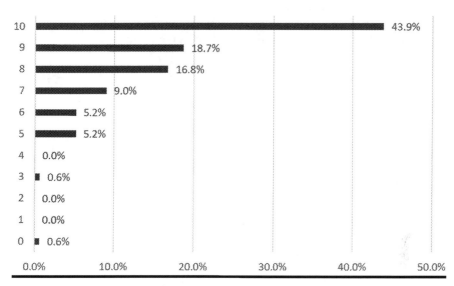

Figure 11.5 Likelihood of recommendation of MOOC in introduction to programming by participants (n = 155).

for its characterization through three sentences, and request suggestions for future editions.

With regard to the likelihood of recommending the course on a scale of 0–10, where zero (0) is not at all likely and 10 is extremely likely, The most frequent response was 10 (extremely likely), with 43.9% of the responses, followed by evaluation 9 with 18.7% responses and evaluation 8 with 16.8% of the responses (Figure 11.5).

As with the MOOC in Sustainable Tourism, three sentences were requested that best characterized the Introduction to Programming MOOC course. We received 268 sentences/expressions. Of these, only three contained comments with negative criticism related to its duration, all the other comments reported positive aspects, namely: 47 comments focusing on the development of skills in students, 17 comments listing various adjectives to the overall course, and 218 comments listing positive ratings on various aspects of the course (Table 11.2).

In this survey, students were also asked for suggestions for future editions. A total of 58 comments were received, of which we leave some examples: "none"; "nothing to say"; "nothing, keep going"; "more editions"; "maybe more courses with access to ECTs"; "more courses similar to this one for Phyton, PHP"; "please IPT, keep the same actions"; "more courses like this"; "module 2"; "repeat"; "training in Phyton"; "training in other programming languages"; "I believe that it would be an enormous added value to continue this path of learning programming"; "The evaluations should have at least 3 attempts, which is what happens in the different MOOCs in which I participated"; "More courses on programming. Also, a longer duration of the course would be great"; "Other continuity trainings programming microcontrollers".

Table 11.2 Analysis of the Sentences Prepared by the Participants to Characterize the MOOC in Introduction to Programming

Category	Examples of Expressions Used in this Category (with Expressions and Adjectives):	Number of Sentences/ Adjectives
Objectivity	"Practical course"; "clarity"; "teacher with clear and straightforward language"; "clear videos"; "matter exposed in a simple way"; "practical"; "simple"; "very practical assessment"; "concise"; "simple and clear".	39
Rating	"good course"; "very good"; "good explanations"; "good software"; "I liked it"; "I liked it very much"; "I enjoyed working"; "recommended"; "excellent course"; "I'm pleased"; "it was awesome"; "I'm loving it"; "the course is fascinating"; "excellent tool", "excellent quality"; "excellent initiation"; "excellent".	59
Interest	"quite interesting"; "interesting course"; "arouses interest"; "extremely interesting".	16
Easiness	"Facilitates learning"; "ease of interaction"; "facilitates learning"; "easy language"; "easy understanding"; "user-friendly videos".	14
Accessibility	"Accessible for those just starting out"; "the exercises are accessible"; "well-built and accessible"; "simple and accessible"; "good accessibility".	14
Structuring	"Well-structured explanations"; "well-structured course"; "very well structured"; "the structure/ order is good"; "the course is very well structured"; "well organised and structured".	12
Adequacy	"Suitable for those just starting out"; "excellent for those wanting to get started"; "useful for getting started programming"; "for those wanting to get started"; "excellent first approach"; "essential for those wanting to get started"; "useful as an introductory mechanism to programming".	11
Organization	"Well organised"; "well organised course", "well organised material".	7

(Continued)

Table 11.2 (Continued)

Category	Examples of Expressions Used in this Category (with Expressions and Adjectives):	Number of Sentences/ Adjectives
Usefulness	"A different approach, very useful"; "help about programming language"; "very useful and advised a lot of colleagues and friends to watch and do"; "useful for learning programming".	10
Intuition	"Intuitive tools"; "easy and intuitive"; "accessible and intuitive tools"; "intuitive teaching, very intuitive Algorithmi platform".	6
Other	"gave me some tips and ideas"; "comfortable"; "provides various resources"; "very pertinent"; "congratulations to the trainer"; "introduces new knowledge"; "exceptional service provided to HUMANITY"; "adapted to all audiences"; "full of stimulating content"; "it's delightful"; "innovative"; "explains the basics of programming in an enlightening way"; "educational videos"; "A course of real professionalism"; "The time provided for the completion of the course is quite ample, which allows it to be tailored to each student"; "Effective in passing on concepts and implementing them".	30

11.5 MOOCs in Health: A Case Study Based on the Nursing School of Porto Experience

Society is facing new challenges posed by the growing aging population and subsequent increase in noncommunicable diseases (NCDs) (WHO, 2019a). According to the World Health Organization (WHO, 2019a), the five most prevalent NCDs are heart disease, stroke, cancer, diabetes, and chronic lung disease, responsible for almost 70% of all deaths worldwide. In the European, region deaths by these NCDs reach 86% (WHO, 2019b).

In view of the growing aging population and the increasing prevalence of NCDs, healthcare systems, professionals, and higher education institutions are prompted to develop new strategies to reduce mortality and morbidity and enhance the quality of life of NCD patients while preserving healthcare systems' sustainability. These challenges call for innovation in healthcare services where the healthcare professionals' upskilling and reskilling are critical.

Lifelong learning is one of the strategies available and widely used by healthcare professionals to keep up-to-date about prevention, diagnosis, interventions, and expected outcomes. Lifelong learning was traditionally delivered through in-service training, universities, or educational institutions. The 21st-century healthcare demands urge professionals to be certified and up-to-date in the practice core fields as a way to ensure the safety and quality of the healthcare provided. Access to a certified high-quality lifelong learning digital education in a globalization era responds to time and financial constraints and familiar management challenges.

Digital learning content for healthcare professionals is emerging and evolving, envisioning to complement rather than replace traditional methods of delivering continued health education and in-service training (WHO, 2019c).

In line with the exponential increase in the number of trainees enrolled in MOOCs in several areas, The Report by Class Central, 2021, refers to 220 million apprenticeships (about 300,000 trainees in 2012) (Shah, 2021). Moreover, the diversity of MOOCs available in the health area has increased; however, it still represents a small part of the set of available MOOCs, about 2.7% of the total.

Therefore, there is a need for greater attention to this structuring area of modern society. However, specific constraints, such as the need for constant updating and the imperative to introduce advanced technology (such as virtual simulation), have limited the development of this type of course.

As stated by Rowe et al. (2019), health education requires a design approach different from the predominant form of MOOCs, namely, concerning the evaluation of decision-making processes or the need for more interactive learning dynamics, as suggested by Moriates et al. (2019).

Nowadays, the massive use of ICT and high technological literacy of young generations of healthcare providers contribute to the perceived usefulness and intention to adopt new pedagogical approaches aiming to facilitate learning in undergraduate students and in lifelong learning education (Padilha et al., 2018; Padilha et al., 2021).

The use of digital platforms allows students and healthcare professionals to access content in several formats, namely in asynchronous layouts, enabling the required pedagogical autonomy and personal time management. Furthermore, when complemented with interactive technologies for discussion, this strategy fosters active learning.

In the 21st century, the teaching and learning methodologies focused on exposure, repetition, and memorization are no longer challenging and are prompting the development of innovative teaching and learning methods using ICT tools. The attention is focused on the development of strategies targeted at active learning, in which the teacher is both a promoter and a facilitator of the learning process, helping healthcare professionals to learn from experiences and contextualized environments, thus meeting personal expectations and boosting motivation to learn (AlRuthia et al., 2019; Woods & Rosenberg, 2016; Scott et al., 2014; Hoke & Robbins, 2005).

The WHO recommends the digital provision of training and educational content for health workers via mobile devices/mLearning to complement continuous health education and in-service training (WHO, 2019c).

In this context, in 2018, the Nursing School of Porto, envisioning the setting up of an effective and innovative response to the nurses' challenges to keep up-to-date with noncommunicable diseases management, conducted a pilot study regarding the creation of a Massive Open Online Course, co-financed by the European Regional Development Fund (FEDER) and national fund COMPETE2020 (POCI-01-0145-FEDER-023342). This MOOC, called "Ecare-COPD", aimed to develop nurses' competencies to support the development of patient skills in the self-management of Chronic Obstructive Pulmonary Disease (COPD). COPD poses a substantial burden worldwide and, in 2020, was already the third leading cause of death.

In order to confirm the designed training model and considering that the model was ready for full deployment alongside the need to respond to the pandemic context experienced between 2020 and 2022, a new course was developed, now targeted at health professionals. This course aimed to deepen these professionals' skills to optimize the provision and management of care for COVID-19 patients, which will be described later in this chapter.

The production of MOOCs – both cases described below – followed the Technology Readiness Levels (TRL) (Moorhouse, 2012) are used here as a reference for understanding the evolution of this technology-based process.

The conceptual diffusion of technology is well portrayed in the work of Schatzberg (2018), who states that "the definition of technology is a mess" (p. 1). Thus, following, once again, Schatzberg (2018), technology is considered a set of practices used to transform the material world, overcoming the difficult task of defining barriers between technology and its based production processes, of which MOOCs are a good example.

11.5.1 The Ecare-COPD Training Program

The Ecare-COPD MOOC was developed based on a research study (Padilha, 2013, 2017) that enabled to understand the need to provide nurses with skills for the empowerment of patients regarding self-management of COPD and thus, listing several strategies for its implementation (TRL 1–4) (Padilha (2013); Padilha et al. (2017)).

To validate the concept in a relevant environment, the Ecare-COPD MOOC was created in three levels, based on expert opinion using the Focus group approach and tested by beta-testers (TRL 5) after the initial development phase.

After these preparatory phases, a prototype was created, demonstrating the technology in a relevant environment (TRL 6), hosted by the Portuguese National Agency for Science and Technology (FCT), which provides Portuguese institutions with an e-learning platform to promote MOOC creation and delivery.

At an initial level, the course was structured for undergraduate students, at an intermediate level for general nurses, and an advanced level for specialized rehabilitation nurses.

The three-level course was divided into 19 learning modules, each answering specific learning goals. Learning modules were organized into several lessons, which were supported by text, multimedia, clinical virtual simulation activities, and references. The multimedia contents focused on the major goals and topics of the training program, each lasting an average of 5.06 minutes (Padilha et al., 2021).

One of the most striking innovations of this MOOC was the creation of gamification components made available through an embedded clinical virtual simulator (CVS) named Body Interact®. The use of CVS allowed the user to practice decision-making skills based on the knowledge addressed in the other contents created. These scenarios were made available progressively and were dynamic over the learning experience.

This experience showed that participants rated the easiness and global quality of the course with an average score of 4.70 (SD = 0.31), and usefulness and intention to use in the future the MOOC´s with an average score of 4.73 (SD = 0.34) on a 5-point Likert scale (where 1 represented the worst opinion and 5 the best opinion regarding the item analyzed), proving to be operational in a real environment (TRL 7).

The development phase was completed and qualified by participants (TRL 8), evidencing nurses with more qualifications, experience, and age as those rating higher on the MOOC for easiness and global quality of the course (see details in Padilha et al., 2021).

11.5.2 The Ecare-COVID19 Professional Update Program

In 2020, the COVID-19 outbreak posed tremendous challenges to our society. Healthcare professionals were under extreme burden and undergoing everyday new challenges to keep up-to-date while responding to the global health emergency. The over workload and the restrictions imposed by the confinements transformed the way of accessing lifelong learning by healthcare professionals. In this context, and with the additional aim of testing the development method created in the pilot study described above (TRL 9) in an operational environment, a MOOC – Ecare-COVID19 – was developed and made available.

Ecare-COVID19 was designed and developed with the collaboration of experts from different knowledge backgrounds in the healthcare field. This MOOC was made available directed for clinical diagnosis and treatment of COVID, in the Portuguese language.

Learning modules were organized into several lessons. Lessons were supported by text, multimedia, a clinical virtual simulator, and references. This MOOC consisted of 10 modules with 39 lessons supported by video lasting an average of 7.5 minutes. Participants had an estimated workload of 35 hours to complete this MOOC.

The Ecare-COVID19 MOOC was completed by 847 participants (32.2% of the 2629 healthcare professionals enrolled in the MOOC). In this MOOC, the easiness, usefulness, and intention to use it in future lifelong learning were rated with an average of 4.4 (SD ± 0.7) and with satisfaction of 4.5 (SD ± 0.7) on a 5-point

Likert scale (where 1 represented the worst opinion and 5 the best opinion regarding the item analyzed). Regarding knowledge retention, we compared the level of knowledge before and after the MOOC and found that MOOC was effective in knowledge retention regarding the COVID-19 diagnosis, treatment, and management (t795 = 58.5; P < 0.001; d = 0.19).

11.5.3 Further Developments

The system's effectiveness was proven in an operational environment based on the success of the development and impact of the above-described MOOCs. Following these results, the Nursing School of Porto will deepen the development of this typology of courses in a structure called IP Alliance – Integrated Platform for Lifelong Learning and Training of Healthcare Professionals, funded by the NextGenerationEU Programme.

This collaborative alliance was built based on our past experience and we will work on the responses to some of the biggest societal challenges in health determinants by promoting reskilling and upskilling of healthcare professionals, focusing on the leading global health challenges.

Mainly directed at physicians, nurses, and technicians in clinical diagnostic and laboratory, the IP Alliance presents itself as an innovative and disruptive multidisciplinary, multiprofessional, and know-how sharing proposal between partners. It intends to create the conditions for responding to what the WHO defined as "Slow Motion Disaster": noncommunicable diseases (NCDs), also known as chronic diseases. NCDs currently represent around 86% of deaths in Europe and substantial losses in the quality of life of citizens.

In fact, the constant advancements in scientific knowledge in health have repercussions on diagnosis, treatment, and intervention, requiring innovation in health services and health professionals updating on the conversion and updating of skills (reskilling and upskilling). These societal challenges are also at the origin of the need for constant adaptation of the Higher Education Institutions' internal ecosystem to the emerging training demands of health professionals and citizens. Thus, this Alliance intends to develop and make available new lifelong training courses of interprofessional nature aimed at training health professionals to contribute to the control of some of the most prevalent noncommunicable diseases and to be responsive to the needs for increasing quality, safety, and sustainability of National Healthcare Systems.

11.6 Conclusions

Internationally, we can see that the level of maturity of using MOOC is different from context to context. The well-known MOOC providers are operating for about a decade and have a bigger maturity in this field. The business model of MOOC is quite clear for the higher education institutions that started this process and see the added value to embracing this pedagogical approach, despite the reasons to do it.

Analyzing the case studies presented, we can consider that we are facing an initial level of maturity in the Portuguese reality. However, compared to the organization's initiative (Universidade Aberta, Instituto Politécnico de Leiria, and Instituto Superior Técnico), we noticed that MOOCs offered at NAU platforms that aimed at the institution's target public have a higher number of enrolments. Furthermore, those MOOCs that imply a lower effort of hours obtain a higher number of certifications. For instance, IPT obtained 35.8% of certification on the MOOC with 29 hours and the NSP's MOOC with 35 hours the number was quite similar (32.2%), while the IPT MOOC with 128 hours of effort had only 8.6% of certificates issued.

The experiences taken in NAU platform seem to be more aligned with an institutional strategy to reach more students and new target audiences that might, in the future, become campus students. The numbers also show that most of the learners are working professionals that need to reskill or upskill their competences and, therefore, we are reaching learners different from the traditional ones we have on campus. Moreover, if we aim to experiment with new learning approaches, the NAU platform seems to be a better option because it reaches a broader group of people. In fact, in the described cases, satisfaction with the MOOC training experience is quite positive, exceeding 4 points on a scale of 1–5.

It is relevant that most trainees are employed, which shows that the contents addressed meet the needs of these professionals. This can be a way to enrich and contribute to the lifelong learning that higher education institutions can provide to former students or even to professionals in their field, that want to be up to date in their knowledge.

Summing up, in terms of sustainability, the effort to invest in an institutional platform will probably enlarge the costs with more human resources, IT infrastructure, and services around it, to build courses and maintain the infrastructure. At the same time, the reach in terms of students is much smaller in this case, putting a bigger stress on the goals that the institution might want to achieve. Consequently, using a platform like NAU might be more aligned with the typical goals that are assumed when moving toward the use of MOOC, allowing the institution to focus its resources on the development of courses, and, therefore, having a more efficient approach, that will allow an easier way to achieve the desired sustainability.

References

AlRuthia, Y., Alhawas, S., Alodaibi, F., et al. (2019). The use of active learning strategies in healthcare colleges in the Middle East. *BMC Medical Education* 19(143), 1–10. https://doi.org/10.1186/s12909-019-1580-4

Bastos, G., Cabral, P.B., & Rocio, V. (2019). Social engagement and motivation in a MOOC on school libraries. *ICERI2018 Proceedings 11th annual International*

Conference of Education, Research and Innovation. (pp. 6690–6695). http://hdl.handle.net/10400.2/9278

Butler, M., & Morgan, M. (2007). Learning challenges faced by novice programming students studying high level and low feedback concepts. *Proceedings of ASCILATE 2007* (pp. 99–107). ASCILATE.

Class Central (2019). Online Degrees Slowdown: A Review of MOOC Stats and Trends in 2019. https://www.classcentral.com/report/moocs-stats-and-trends-2019/

Class Central (2021). A Decade of MOOCs: A Review of MOOC Stats and Trends in 2021. https://www.classcentral.com/report/moocs-stats-and-trends-2021/

Dias, P. (2021). *Using gamification to increase learners' engagement in MOOCs*. [Master Dissertation, Instituto Superior Técnico]. Campus Repository. https://scholar.tecnico.ulisboa.pt/records/y4aw4C5IUje0wWgNFso9FKWNU6qhu6INQP8t?lang=pt

EADTU (2016). Comparing Institutional MOOC strategies - status report based on a mapping survey conducted in October - December 2015. http://eadtu.eu/images/publicaties/Comparing_Institutional_MOOC_strategies.pdf

EdX (2022). Important changes at edX. https://support.edx.org/hc/en-us/articles/4411774304919-Important-changes-at-edX

Gonçalves, V. C. (2019). *Massive Open Online Course (MOOC) como recurso de formação em Bibliotecas Universitárias: um estudo de caso no Politécnico de Leiria*. [Master Dissertation, University of Minho]. Campus Repository. https://hdl.handle.net/1822/63676

Hoke, M., & Robbins, L. (2005). The impact of active learning on nursing students' clinical success. *Journal of Holistic Nursing*, 23(3), 348–355. https://doi.org/10.1177/0898010105277648

Jenkins, T. (2002). On the difficulty of learning to program. *Proceedings of the 3rd Annual Conference of the LTSN Centre for Information and Computer Science* (pp. 65–71). LTSN-ICS.

Lahtinen, E., Mutka, K., & Jarvinen, H. (2005). A Study of the difficulties of novice programmers. *Proceedings of the 10th Annual SIGCSE Conference on Innovation and Technology in Computer ITiCSE'05* (pp. 14–18). Association for Computing Machinery.

Manso, A., Marques, C. G., & Santos, P. (2018). Algoritmi: sistema de informação para apoio à aprendizagem de programação. In J. M. Dodero, C. G. Marques, & I. Ruiz (Eds.), *Proceedings of the 2018 International Symposium on Computers in Education*. IEEE.

Moorhouse, D. J. (2012). Detailed definitions and guidance for application. *Journal of Aircraft*, 39(1), 190–192. https://doi.org/10.2514/2.2916

Moriates, C. et al. (2019). Using interactive learning modules to teach value-based health care to health professions trainees across the United States. *Academic Medicine*, 94(9), 1332–1336. https://doi.org/10.1097/ACM.0000000000002670

Padilha, J. Miguel. (2013). *Promotion of self-management in patients with COPD: a course of action-research*. [Doctoral dissertation, Portuguese Catholic University]. Campus Repository. http://hdl.handle.net/10400.14/14958 (inPortuguese).

Padilha, J. M., de Sousa, P. A. F., & Pereira, F. M. S. (2017). Nursing clinical practice changes to improve self-management in chronic obstructive pulmonary disease. *International Nursing Review* 65(1), 122–130. https://doi.org/10.1111/inr.12366

Padilha, J. M., Machado, P. P., Ribeiro, A. L., Ribeiro, R., Vieira, F., & Costa, P. (2021). Easiness, usefulness and intention to use a MOOC in nursing. *Nurse Educ Today*, 97(104705), 1–7. https://doi.org/10.1016/j.nedt.2020.104705

Padilha, J. M., Machado, P. P., Ribeiro, A. L., et al. (2018). Clinical virtual simulation in nursing education. *Clinical Simulation in Nursing*, 15(C), 13–18. https://doi.org/10.1016/j.ecns.2017.09.005

Rhoads, R. A. (2015). *MOOCs, High Technology, and Higher Learning*. Johns Hopkins University Press.

Rowe, M., Osadnik, C. R., Pritchard, S., & Maloney, S. (2019). These may not be the courses you are seeking: A systematic review of open online courses in health professions education. *BMC Medical Education*, 19(356), 1–12. https://doi.org/10.1186/s12909-019-1774-9

Schatzberg, E. (2018). *Technology: Critical History of a Concept*. The University of Chicago Press.

Scott, F., Sarah, L. Eddy, M., et al. (2014). Active learning increases student performance in science, engineering, and mathematics. *PNAS – Proceedings of the National Academy of Sciences of the USA*, 111(23), 8410–8415. https://doi.org/10.1073/pnas.1319030111

Shah, D. (2021, December 14). A Decade of MOOCs: A Review of MOOC Stats and Trends in 2021. The Report by Class Central. https://www.classcentral.com/report/moocs-stats-and-trends-2021/

Woods, M., & Rosenberg, M. E. (2016). Educational tools: Thinking outside the box. *Clinical Journal of the American Society of Nephrology*, 11(3), 518–526. https://doi.org/10.2215/CJN.02570315

World Health Organization (2019a). Noncommunicable diseases and their risk factors. Major NCDs and their risk factors. Retrieved December 26, 2019, https://www.who.int/ncds/introduction/en/

World Health Organization (2019b). Noncommeunicable diseases. Retrieved December 26, 2019 http://www.euro.who.int/en/health-topics/noncommunicable-diseases

World Health Organization (2019c). *WHO Guideline: Recommendations on Digital Interventions for Health System Strengthening*. World Health Organization.

Yin, R. K. (2014). *Case Study Research: Design and Methods* (5th ed.). Sage Publications.

Index

Pages in *italics* refer to figures and pages in **bold** refer to tables.

A

Accounting education, 144–147, 150–154, 158, **160**, 164, 166, 174–175, 177
Adaptive learning, 213, 230–233
Adaptive platforms, 230, 232–233
Adequacy, **250**
Algorithmi application, 248
Artificial intelligence, 213–219, 224–225, **227–228**, 230–233
Attitudes, 49, 145, 147, **160**, 176
Augmented reality, **227–228**, 230–233

B

Bibliometric analysis, 122, 125–126, 131, 134, 150–151, 158, 217–218, 225
Biopsychosocial, 98
BYOD, 86

C

Chatbot, 229–233
Citizenship, 122–124, 138–139
Clarity, 245, **247**
Classrooms, 34
Collaborations, 151, 171
Competencies, 43, 146, 175–176
Complex computational calculus, 248
Compliance, 145, 169
Computer-assisted instruction, 230–233
Conceptual structure of knowledge, 163–164, 175
Constructive, 35
Course structure, **246**
Covid-19, 11, 122, 124–126, 134, 136–139
Critical thinking, 146, **160**, 176
Cyberbullying, 97

D

Daily routines, 98
Dependencies, 98
Digital health, 52–53, *54*
Digital learning pedagogies, 37
Digital learning, 189, 192, 206, 209
Digital literacy, 11
Digital pedagogical, 11
Digital safety, 51
Digital teaching, 189, 203
Digital technologies, 212, **228**

E

Eco-friendly, 83
Economic cooperation, 48
Educational strategies, 122–123, 125, **127**, 131, 134, 136, 139
Educational technologies, 212
Educational, 34
E-learning, 103
Emotionally, 99
European DIGCOMP, 46, 47–55
Experiential learning, 146, 174, 180

F

Face-to-face, 98

G

Global sustainability, 78
Global university, 83
Graves' model, 80
Group-based activities, 91

259

H

Higher education, 10–18, 24, 29, 188–182, 196–198, 213–219, 224–225, **227–228**, 230–233

I

ICT, 96, 122–123, 136–139
Innovation, 12, 122–123, 139
Integral education, 176
Intellectual structure of knowledge, 164
Intelligent tutoring systems, 230, 234
Interdisciplinary, 13
International mobility, 188–192, 196, 202, *220*
Internationalization, 192, 194–195, 203–204, 206
Introduction to programming, 242, 248–249, **250**

K

Knowledge, 12, 49

L

Leadership, 145, 155, 174, 176
Learning, 11, 122, 124–125, 137–139
LMS, 88–90

M

Machine learning, 212–215, **228**, 231–232
Market-proficient, 78
Micro-credentials, 205
Mobility actions, 196, 199–106
Mobility programmes, 192, 195, 203, 205–207
Modularization, 248
Moocs (massive open online courses), 84–85, 230, 232–233, 238–240

N

Negative criticism, **247**

O

Offline extended classroom, 36
Online learning, 36, 136–137

P

Paradigm, 214
Pedagogic, 103
Pedagogical orientation, 11
Pedagogical practices, 11
Planning, 102
Policies, 83

Q

Quality of life, 122–124, 138

R

Robotics, 230, 232–233

S

Self-regulated learning, 138–139
Sequential processing, 248
Skilled professionals, 78
Skills, 49, 145–150, 158, **159**, 161, 164, 166, 174–176
Smart and sustainable cities, 121–123, 126, 131
Social engineering, 71
Social inclusion, 47, 50–51
Social psychology, 96
Social structure of knowledge, 169
Stakeholders, 72
Sustainable cities, 122, 124–126, 134
Sustainable development, 134, 136
Sustainable digital education, 35
Sustainable tourism, 242, 244–249
Systematic literature review, 188–189
System-theoretic accident model, 51

T

Teaching, 11
Teaching–learning, 80
Techniques, 10
Technological skills, 145, 176
Transdisciplinary, 102
Transformation, *81*

U

Underpinning, 51

V

Virtual internationalization, **190**, 206
Virtual mobility, 188, **190**, 206, 209

W

Well-being, 71

Printed in the United States
by Baker & Taylor Publisher Services